A
Lifelong
Call
to Learn

A
Lifelong
to Call
Learn

Approaches to Continuing
Education for Church Leaders

EDITED BY

Robert E. Reber
& D. Bruce Roberts

Abingdon Press
Nashville

A LIFELONG CALL TO LEARN
APPROACHES TO CONTINUING EDUCATION FOR CHURCH LEADERS

Library of Congress Cataloging in Publication Data

A lifelong call to learn: approaches to continuing education for church leaders/edited by Robert E. Reber & D. Bruce Roberts.
   p. cm.
   ISBN 0-687-07146-1
   1. Clergy—Post-ordination training.   2. Theology—Study and teaching (Continuing education)   I. Reber, Robert Eldred, 1937–   II. Roberts, D. Bruce, 1939–

BV4165 .L54 2001
230'.071'5—dc21   00-046428

00 01 02 03 04 05 06 07 08 09—10 9 8 7 6 5 4 3 2 1

MANUFACTURED IN THE UNITED STATES OF AMERICA

This book is dedicated to the thousands of clergy,
church professionals, and lay leaders from
whom we have learned so much and who
have responded enthusiastically to
the lifelong call to learn.

Contents

Development, Management, and Promotion of Programs

Directions and Resources for the Future

Preface

Why This Book?

It has been more than twenty-five years since the publication of a book that focused on continuing theological education for church professionals, whether clergy or laity. Much has happened since that time. Increasingly, theological schools and conference and retreat centers are giving attention to the ongoing education of religious leaders. Judicatories, congregations, entrepreneurs, and professional societies are sponsoring continuing education programs. In many respects, this educational activity reflects what is going on in the larger society where attention and considerable resources are being devoted to continuing education for professionals, as well as a myriad of other types of adult education courses, workshops, seminars, and conferences for the general public.

This book focuses on the broad arena of continuing education for church professionals and laity, especially those who are committed to lifelong learning. The contributors to this volume offer a variety of perspectives that have emerged from years of experience and reflection on their work with clergy and laity in a variety of programs. As directors of continuing education programs, teachers in adult and professional education, and lifelong learners, all are eager to share their insights and to invite you to be part of the journey of lifelong education. There is no greater educational need in the life of congregations and church organizations today than having a committed, informed, and continually educated leadership. We trust that this book will encourage the emergence of new and helpful understandings and practices related to continuing education programs in the years to come.

Overview of Contents

The first section of this book is devoted to historical perspectives and educational contexts. The three chapters address questions such as:

- What is the current state of continuing theological education?
- What is its mission and purpose?
- What historical developments have led up to the present situation?
- Who has been providing continuing education for clergy and laity?
- Who has been participating and who has been often overlooked?

The next section focuses on theory and research in professional continuing education. Attention is given to a more systemic view of continuing education for church leaders, The authors ask what is involved in the effective teaching of adults, and, more specifically, where and how do religious leaders learn.

The third section discusses current models of continuing education and explores the implications of the involvement of laity in continuing education programs that link faith and daily life, taking seriously the growing religious pluralism in this country. Consideration is given to such questions as who is and should be involved in continuing theological education, and what the content of future programs might be.

The fourth section is on the development, management, and promotion of programs. Donald Guthrie and Ron Cervero assert that continuing education belongs at the center of the institutional mission of churches and seminaries. The essays that follow take up practical concerns, such as assessing the needs and interests of potential participants; the dynamics of ongoing program development and evaluation; effective marketing and promotion of educational offerings; methods of welcoming the whole person into the educational environment; and the risks involved in managing an educational program center.

The final section proposes directions for the future. Ward Cornett III argues that, in order to provide arenas for moral deliberation, religious communities must develop their educational programs in partnership with the larger society. Mike and John Maus consider the implications of new and emerging technologies for the future of education in and by churches. The final chapter seeks to summarize what has been said and to identify overriding challenges for the future.

Acknowledgments

It is only because of the collaboration and encouragement of many colleagues and friends that this volume has come to print. Several have given unstintingly of their time and have contributed chapters. We are deeply grateful to the many members of the Society for the Advancement for Continuing Education for Ministry (SACEM) who kept insisting that we needed to get this book done. At the annual gatherings we have been stimulated by discussions with directors of continuing education programs from all over North America, from mainline Protestant, Evangelical, and Roman Catholic seminaries, conference and retreat centers, denominational offices, and educational centers. The Society has truly been, for us, a forum of professional support and reflection on theory and practice in continuing theological education. Another important arena has been the Colleague Program for New Directors of Continuing Theological Education, a program developed under the auspices of Auburn Theological Seminary and funded during the past five years by the Henry Luce Foundation. The program has given the editors of this volume many opportunities to test our ideas with newcomers to the field. We owe considerable thanks to the General Board of Higher Education and Ministry of The United Methodist Church for its enthusiasm and support of this publishing venture. Its Committee on Continuing Education for Ministry and its director, the Reverend Lynne Scott, endorsed this book project from its very beginning.

Finally, we wish to express our thanks to the two institutions that have provided us an arena for our own work as continuing theological educators, Auburn Theological Seminary in New York City and Christian Theological Seminary in Indianapolis. Both have provided time for study and writing and have affirmed the importance of redefining continuing theological education and its centrality to the life of the church.

Robert E. Reber, New York
D. Bruce Roberts, Indianapolis

List of Contributors

GEORGE BROWN is G.W. and Eddie Haworth Professor of Christian Education and Associate Dean at Western Theological Seminary in Holland, Michigan. He directs the program of continuing education and is also director of Doctor of Ministry and Master of Divinity Degree programs. He teaches courses in Christian Education with an emphasis on adult education and curriculum.

RONALD M. CERVERO is a professor in the Department of Adult Education at the University of Georgia. He has published extensively in adult education, with emphasis on continuing education for the professions and the politics of adult education. His books include *Effective Continuing Education for Professionals* and *Planning Responsibly for Adult Education: A Guide to Negotiating Power and Interests* (with Arthur Wilson).

WARD CORNETT III is director of continuing education at Trinity Lutheran Seminary, Columbus, Ohio, and Region 6 of the Evangelical Lutheran Church in America, positions that he has held for six years. Ordained in 1979, he has previously served congregations in Washington, D.C., Pittsburgh, Pennsylvania, and St. Joseph, Michigan.

CYNTHIA CROWNER is the Director of Kirkridge, a fifty-eight-year-old ecumenical retreat and study center in northeastern Pennsylvania. Kirkridge offers more than fifty programs annually in the areas of cutting edge theology, church renewal, peace and justice, ecospirituality, personal growth, and spirituality and the arts. Cindy is an ordained Presbyterian minister.

DONALD C. GUTHRIE is Dean of Academic Administration at Covenant Theological Seminary in St. Louis. He also serves as an Assistant Professor of Christian Education and as the Director of the Doctor of Ministry program. Previously, he served as Director of Training for the campus ministry of the Coalition for Christian Outreach in Pittsburgh.

WILLIAM LORD is the Director of Continuing Education and Development at the Toronto School of Theology in Ontario, Canada. Since 1977 he has been a member of SACEM and has served as President and Secretary. He has conducted and directed research projects on clergy and their needs for lifelong learning.

JOHN MAUS has his own networking and Internet software company, CM Flex Systems, and has been playing with computers in their evolving forms for the past twenty years. He is a part-time student of applied physics and a full-time student of computer and software innovations.

MIKE MAUS is Director of Communications of the American Bible Society, a former NBC News political correspondent, anchorman, and former Associate General Secretary of the National Council of Churches. He taught communications and journalism at Macalester College and the City College of New York.

MARVIN T. MORGAN is director of continuing education and the certificate program at the Interdenominational Theological Center in Atlanta. He has served as a United Church of Christ pastor for twenty-six years and has been in higher education for the past eight years. The certificate program is currently operating in forty-four cities in the United States, Canada, and the Caribbean. Six hundred and eighty-eight students have completed the program.

CAROLYN HENNINGER OEHLER is executive director of Scarritt-Bennett Center, a conference, retreat, and educational center in Nashville. She is a writer, teacher, and seminar leader. Recent publications include "Lucy Rider Meyer" in *Women Building Chicago 1790–1990: A Biographical Dictionary*, "Steps Toward Building Wholeness: Learning and Repentance," and "The Journey Is Our Home."

RODNEY PARROTT is Professor of New Testament and Disciples' Studies at the Disciples Seminary Foundation in Claremont, California. From 1979 to 1999, he served as Assistant Dean and, more recently, as Associate Dean of the seminary, positions that include responsibilities for continuing education. He has worked with the seminary's extension programs for continuing education in eight states.

ROBERT E. REBER is dean of Auburn Theological Seminary in New York City and the director of its continuing education and inter-religious programs. For twenty-eight years he has developed educational programs with clergy and laity in denominational, ecumenical, and multireligious settings. He is the author of *Linking Faith and Daily Life* and articles on professional and adult religious education.

D. BRUCE ROBERTS is Director of the Indiana Clergy Peer Group Study Program and Professor of Christian Ministries, Christian Theological Seminary, Indianapolis. For the past twenty-eight years, he has worked in graduate theological education as a teacher of adult education, congregational studies, and field education supervision. He was director of continuing education at CTS for eighteen years.

MARK ROUCH was for ten years Director of the Intentional Growth Center, Lake Junaluska, North Carolina. He has been a United Methodist pastor and Director of Continuing Education, The United Methodist Church Board of Ordained Ministry. A founding member and former president of the Society for the

Advancement of Continuing Education for Ministry, he is the author of *Competent Ministry: A Guide to Effective Continuing Education.*

DORIS J. RUDY was secretary, administrative coordinator, and then director of the continuing education program and summer school at Garrett-Evangelical Theological Seminary, Evanston, Illinois, for twenty years. The first seminar she attended after joining the staff in 1979 was on marketing. She had on-the-job training in risk management.

SALLY SIMMEL has been engaged in education and theological reflection with laity for many years, helping lay Christians discern God's activity in the world and their call to be cocreators with God. She is Director for Ministry in Daily Life for the Evangelical Lutheran Church in America, and has written for *Faith at Work, Lutheran Women Today,* the *Public Religion Project* and distance learning resources for the Evangelical Lutheran Church of America (ELCA).

DOUGLAS E. WINGEIER, emeritus professor of practical theology, Garrett-Evangelical Theological Seminary, taught Christian education and church administration 1970–1998. He was also director of continuing education and director of the Doctor of Ministry program. He is the author of *Working Out Your Own Beliefs* and *Eight Ways to Become Christian.*

Historical Perspectives and Educational Contexts

Chapter 1

From Yesterday to Today in Continuing Education

Mark Rouch

"Let me show you my favorite nude." My parents were even more startled than I by this suggestion from our pastor. The setting, however, was New York City's Metropolitan Museum of Art and the "nude," as it turned out, was a lovely piece of Greek sculpture. I was fifteen and we were attending the New York World's Fair. Our pastor and his wife were in Manhattan because he was enrolled in Union Theological Seminary's summer school. The year was 1940.

This personal incident illustrates that long before a widespread movement in support of continuing education programs for ministry gained momentum, there were individual clergy who took responsibility for their continued learning and agencies that provided outstanding program opportunities.

However, in the early 1960s in Protestantism and the 1970s in Roman Catholicism, a continuing education movement began that was to have far-reaching effects in the United States and Canada— and beyond. Never centered in a single organization—in fact, never tightly organized at all—it nevertheless has been a self-conscious movement involving a network of persons focused upon a common enterprise and centered in several organizational structures.

The publication in 1960 of Dr. Connolly Gamble's *Continuing Theological Education of the American Minister* provided the spark that began the movement.[1] Prior to that time there had been an acceleration of continuing education programs[2] including such pioneering ventures as the Tower Room Scholars at Union

Theological Seminary in Virginia, developed by Dr. Gamble, and the Institute for Advanced Pastoral Studies, Bloomfield Hills, Michigan, founded by Dr. Reuel Howe.

Dr. Gamble reported, however, that a surprising amount of continuing education was being developed. A questionnaire had been sent to 500 agencies. Their response indicated that 95 seminaries, 35 colleges and universities, 15 conference centers, and 10 pastoral institutes offered some sort of continuing education programs for clergy. These findings created a lively discussion among church leaders, and led to a series of events which resulted in the founding of the Society for the Advancement of Continuing Education for Ministry in 1968.

The Society for the Advancement of Continuing Education for Ministry

In 1964, the Department of the Ministry of the National Council of Churches convened a consultation at Andover Newton Seminary with Dr. Gamble as chair. Representatives came from a large number of groups, including seminary faculties, denominational offices, independent continuing education agencies, government agencies, and many others. It was, in fact, described as "the most widely diversified group ever to focus upon the continuing education of a single profession."[3]

One recommendation of the consultation was that the National Council of Churches Department of the Ministry (NCCDOM) establish a committee on continuing education. The committee was organized and for the next several years became an active arena of discussion of issues and new developments in the field. Another recommendation was that a second consultation be called.

That consultation met in 1965 at the Center for Continuing Education of the University of Chicago. Some one hundred continuing educators assembled to consider emerging issues and developments. One recommendation from this consultation was that a series of learning events be held especially for continuing educators in ministry. This led to the third major event antecedent to the formation of SACEM.

Planned by the NCCDOM Committee on Continuing Education,

a seminar for continuing educators was held the following year at the Kellogg Center for Continuing Education, Michigan State University. Developed in cooperation with the staff of the center, it was a lively learning event which expanded the awareness of many of those attending. At the close, the group convened itself as a business session and decided that a society of continuing educators for ministry should be formed. A committee was named to draw up a set of bylaws, recommend a name, and bring a report to a second seminar the following year.

In 1967, at the Center for Continuing Education, Syracuse University (in sweltering heat with no air-conditioning), SACEM was established during the business meeting when the committee's report was accepted. Bylaws were adopted and the name selected, with one emendation, from the committee proposal. Proposed was Society for the Advancement of Continuing Education of the Ministry. "The" was dropped to become "Continuing Education for Ministry"—a small but highly significant change. The majority sentiment was that the new society should focus on the whole ministry of the church, including the work of nonordained professionals in ministry, as well as laity.

A fourfold statement of purpose was adopted and remains unchanged to this day, guiding the work of SACEM. In summary, the four tasks are:

- To bring together regularly persons concerned for ministry so that they might share ideas and grow as professionals in the field;
- To identify issues which affect the advancement of continuing education for ministry and to develop strategies to address them;
- To advocate for continuing education for ministry;
- To conduct and encourage others to conduct relevant research.

Thus, SACEM was under way. A board was elected and Connolly Gamble enthusiastically selected as the first president. The first annual general meeting of the society was held in 1968 in Clayton, Missouri, a suburb of St. Louis, with a focus on the case study method in continuing education.

Each year since, a general meeting of the Society has been held in widely diverse locations, each with a theme focused on some significant concern of the Society. Planning committees have included members from the area where the meeting has been held; members of the SACEM board and, in more recent years, denominational continuing education officials. Meetings have been planned as learning events for those attending, but always a significant function has been networking and the informal exchange of ideas.

Soon after its establishment, the Society decided that at least part-time executive leadership would be needed, and Dr. Gamble was chosen for this position. Continuing his work at Union Theological Seminary in Virginia, and later as a member of the American Baptist continuing education staff, he served as part-time executive secretary of SACEM until 1987. In that year, Patricia Cremins, then on the continuing education staff of the University of Hartford, assumed the position. At the dinner honoring Dr. Gamble at the annual meeting in 1987, tribute was paid to his creative work with the Society. In 1989, it became necessary, for financial reasons, to discontinue the executive secretary position, at least temporarily, and to divide responsibilities among members of the Board. This plan has worked out well.

From early on, Canadian educators were involved in SACEM. Dr. Robert Oliver, Director of Continuing Education, Toronto School of Theology, became a member in the late-1960s and was elected to the Board in 1971, later serving as president in 1975–76. In 1980, a major consultation of Canadian leaders was called by the Coordinating Committee on Theological Education in Canada. It was decided that "SACEM should be the continuing foundation for an enlarged and enhanced effort in Canada which could extend the work already begun under its leadership."[4] By that time, however, Canadian participation in SACEM and its leadership had become a *de facto* reality and an annual meeting had been held at the Ontario Institute for Studies in Education (OISE) in Toronto in 1977.

Not all of SACEM's one hundred sixty-nine charter members retained their membership; nevertheless, the membership remained strong and fairly stable until the late-1980s when the

Society began to see a marked decline. Since the major financial support of the organization came from membership fees, the decline in membership created serious financial problems, which was a major consideration in the decision to discontinue the executive secretary position.

The low point in terms of membership, finances, and morale was in 1990. At that time, several decisions were made which had long-range implications for the organization and effected a turnaround in its membership and finances. The first involved not only discontinuance of the executive secretary position, but also the distribution of responsibilities among members of the Board. Fearful at first, the group soon began to feel new enthusiasm as it engaged in the new tasks, and a fresh *esprit de corps* developed.

A second decision was to seek closer relationships with denominational continuing education personnel. Included was the hope that denominational groups of continuing educators might be called together for meetings in conjunction with the SACEM annual meetings. This plan worked well; concomitantly, membership began to grow and finances strengthen.

The dissemination of information has been one of the major services which SACEM has provided to its members and others through the years. For three years, the Committee on Continuing Education of the NCCDOM published compendious listings of continuing education programs. SACEM took over the project in 1972 and published study guides for five regions of the United States, which included information concerning program agencies, the kinds of continuing education programs they offered, and how to get in touch with them. Some fifty thousand were distributed each year. In 1976, a simpler format was adopted. The publication of the guides was discontinued in 1985.

When Connolly Gamble became executive secretary, he began publication of a newsletter which contained information about members' activities; listing of new members; and word of new relevant publications, including those by SACEM members. In 1983, the newsletter was replaced by *The Continuing Educator,* a journal that continues to provide substantive articles, reports of annual meeting presentations, and book reviews. Another information service which has been gaining increasing importance since its inception in recent years is a SACEM web page on the Internet.

The development of educational events for members, in addition to the annual meeting, is another service provided by the organization. In 1972, a seminar on "The Effects of Justice, Liberation, and Development for Continuing Education for Ministry" was held. Between 1976 and 1978 there were four seminars on "Motivation for Continuing Education" in several regions of the United States that involved members of NOCERCC in the planning committee. In 1978, an event entitled "New Perspectives on Adulthood" took place. Sessions for new practitioners in continuing education have been held in connection with recent SACEM annual meetings, both to orient them to SACEM and to provide basic training for their work.

Another major activity of SACEM has been support of research by its members and the fostering of research by others in accord with its fourth basic purpose. Attention will be given to that activity in connection with a broader discussion of research.

The SACEM has actively pursued connections with other organizations devoted to continuing education for ministry. The officers and executive secretary of SACEM have maintained active contact with a number of these organizations. They include the Association of Clinical Pastoral Education; Association of Theological Schools; Action-training Coalition; Ecumenical Continuing Education Team; Association for Creative Change; and others.

Perhaps the most significant of these contacts has been with the National Organization for Continuing Education of Roman Catholic Clergy (NOCERCC).[5] To that organization we now turn. Its founding in 1973 was one of the landmark events in the continuing education for ministry movement.

National Organization for the Continuing Education of Roman Catholic Clergy

As with SACEM, NOCERCC did not appear on the scene full blown; significant antecedents led to its formation. Vatican II had seen and enunciated a new vision of the church, which led to profound changes in the church's organizational life. Out of that ferment, two organizations were formed in the United States which were to have significant impact on the continuing education movement: the National Council of Catholic Bishops (NCCB) in 1966, and the National Federation of Priests Councils (NFPC) in 1968.

In 1972, the NCCB issued "The Program of Continuing Education for Priests" which outlined the importance of continuing education for priests; urged each diocese to appoint a director of continuing education, and recommended the formation of a national organization to coordinate continuing education developments. Also in that year, the NFPC charged its own continuing education committee to prepare for a national meeting to form an ongoing organization. Interestingly, the leaders of both groups have insisted that the occurrence of the two events in the same year was purely coincidental.

In February, 1973, more than one hundred diocesan directors of continuing education and others met at the University of Notre Dame and, following serious discussion, decided to form an organization on the spot, adopted bylaws, and elected a Board and officers. Thus, NOCERCC became a reality.

The first president was the Reverend Joseph Voor of the Louisville Archdiocese. Early in his presidency, Fr. Voor contacted SACEM and was elected to its Board 1973–1976. In a personal letter to this writer, Fr. Voor said, "My involvement with SACEM was my first venture into ecumenism as called for by Vatican II and really helped me to realize that we are brothers in Christ."

Thus began a lively contact, which continued for a number of years. Dr. Gamble attended the NOCERCC Board, at their invitation, nine of his ten years as executive secretary; NOCERCC president, the Reverend Jim Dunning, met with SACEM in 1977, and conversations began which led to a joint meeting of the two boards in 1978. After the mid-1980s, contact between the two organizations waned, probably more through preoccupation with their own affairs than any explicit intent. SACEM minutes reflect at several points a desire to resume the contact.

Striking similarities have existed between the two organizations. Both have held annual meetings focused on relevant themes. In fact, the lists of meeting subjects addressed at the meetings of the two organizations are so similar that, with substitution of certain clerical terms, they could be interchangeable between the two groups! Both have published newsletters regularly. Both have struggled to maintain steady membership numbers, although because of the structure of the organization in relation to the dioceses, maintaining memberships has perhaps been easier for NOCERCC. In 1998, NOCERCC reported membership of one hundred fifty-three United States dioceses from among one hundred seventy-seven. Opening the organization to representatives from religious communities and retreat centers has added to the membership potential. The parallel continues with NOCERCC employment of a part-time executive director, the Reverend James Dunning, in 1979. However, in the case of NOCERCC, the position has become full time while being eliminated from the SACEM.

The Adult Education Movement

One antecedent is common to both SACEM and NOCERCC—the adult education movement. Perhaps it would be more apt to refer to it as "fertile soil" rather than as "antecedent." With roots in Europe, the adult education movement in the United States began in the late nineteenth century with the Chautauqua Movement, the YMCA, Extension Services of Land Grant Universities, and other agencies and movements. By the 1960s the movement had become widespread in the United States and Canada; millions of adults were involved in educational programs; and departments of adult education established in many major universities. Seminal leaders in this period, such as Malcolm Knowles at Boston University and North Carolina State University, Alan Knox at Columbia University, Cyril Houle at the University of Chicago, and Alan Tough at the Ontario Institute for Studies in Education (OISE) in Toronto had considerable influence on the continuing education for ministry movement. They presented papers at consultations, leaders in the movement studied with them, and their books and articles were widely read. In addition, their work fed the movement indirectly through their influence within the wider adult education movement. In short, the continuing education for ministry movement would have been inconceivable aside from the adult education movement.

Research

From very early in the continuing education for ministry movement until the present, research has played a significant role. Dr. Gamble's 1960 study was the first significant effort. In 1964, the Ministers Life and Casualty Insurance Company cosponsored with the NCCDOM the "Clergy Support Study." The Study was repeated in 1969, but this time included additional questions concerning continuing education. The responses were analyzed and reported by the Ministry Studies Board.

In 1965, the Association of Theological Schools and the NCC-DOM jointly created the Ministry Studies Board (MSB) and at the beginning in 1966, Dr. Edgar Mills became director. Until 1972, when it was merged with the NCCDOM, the Board carried out a significant amount of research, much of which was published in books and documents which had major impact on the movement. One such book was *Stress in the Ministry* by Mills and John Koval, 1971. Another was *Ex-Pastors: Why Men Leave the Parish Ministry.*[6] Between 1967 and 1969, the MSB also published twelve issues of a monograph series entitled "Ministry Studies." The MSB, with Dr. Mills's leadership, provided sound, scientifically based social research. Its demise was a loss to the field.

From the beginning, SACEM has had an active committee on research. It has supported research by SACEM members, as well as promoting relevant research by others, including doctoral candidates. Research supported by SACEM has fallen largely into several categories—participation of clergy in continuing education, both the degree of participation and the settings; the effect of their participation; and the needs that clergy experience related to continuing education.

One of the major research projects carried out by SACEM was focused on needs assessment instruments and processes and will be discussed below. In 1984, a major study was made of continuing education involvement of some fifty-four hundred clergy in twelve denominations. A study was made of clergy who had earned the Doctor of Ministry degree, the results of which were reported to the annual meeting in 1982. More recent studies include continuing education in colleague groups and spiritual growth needs of clergy in midlife. Tracing two major strands of development will complete our survey of continuing education: (1) the agencies which have provided resources services, primarily programs; and (2) individuals as they have engaged in their own continuing education.

Educational Resource Agencies

Denominational Judicatories

In the 1960s and 1970s, national denominational agencies provided a substantial number of program opportunities, but many fewer since then. One of the pioneering denominational programs was the Young Pastors Schools, sponsored by the United Presbyterian Church, USA, in which clergy, during the first few years after seminary, participated in a succession of three five-day seminars, the third with their spouses. There was a great deal of openness and freedom to examine the personal and professional issues they had encountered in this entry period. The Lutheran Church of America sponsored five-day seminars in various parts of the country, providing opportunities for clergy to engage in theological reflection in a small-group setting in which personal and relational issues could be examined openly. In 1987, NOCERCC sponsored a series of seminars, "A Shepherd's Care: Reflections on the Changing Role of the Pastor."

The Ecumenical Continuing Education Team should be mentioned in connection with denominational agencies. In the 1960s and 1970s, the major denominations all had at least one full-time staff person in continuing education, in a few cases, more than one. These staff members were drawn together in various groups, such as the NCCDOM Continuing Education Committee and SACEM. However, in the late-1960s, they decided to form their own group meeting which convened annually and allowed them to share ideas, to shape their own learning events, and to support each other in what was sometimes a lonely job. As long as denominations had full-time staff members, the team remained strong. As staffs shrank and many had multiple responsibilities, the team met less frequently and with fewer participants. A small group gathered in conjunction with the SACEM annual meeting in 1987; the last note of a meeting recorded in the SACEM minutes was in 1989. However, with the renewed relation of SACEM to denominational continuing education staffs, contact among this group is now increasing once again.

Gradually denominational programming has shifted to middle judicatories, but this has not reversed the trend toward a reduction of programming. A few judicatories, such as the United Methodist North Indiana Annual Conference, still offer a full range of opportunities. One reason for the reduction in program sponsorship has been the shifting of available funds to scholarship assistance to enable clergy to participate in continuing education programs of their own choosing.

Seminaries

In the beginning of the movement, seminary programs multiplied rapidly. Most seminaries of major Protestant denominations employed full- or part-time directors and almost without exception had faculty committees of continuing education. As the Doctor of Ministry degree has gained prominence and many seminary budgets have become more limited, programming has gradually waned. There are, however, seminaries that have continued to provide full, well-rounded programs: Princeton Theological Seminary; Duke Divinity School; Garrett-Evangelical Seminary; Toronto School of Theology; and others.

Several institutions which offer active continuing education programs fall into this category, but with a difference. Two are Auburn Theological Seminary in New York City and Hartford Seminary Foundation in Connecticut. Auburn has not offered degrees since it moved to the campus of Union in New York City in 1939; Hartford offers a limited degree program, but no longer offers a basic seminary degree. Both agencies sponsor continuing education based on research and analysis of the needs of the church and its ministry. A third institution in this category is the Scarritt-Bennett Center in Nashville. For many years, as Scarritt College, it had been a degree-granting institution primarily for lay professional workers in the United Methodist Church. Early in the 1970s, it began a transition, first with the establishment of a Center of

Continuing Education directed by Dr. Robert Reber; finally ending its degree program in 1980, it has become a center sponsored by the Women's Division of United Methodist Board of Global Ministries, which offers learning events for both clergy and laity

Most seminary programming has been designed to draw the participant to the school for a period of time; however, some schools have made provision for faculty to meet with groups in the field. Another exception to residence programs deserves special mention. There are a few schools that simply provide enrollees with books on library loan, accompanied by a study guide. The user enrolls in a particular guide and books are sent to him or her successively, according to the guide's design. The original program was developed by Dr. Gamble at Union in Richmond; at its height, it made available some seventy-five guides. The other major program was at Perkins School of Theology, Southern Methodist University. The Perkins program made it possible for a study group to contract for the use of a guide and at the end of the period of study, Perkins would provide a professor to meet with the group for a day.

The Doctor of Ministry Degree

One of the pioneer ventures in continuing education in the early 1960s was the Doctor of Scientific Theology degree (an interesting title!) and a comparable Masters degree at San Francisco Theological Seminary, designed primarily by Dr. Henry Adams. The degree was promoted as a break with traditional theological degree programs and shifted the arena of learning from academy to the parish or other venues of ministry. One of Henry Adams's frequently expressed phrases was "learning ministry from the practice of ministry." From the beginning, a backlog of persons waited for admission into one of these degree programs.

Other seminaries quickly saw the potential of such a degree programs and announced what came to be known as the Doctor of Ministry degree. At a consultation of United Methodist continuing educators in 1973 Dr. Marvin Taylor, then a staff member of the ATS, announced that 70 percent of ATS accredited seminaries either were offering or had definite plans to offer the degree.

Enrollees increased along with the number of programs. In 1988, 6,077 were enrolled; in 1992, 7,274; in 1998, 8,356. As of this writing, 113 accredited schools offer a Doctor of Ministry degree. [7]

Among continuing educators there has been ongoing discussion of the value of the Doctor of Ministry degree as continuing education. Critics claim that the temptation of status resulting from the title of "doctor" interferes with the educational value of such programs. Others assert that once one is enrolled in a program, one finds that the possibility of adjusting the learning program to changing needs is too limited, and the financial cost is often too heavy. On the other hand, advocates reply that the programs are helpful because they focus on questions of professional practice, encourage planned continuing education to reach well-defined goals, and, in most cases, utilize peer group approaches that often become an important means of support for participants. Whatever the pros and cons, it is obvious that the Doctor of Ministry degree continues to attract an increasing number of clergy for at least a portion of their continuing education.

Independent Agencies

Independent institutions and retreat centers have served a relatively small percentage of those seeking continuing education. Yet, some of these offer the most creative programming. A primary instance was the Institute for Advanced Pastoral Studies, mentioned above as one of the early pioneer institutions. Another, although with some denominational affiliation, was the Disciples Divinity House at Yale, directed by Parker Rossman. Still a third was the Interpreter's House at Lake Junaluska, North Carolina, directed by Carlyle Marney. These three programs have gone by the wayside partly because the competition for warm bodies and continuing education dollars has increased and partly because they were too dependent upon a charismatic individual for their survival.

Others remain strong and well rounded. Kirkridge, located in the beautiful Delaware River Valley of eastern Pennsylvania, has since its founding, offered creative and cutting edge continuing education for both clergy and laity. The Alban Institute, in Washington, D.C., features experimental programming, the results

31

of which have been written, published, and offered to the church. The Institute has maintained a staff of program leaders available to assist groups wanting to make use of the programs it has developed. Still another is Pendle Hill near Philadelphia, with a strong Quaker history and tradition, offering both short-term and semester study periods. Used widely by members of the Society of Friends, it has also provided an unusual opportunity for clergy and laity of other denominations, including Roman Catholics, to experience continuing education designed to touch both mind and spirit. There are other such centers.

Associations of Program Centers

Perhaps the most widely used program agencies in this category have been centers for Clinical Pastoral Education (CPE). Initiated by Anton Boisen and others in the early 1900s, these programs were originally based almost entirely in medical institutions and were primarily for the benefit of seminarians. Gradually, however, more and more centers became oriented to the needs of those out of seminary and engaged in ministry. Over the years, clinical pastoral educators and centers had congealed into four basic groupings, but in 1967, came together to form the Association of Clinical Pastoral Education (ACPE) which has remained the central agency for furtherance of the movement and accreditation of educators and centers. Records have not been kept by the Association of the total number of practicing church professionals in CPE programs at any one time, but they are known to be in the thousands. At the time of this writing, there are four hundred and eighty-one accredited centers almost all of which include enrollees who are engaged professionally in ministry. Although in the beginning the venue and focus of all programs was hospitals and other medical institutions, the range of institutions over the years has expanded greatly, including several in urban centers in which the primary venue is the parish.[8]

Spiritual Growth/Formation Centers

These will be discussed in connection with a shift in the perception of the nature of ministry described below.

Action Training Centers

In the 1960s many church leaders, including some continuing educators, believed that the church was not making an adequate response to the nation's social crises, especially in urban areas. One result was the establishment of what came to be known as action training centers. The training they provided, involved, among other things, a "plunge" into deteriorated areas of cities. Participants were given a small amount of money and sent out on their own for several days, then to return to reflect on the experience and its implications for ministry. At the height of this movement there were some twenty centers located in various parts of the United States. In 1968, at the instigation of some of their directors and several interdenominational church groups, Protestant and Roman Catholic, a meeting was held at which the action training coalition was formed. Gradually as the church turned its attention to other concerns, the number of centers decreased until at present, to this writer's knowledge, no programs remain—except, possibly, at New York Theological Seminary in New York City where work of this nature continues.

Many agencies not mentioned here have offered continuing education opportunities to persons in ministry: colleges and universities, public libraries, human relations training agencies, such as those which sprang from the National Training Laboratories, and others.

Individual Involvement in Continuing Education

We turn now to the second major strand of development: the individual's own involvement in continuing education. Before looking at this matter statistically, it is important to see it in the larger context of a shift in the understanding of the nature of ministry which has taken place within the period of this survey.

Early in the 1960s much attention was given by leaders in continuing education to the concept of ministry as a profession. Leaders in adult education, such as Cyril Houle at the University of Chicago, were focusing on the nature of the continuing education of professionals. It was natural to think also of continuing education for ministry in those terms. In 1968 Abingdon Press published a book by James Glasse entitled *Profession: Minister.* In that same year, Edgar Mills presented a major paper on ministry as a profession to a United Methodist consultation on continuing education. In my book, *Competent Ministry: A Guide to Effective Continuing Education,*[9] published five years later, I interpreted competence largely in terms of professional practice based on the historic understanding of the professional as one who masters a particular area of knowledge and skill and makes that expertise available to a particular segment of society.

The concept of career is closely related to the concept of profession and in this period, much attention was given to the dynamics of ministerial career, informed by such career psychologists as Dr. Donald Soper at Columbia University. One outcome of this concern was the career stage seminars developed by the United Presbyterian Church, USA, the United Methodist Church, and others.

It was out of this focus on career that a group of agencies known as Church Career Development Centers were established. Dr. Edward Golden, Director of the United Presbyterian Interboard Office of Personnel Service, envisioned "...the possibility of career centers where testing and counseling services could enable ministers to take charge of their own careers and make more informed career decisions."[10] A pilot center was established in Princeton, New Jersey, with Dr. Thomas Brown, a trained career counselor (later president of SACEM) as director. The project was successful and became the first of a group of Church Career Development Centers across the United States. These centers were brought together in the Church Career Development Council (CCDC) in 1969 in Philadelphia. The Council had both denominational and center directors as members and became the primary agency to further the movement and to accredit both the centers and their counseling staffs.

The centers have served the purpose not only of providing counsel concerning future career direction, but also of enabling participants, especially those who had decided to remain in a ministerial career, to develop more effective personal continuing education programs. In fact, the American Baptist Centers for Ministry, which were members of the CCDC, had individuals in the same staff who did career counseling and others available for continuing education counseling. "Ministry Development Council" has replaced "Church Career Development Council" as the name of the umbrella organization, reflecting to a degree the shift about to be noted.

Over time, the emphasis on ministry as a profession lessened. A substantial number of church leaders, including continuing educators, began to fear that the true nature of ministry was being eroded by professionalism and that the emphasis on career and career dynamics was leading to careerism. (In this writer's view, nothing in the true understanding of either profession or career leads necessarily in that direction. Rather, the shift probably was fostered more by increased membership and competitiveness among clergy.)

As focus on profession waned, a new emphasis on spirituality in ministry began to emerge. This shift was probably caused by the rise in a new, general interest across the churches in spiritual growth, or spiritual formation.

In response to this shift, a number of centers and programs have been established, which focus on spiritual formation. One of the first and most prominent is Shalem in Washington, D.C., directed by Dr. Tilden Edwards, an early member of SACEM and its Board. Epiphany Associates was established in 1979, with centers in both Pittsburgh and Indianapolis. The Academy of Spiritual Formation is sponsored by the United Methodist Church with centers in Alabama, California, and Wisconsin. There are others, some sponsored by Roman Catholics, some by Protestants, but all ecumenically open. No figures are available for the number of clergy who have participated in this group of programs, but they would be in the thousands.

Numerically, participation of clergy in their own continuing education is difficult to estimate. However, there is little question that over the period covered in this survey, the numbers have increased dramatically. The Clergy Support Study of 1973 showed that 34 percent of those responding had taken part in a continuing education event of at least three days within the previous two years; Dr. Gamble's 1982 study showed that 75 percent of those responding had engaged in learning away from home in the year surveyed. While the figures are not exactly comparable, they show an encouraging increase. What the figures would be today is impossible to determine, but it is likely that they are continuing to increase.

In *Competent Ministry*, I defined continuing education as "an individual's personally designed learning program which begins when formal education ends and continues throughout a career and beyond. An unfolding process, it links together study and reflection and participation in organized group events."[11] When continuing education is viewed broadly in this way, the question of the number of those participating changes. I continue to believe that while the number who enroll each year in one kind of continuing education program or another may be quite high, the number who engage in a well-planned program of learning designed to meet their needs is much lower. Exceptions to this, of course, would be those enrolled in a Doctor of Ministry degree or in a structured learning program such as CPE, but even in those cases, it would be true only for the time in the program, although it is hoped that patterns of planned learning established in such programs might continue after they have ended.

One organization that has urged the planning of a personal program of learning for its members is the Academy of Parish Clergy. Dr. Granger Westberg wrote an article published in *The Christian Century* in the mid-1960s entitled "Why Not an Academy of Parish Clergy." He had proposed an organization founded on the pattern of the Academy of General Practice for physicians and in 1968 in Houston, Texas, such an academy was organized. Based on the concept that the clergyperson should take responsibility for his or her own continuing education, rather than being dependent on schools or denominational agencies, the Academy developed suggestions and procedures for enabling this to happen, including a needs assessment process to be conducted with the help of a chosen colleague in ministry and in the setting of the congregation. The Academy has never claimed a large percentage of the total number of ordained clergy as members, but has been a distinct and important voice in the continuing education movement.

Needs Assessment

As the idea that continuing education should be understood as the individual's participation in a personally planned learning program became more widespread, it was evident that it was important that an individual's learning program be developed on the basis of well-defined learning needs. Accordingly, groups and individuals began to develop needs assessment instruments and procedures which were quite widely used in the 1970s and 1980s. One of the most ambitious and extensive research projects carried out by SACEM focused on analysis of the various needs assessment instruments to determine which were the most effective. Among other things, it was determined that the most beneficial were those in which the clergyperson was the sole beneficiary. It was also determined that the degree of follow-through, once needs were determined, was enhanced by support of judicatory officials and colleagues.

The constraints of a chapter such as this have required that many developments in continuing education for ministry be either shortchanged or omitted. It should be realized also, that while much of the above has focused on organizations, the real history of the movement has been in the creative and devoted effort given to it by many, many individuals.

When Shakespeare in *The Tempest* has Antonio say that "what's past is prologue," it is obvious that he is not referring to affairs such as we have described here. Nevertheless, one might hope that his words apply. It is fitting that this chapter come at the first of this book, not only to provide background, but also to make evident what rich soil has been prepared for future growth. And, indeed, the chapters which lie ahead will show what new life and energy—and new horizons—are now present in this movement. Surely, "what's past is prologue."

References

1. Published by Union Theological Seminary, Richmond, Virginia.

2. From this point, when the term "continuing education" is used, it denotes "continuing education for ministry," unless otherwise noted.

3. Unidentified quotation, p. 5, is from "The SACEM Story," 1987, an unpublished paper written by Dr. Connolly Gamble. This extensive paper, commissioned and distributed by SACEM, has been an invaluable resource in the preparation of this chapter and is a significant document for SACEM's history from its inception to 1987. Used by Dr. Gamble's permission.

4. Ibid., p. 44.

5. Much of the information concerning NOCERCC is taken from Joseph M. White, "A Work Never Finished," an unpublished document circulated by NOCERCC, 1997.

6. Edgar Mills, Gerald Judd, and Genevieve Burch. *Ex-Pastors: Why Men Leave the Parish Ministry* (Pilgrim, Ohio: Pilgrim Press, 1970).

7. Figures from a personal report to the writer by the ATS office, June, 1999.

8. Charles E. Hall, *Head and Heart*, Journal of Pastoral Care Publications, 1992, p. 164. This book is a helpful resource for the history of the movement, written by one who was, for many years, executive of the ACPE.

9. Mark Rouch, *Competent Ministry: A Guide to Effective Continuing Education* (Nashville: Abingdon Press, 1974). See especially chapter 3.

10. From an unpublished paper, "CCDC: The Beginning" by the Reverend James Gunn, written for the Church Career Development Council, 1984. At the time of writing, Gunn was the Executive for Professional Church Leadership, the National Council of Churches (formerly NCCDOM).

11. Mark Rouch, *Competent Ministry*, pp. 16-17.

Chapter 2

Educating Out of the Future: Where Are We Headed in Continuing Theological Education?

Robert E. Reber

The ambiguity of this chapter's title is deliberate and expresses the ambivalence I have about the directions in which continuing and adult theological education programs seem to be heading. We can educate church leaders for the future or we can educate them without regard for the future and, therefore, find our efforts increasingly irrelevant and out of touch with life and ministry in the world and the church. We are, in fact, doing both. On the one hand, some programs take seriously what is emerging in the life of the world and the church and the implications that this has for continuing education. On the other hand, one can also identify programs that ignore what is ahead and focus only on the immediate, if pressing, demands of the present, resulting in a simplistic, short-term approach.

I remember well my first meeting of the Society for the Advancement of Continuing Education for Ministry (SACEM) in 1972. The opening address was given by the director of professional medical education of a leading medical school in this country. His thesis was: There is not a shred of evidence to suggest that mandatory continuing education of physicians leads to any qualitative difference in the practice of medicine. His comment continues to haunt me after twenty-five years, especially since some have sought through legislation to make continuing education mandatory, an effort that has been misguided and has failed for the most part. To a large extent, I think his judgment reflects the past and current state of much continuing education for religious professionals. In fact, a more recent study found that "70 to 75 percent of the members of three professions who participated in formal educational programs reported little or no change after the implementation of mandatory continuing education." The participants were physicians, health care professionals, and certified public accountants. Ronald Cervero says that "although mandatory continuing education is touted as an effective way to foster participation, the evidence shows a relatively weak effect" (Cervero, 1988, p. 73).

Twenty-one years ago, Mark Rouch, who for a number of years the national staff person at the Board of Higher Education and Ministry of the United Methodist Church and worked full time on continuing education for clergy, gave a lecture. The title of the address was "Continuing Education as a Subversive Activity." Mark maintained that "all education is, by its nature, subversive—continuing education no less than any other education. In fact, when true to itself, continuing education may be the most subversive of all." He said that our business is to subvert, "to destroy—in terms of the Latin root, to turn upside down—every fragmented, inadequate view of truth. Looked at another way, our business is to subvert every block to human growth in those persons for whom we have responsibility in education for ministry." Obviously, Mark's commitment to continuing education as a subversive activity is based on an assumption that continuing education for ministry can make a difference. I believe this also. That is why I have devoted much of my professional life to continuing theological education for clergy and laity.

However, I live constantly with the question: Are our efforts in continuing education for clergy and laity bringing about any qualitative difference in the lives of persons, and in the practice of ministry and mission in congregations and other diverse settings? We have a responsibility to ask ourselves this question. The answers may not be clear, and may be hard to get, but we owe it to ourselves to continue asking. Considerable resources have been made available by denominations, judicatories, seminaries, congregations, foundations, and individuals. The least that we can do is to be honest about what we know and do not know, or refuse to find out, and hold each other accountable.

Clearly, a tension exists between my ideal, following Rouch, that education subverts our inadequate understandings and the reality, described by Cervero and the keynote speaker, that continuing education has no measurable influence on performance. I ask you to keep this tension in mind as I address three questions in the remainder of this chapter:

- What is the current state of continuing theological education for clergy and laity?
- What should the future be?
- What are questions that we all need to struggle with?

My answers, of course, unavoidably will reflect my own experiences. Your perspective will be different and I invite you to keep your experiences in mind as we join in a dialogue about how to educate out of the future.

What Is the Current State of Continuing Theological Education for Clergy and Laity?

First, continuing theological education is still at a real disadvantage in the church's educational ecology. It is still not a part of the top educational priorities of most, if not all, denominations, judicatories, and seminaries in this country. In fact, recognition of its importance has been slipping in recent years. Consider that fifteen years ago most mainline denominations had a full-time staff person responsible for continuing education for ministry at the national level. Now only one, the Evangelical Lutheran Church in America, has a full-time person. In addition, directors of continuing education continue to be the last hired and the first to go at many seminaries. They are probably the most marginalized group within the institution, and often the only staff members whose courses must pay for themselves. Continuing education for clergy and laity is the least subsidized educational enterprise in all of seminary education and church education in general.

Second, the Lone Ranger image continues to dominate the field of continuing education. We are still asked to believe that pastors or lay leaders, who come to one day to two week events offered by our institutions and centers, will bring about change, both personally and corporately. We expect that an individual can return to home base and make a difference. Lack of accountability, recognition, and reward for participation in continuing education for clergy and laity further reinforces this Lone Ranger image.

Third, the offerings in continuing education are becoming shorter and shorter across the country. Three years ago, there were several centers at which five-day programs were the norm. Today, most programs are limited to forty-eight hours or less. Longer programs do not guarantee that participants learn more. However, I am convinced that longer programs do offer a greater possibility for sustainable growth. There are many forces that encourage shorter programs: lack of recognition and reward, quick-fix mentality, resistance to give much time, family pressures where both spouses are working outside the home, and so forth.

Fourth, continuing education offerings tend to focus more on the "how to" and promise practical helps. This is what folks will buy and is in part driven by pressing needs and a desire to make an immediate difference in facing different situations, personally, in the congregation, and to some extent, in the society. On the one hand, the demand for readily applicable programs is quite understandable and deserves a sympathetic hearing. All of us are driven by a sense of immediacy and want programs we attend to make an immediate difference in some aspect of our professional and personal lives. On the other hand, a dangerous and highly functionalist view of church life and ministry may result. Serious questions about the nature and purpose of the church, ministry, and mission must be addressed, but require more substantive reflection and offer less immediate gratification. In short programs, issues of how people learn and how systems change are necessarily ignored. So, caught in this cycle, our offerings get narrower and narrower in focus and, in the end, we cannot deliver what we promise: a qualitative difference in the lives of persons and their practice of ministry and mission.

Fifth, in continuing education for clergy and laity we tend to offer what we think is best for the constituencies to be served. By "we," I mean directors of continuing education, seminary faculty, and entrepreneurs. We should offer what our experience, study, scholarship, and commitment tell us may be best in terms of leadership, content, and practice. Delivery systems usually mean people

come to the centers for relatively short periods of time to participate in programs that we publicize. Sometimes we go out there,
that is to local communities where groups of clergy and church
professionals gather and occasionally include laypeople. It is the
exception to the rule, however, when representatives of the constituencies to be served are involved in planning particular programs that are to be offered. Most likely, this does not happen
because nobody wants to pay for the staff time to do it and we do
not see the planning process itself as educational. It is probably the
major reason why programs are canceled.

Sixth, much of continuing education is market driven. What will
"sell" is given top priority. This often comes from the demand that
program income cover not only direct costs but institutional overhead in terms of staff and facilities. I believe it is accurate to say
that continuing education for clergy and laity is the only educational enterprise that is often asked to "pay its own way." With this
limitation, it is tough to be creative, to take risks, to be inclusive, in
terms of class and race, to move beyond "big" names (who usually
demand big fees), and to wrestle with what will make a qualitative
difference in the lives of persons, institutions, and societies.

Seventh, most people who spend time professionally directing
continuing education centers for clergy and laity do so by accident,
circumstance, and surprise. Some see it as a calling, but many consider it a way station on the road to something else. Over the years
this has changed somewhat because of the work of professional
organizations like SACEM or the National Organization for
Continuing Education of Roman Catholic Clergy. Also, the work of
the American Association of Adult and Continuing Education has
sought to bring standards of training and professionalism to the
field. Auburn Theological Seminary's Colleague Program for New
Directors of Continuing Theological Education certainly indicates
an eagerness by seminaries and independent centers and their new
directors of continuing education to change this. Funded by the
Henry Luce Foundation, this program provides on-the-job training
program for new directors over a period of eighteen months.
Participants come to four three-day modules and work intentionally on different issues in their job settings. Even though denomi-

nations seem to be giving less importance to continuing education for clergy, some seminaries and independent centers are not. There is an eagerness to have trained and professional directors. However, it is also clear that many places have a long way to go in developing mission statements and policies that place continuing theological education for clergy and laity at the heart of institutional life, and taking responsibility to partner with clergy and laity for at least forty years of ongoing education!

What Should the Future of Continuing Education for Clergy and Laity Be?

My comments about the current state of continuing education for clergy and laity tend to be rather bleak, and a Northeast bias is evident. In relation to each of the seven points I made above, there are exceptions and signs of hope. However, the generalizations still stand. We must move into the future, keeping in mind our current weaknesses and keeping alive our hope.

First and foremost, continuing education in the future must regain its "subversive" quality. It should seek to subvert our limited, fragmented, and distorted views of truth. It should take on seriously the theological task of faith seeking understanding. I do not mean this in any narrow academic sense, but in the larger sense of offering opportunities for pastors and laity to examine the life of faith from biblical, theological, historical, and missional perspectives. Education cannot be subversive unless it addresses the whole person and the context in which he or she lives, works and ministers; and invites persons into situations where learning and growth are possible.

Second, continuing education for ministry should be front and center in the life of denominations, congregations, theological centers, and seminaries. This requires a careful examination of mission statements and policies of our institutions. If it is merely an add-on, it will be a weak and insignificant enterprise. I think all of us are being challenged to see how we can be theological resource centers for the church and larger community. Yes, there is a primary responsibility for the education of clergy and church professionals at the Master of Divinity level, but also a serious mandate to consider what resources we might bring to bear in the ongoing education of clergy and laity. Much of higher education is already doing this. Our country went through a major change in the 1970s when, for the first time in our history, more people above the age of eighteen than below the age of eighteen became enrolled in educational institutions of all kinds. This is a major reason for the growth of adult and continuing education programs, in the context of higher education. Increasingly, a criterion for funding all sorts of schools may be, "To what extent does an institution serve the society on a lifelong basis?" Should we not bring that same criterion to bear on our own programs, as educational centers in the life of the church?

Third, ecumenical and inter-religious perspectives should inform our work in continuing education for clergy and laity. What opportunities are there for ecumenical and inter-religious collaboration? In my experience, they are almost endless. Ecumenical and inter-religious collaboration is vitally important to the future of continuing theological education. There are many reasons why we should *not* operate in isolation. We have a biblical and theological mandate to work toward, and manifest, the unity of the church and of humankind. Our parochialism betrays the gospel and mirrors rather than disputes the conditions of a fractured community, world, and church. If we believe that God wills the unity of the church and humankind, it should be evident in our work as directors of continuing theological education. We need to network with other churches, denominations, civic organizations, and educational institutions, in order to have a clearer picture of the particular communities in which we have been called to work; to avoid unnecessary duplication and expenditure of resources; to build stronger educational programs that make a difference in the lives of laity and clergy; and to give us contacts and more effective ownership on the part of constituencies we wish to serve.

Where I work, we take this with utmost seriousness. At present, we collaborate with thirty-three different organizations and institutions in planning and carrying out our educational programs. I had no idea of the number until someone recently asked me this question and I sat down and counted them. We are collaborating with other seminaries, ecumenical and inter-religious organizations, universities, denominations, judicatories, congregations, and independent centers. In many cases, we have taken the initiative and, in others, our partners approached us. When an idea for a program pops into our heads, we ask, "Who else can we work with?" In a recent evaluation of Auburn's educational programs, the outside evaluator said, "My sense is that the central idea of Auburn is to serve as a broker among the many competing stakeholders in the ongoing societal conversations about the role that religion and spirituality can play in creating a better world for all peoples. In being a broker across multiple differences, Auburn sees that education is both a struggle for meaning and power."

I do not tell you this because Auburn is the best example, or something that anybody else should imitate. Each situation is different. I contend, however, that none of us can afford to operate as the Lone Ranger, and somehow think that we can sit in our offices, institutions, or centers, and decide what is best for the church, or for the larger community. We need partners. If you undertake the work of collaboration, doors will open that you never dreamed of and, only, a few will close.

We must be willing to risk with partners for the future. I believe that God is calling us to work, to educate, across multiple differences in our communities and world. This may mean with other denominations; with persons and organizations outside the church; with different religious communities, that may be Jewish, Muslim, Hindu, or Buddhist; with different racial/ethnic and social/economic groups; with persons of different sexual orientations; and with different age groups, be they young, middle aged, or older adults. It is also time for us to come out of our religious hideaways and witness in public life to what our religious faith means and stands for. The stakes are too high in civil society to back off from the public square. The quality of life, of civil discourse, even the survival of the planet, depends upon all of us doing our part educationally to bring about change in people's lives, in our churches, and the society at large.

Fourth, a systemic approach is required to move beyond the apathy (sometimes resistance) and lack of valuing the ongoing education of clergy and laity. Appreciation, affirmation, and reward are critical to changing the current climate. In a recent report adopted by the Evangelical Lutheran Church in America, "Life long Learning and Development for Faithful Leaders," there is a commitment to doing this:

> The church envisions...an environment in which intentional continued learning and development are valued and expected, and the rostered [ordained ministers, associates in ministry, deaconesses, and diaconal ministers] leaders enjoy supportive partnerships with their congregations or agencies, colleagues, and the synodical and churchwide expressions of this church. (Evangelical Lutheran Church in America, 1997, p. 2)

To what extent are we serving clergy and increasingly laity on a lifelong basis? Should this be based only on the ability to pay? We hope not. Again, this is a policy and resource issue that needs careful attention.

Many pastors and laypeople are looking for a structure to be provided in which they can engage in continuing education. Many are not going to take a sustained disciplined approach in their learning on their own. Those of us who provide continuing education opportunities need to take a more serious look at this matter. This was one of the key things identified in the Doctor of Ministry Study that Auburn and Hartford seminaries carried out. Clergy in Doctor of Ministry programs tended to view short-term workshops, seminars and courses that are picked by using a shotgun approach as unsatisfactory. They seek in Doctor of Ministry programs "an ordered progression of activities and a discipline that they find it difficult to provide for themselves in the midst of a demanding full-time job" (Carroll and Wheeler, 1987, p. 36). We who are directors of non-degree programs need to take note: Doctor of Ministry participants represent a sizable group of clergy who "find an ordered curriculum, the opportunity to submit work for evaluation, and the discipline of deadlines and requirements, to be important elements in continuing professional learning. Some of these features can be provided outside a degree context as well as within it" (Carroll and Wheeler, p. 36).

Fifth, I believe that continuing education for ministry must involve both clergy and laity. After all, we are all involved in ministry together and need to offer educational programs that inform, enrich, and enable the ministry of all God's people. Again, there will need to be programs that focus on particular needs of clergy, whether this is in worship, preaching, or other areas of professional development. This is also true of laity. For example, Auburn Seminary carries out extensive programs with health care professionals, lawyers and judges, middle managers, and chief executive officers of corporations. It has programs that help laity from many different walks of life consider and reflect upon what it means to live out one's faith in the workplace, at home, and in the larger community.

To involve different constituencies in continuing education for ministry clearly means that the delivery systems have to change. Programs offered Monday through Friday from 9 to 5 are increasingly unattractive for clergy and even more so for laity. If we are to involve members of both groups, the times and days we choose and the formats we follow will have to vary. We also need to cultivate greater flexibility about where we hold programs. Everything will not take place on our turf or in our facilities. In collaboration with others, we may need to offer educational programs in closer proximity to where people work and live.

Finally, there is the whole arena of electronic technology and the super information highway. More and more pastors and laypeople have personal computers with CD-ROMs. They are looking for educational programs that they can use in individual and group settings. Two examples of organizations producing quality materials on CDs are the American Bible Society and the Harvard Center for World Religions. We already have the "electronic church," teleconferencing, and on-line programs on different topics that allow interaction between teacher and student. Those of us in more traditional religious institutions need to be aware of these developments or we will be left behind.

I think the future of continuing education for clergy and laity should mean paying serious attention to the teaching/learning enterprise, no matter what the subject or topic is. How do people learn? How are needs and interests assessed and tested? How does change take place in persons or institutions? What does it mean for the congregation or local church to understand itself as the agency of education? Who is an effective teacher? If learning means change in knowledge, understanding, attitudes, values, and skills, what has to be part of the teaching/learning transaction? There are no easy answers, but we do know some things from research on how adults learn. We need to experiment with different models and evaluate our efforts.

Despite the serious obstacles we face, I am convinced that continuing education for ministry can make a qualitative difference in the lives of individuals and in the churches more generally. I want to pose some questions that I hope we can struggle with together.

Questions for Our Future Work in Continuing Education

(1) Why are clergy reading less and less in all areas? This seems to be true in theological disciplines as well as in reading novels, biographies, poetry, plays, social and political analyses. Why are they giving less and less time to ongoing educational opportunities that have a sustained educational thrust over time?

(2) How might we involve clergy and laity who don't participate in continuing education, whether in structured programs or their own independent study? We tend to get the committed. What do we do about those who are hard to reach?

(3) What can we do to move beyond the undue emphasis on the quick-fixes or "how-tos" of church life? Short workshops on fixing sermons, educational programs, church growth, and spirituality abound. I even saw a workshop advertised on "Preaching in Sound Bytes."

(4) How might we focus more on critical issues about the quality of life on this planet and in the life of the church? So few of our educational offerings take up questions about racism, sexuality, the feminist movement, the pollution of the environment, the quality of health care for all, the ecumenical

      movement, and the growing religious pluralism in American society. Each of us could add issues to this list.

(5) What do we need to do to strengthen and sustain ecumenical collaboration? What are the theological and ecclesial issues that we should be addressing? How might our ecumenical commitments really be incarnational, that is, rooted in reality, in what we do day in and day out?

The future of continuing education for ministry depends on changing the climate, the expectations, the values, the rewards for lifelong learning in the church and the church's educational institutions. We must engage in strategic planning to accomplish this daunting agenda. Recognition of the importance of ongoing learning must permeate every area of professional, denominational, and community life. We cannot just say it is good for others; we must demonstrate in our own lives our involvement in continuing education for ministry and mission, and our willingness to risk and take on the difficult issues facing us in the church and our society. Walter Brueggemann says that "theological education [and I would add continuing theological education] is not about reasonableness and skill and management, all of which may be necessary. Rather, it is about power, insight, vision, courage and freedom of another kind, wrought precisely against the rulers of this age. It is now a question in the church whether faith and resources are available for a radically different reading of reality" (Brueggemann, 1987, pp. 13-14).

Perhaps it would be helpful to end with a story from Robert Greenleaf's childhood, which is mentioned in his book, *Servant Leadership*. It is a story about a dogsled race in his hometown. Most of the boys in the race had big sleds and several dogs. Greenleaf, only five years old, had a small sled and one dog. The course was one mile staked out on the lake. As the race started, the more powerful contenders quickly left small Greenleaf behind. In fact, he hardly looked like he was in the race at all. All went well with the rest until about half-way around, the team that was second started to pass the team that was in the lead. They came too close and the dogs got into a fight. Soon, the other dog teams joined in and little Greenleaf could see one seething mass of kids, sleds, and dogs about one-half mile away. So, he gave them all wide berth and was the only one who finished the race. Looking back as an adult, he concludes: "As I reflect on the many vexing problems and the stresses of our times that complicate their solutions, this simple scene from long ago comes vividly to mind and I draw the obvious moral: no matter how difficult the challenge or how impossible or hopeless the task may seem, if you are reasonably sure of your course—just keep going!" (Greenleaf, 1977, p. 175) If we really believe that we may contribute to the lifelong education of clergy and laity, the unity of the church and humankind, and the quality of life on this planet, we must keep going.

References

J. W. Carroll, and B. G. Wheeler. "Doctor of Ministry Program: History, Summary of Findings, and Recommendations" in *Theological Education*, Spring, 1987, pp. 7-51.

R. M. Cervero. *Effective Continuing Education for Professionals*. San Francisco: Jossey-Bass, 1988.

Evangelical Lutheran Church in America, Division for Ministry. "Lifelong Learning and Development for Faithful Leaders, 1997. "

R. K. Greenleaf. *Servant Leadership: A Journey into the Nature of Legitimate Power and Greatness*. New York: Paulist Press, 1977.

Chapter 3

Providers: Then and Now

William Lord

In 1963, I graduated with a B.D., was ordained, and posted to be the pastor of four small churches in rural Manitoba, about two hours' drive north and west of Winnipeg. My innate curiosity meant that I was destined to be a lifelong learner, and I started early. On the suggestion of one of my early mentors, I took out a subscription to the journal *Theology Today*, because he believed that it was a good thing to keep up with developments in theology. One day, as I sat in my study reading a recent copy, I noticed an ad for a continuing education self-directed reading course from Union Seminary in Richmond, Virginia. Hence, my first connection with a provider of continuing education was born. However, I was not one of their easier customers. With a snail mail service that was no speedier then than now, no sooner had I received the mailing of the course outline, with questions and the books from the library, than they were due back in Richmond. In a letter of special pleading, I asked Connolly Gamble Jr., the Director of Continuing Education, for an extension on the book loan from three weeks to six. As a supportive provider, he made an exception for a student in the hinterland. As an unintended consequence, I learned a lesson about the importance of responding to the learner's needs and context. Only now, many years later, and having crossed the line from consumer to provider, can I begin to understand the depth of that learning.

Many of the comments and observations in this chapter come from my own experience as a pastor, later in a regional office of a denomination serving as a consultant to individuals planning for their continuing learning, and for the past fourteen years as the Director of Continuing Education at the Toronto School of Theology. Over the years, since 1977, when I joined the Society for the Advancement of Continuing Education in Ministry (SACEM), I have come to know many of the pioneers in the field of continuing education in both the secular and the religious worlds.

Some Examples of Early Providers

Robert T. Freirichs, in an article, "A History of the Continuing Education Movement," in the *Drew Gateway* (1976–77), provided a brief but significant overview of some of the very early providers in the field of continuing theological education, and the parallel developments in adult education. He included references from "A History of the Baptists of Illinois," which described a home mission superintendent who gathered together from 1864 onward, groups of seventy to more than two hundred ministers for a two-week program in the old University of Chicago (p. 21) to study Bible exposition, biblical, polemic, and practical theology, and elocution.

Other frontrunners were the land grant universities, who as a part of their Rural Life Movement, began in 1910 to offer courses on their campuses for clergy. This innovation paralleled their efforts in agricultural extension education for farmers and their families.

Another innovation was the establishment in 1929 of the College of Preachers, in Washington, D.C., created especially to provide continuing education in preaching and communications.

Other examples of early providers started up during the 1940s:
- The Summer Institute for Clergy began at Princeton Seminary in 1941, and it continues to attract top-flight leadership and large numbers of participants from several countries to the present.
- The United Presbyterian Church created the Presbyterian Institute of Industrial Relations in Chicago in 1942 to train clergy for urban ministry.
- The Episcopal Church established Roanridge Rural Training Foundation for rural pastors as they attempted to deal with problems of ministry in changing rural communities.
- Like The Episcopal Church in 1945, the American Baptist

Church founded a Rural Church Center, at Green Lake, Wisconsin. Not only did it offer residential courses, but its resources included a lending library and an extension service to pastors.

Contextual Educational Antecedents

A quick review of a few of the secular institutions and movements around the same time, provides us with some insight into the sources of challenge and opportunity that these early providers for continuing theological education experienced from their environment. An early leader in popular adult education and cultural events was the institution of Chautauqua. It began in Western New York State, about 1874, and provided lectures, concerts, and study programs to large numbers of people, many of whom were clergy. It later expanded and traveled across Canada and the United States, and became the source of significant learning locally, for both clergy and laity.

In the Canadian context,[1] one of the first groups to be established was the Workers Education Association. It began its work in Toronto, in 1918, and two years later had increased to units all across the province (Kidd, 1963, pp. 14-15).

Immediately after the end of the First World War, St. Francis Xavier University in Antigonish, Nova Scotia, began a People's School from January to March each winter. Directed especially to farmers, it provided popular courses in arts, science, and agriculture. These were available to anyone who was interested, and there were no entrance requirements or fees.

In the 1950s, three significant secular organizations were formed that were to have a lasting influence on continuing theological education; these were the Adult Education Association, the American Society for Training and Development, and the National Training Laboratory at Bethel, Maine.

Further Advances

In 1939, Auburn Seminary moved from upstate New York, to the campus of Union Theological Seminary, in New York City.

According to the current dean, Robert Reber, a decision was made eventually to use the resources of Auburn to:

(a) do research on the history of theological education and

(b) begin a program in continuing education in consultation with the presbyteries in the state of New York.

Union Theological Seminary in Richmond, Virginia, and Princeton Theological Seminary in Princeton, New Jersey, came on the scene shortly thereafter with their own programs. A growing number of seminaries began to develop summer schools, and institutes, whose curriculum consisted primarily of refresher courses, and/or surveys of the latest trends in theology.

Reuel Howe left the faculty of the Episcopal Divinity School to establish the Institute for Advanced Pastoral Studies, in Bloomfield Hills, Michigan. Its offerings focused on helping clergy and lay leaders to see themselves as whole persons, and not just role players in the bureaucracy of the church.

After two decades of experimentation, clinical pastoral education began to take shape in many different settings and institutions arising out of the vision of Anton Boisen. In clinical pastoral education, continuing education moved from the classroom to the clinical setting.

During the 1960s, Urban Training Centers were developed in more than twenty-five cities across the United States and Canada, to offer training for church life in the urban community, using the urban landscape, rather than the clinical setting, as the basis for contextual learning, and participants engaged with theology on the basis of experience in that setting.

The Plot Thickens

In 1977, I attended my first meeting of the Society for the Advancement of Continuing Education in Ministry (SACEM). I was amazed at the rich and varied mix of those present. The one hundred twenty attendees represented the wide range of relationships to the field. These were the entrepreneurs, individuals who represented independent and denominational centers. These institutions offered programs, in many instances, for both laity and clergy. Others were from institutes such as the one for Advanced

Pastoral Education in Michigan, from Alban, and from career centers. There were staff members from denominational judicatories who had responsibility for planning and/or leading programs. Of course, there were several seminary directors of continuing education present, as well. I was very interested to meet many of the founding members of SACEM at that annual meeting in Toronto. Truly, it was a young organization. Hence, it was natural for me to interview a select group of those who were early providers to catch something of the vision and passion they had for continuing theological education in its formative years.

Some Reflections from Early Providers

One of the great things that is possible when one is analyzing the early history of a movement, is the rich resource of memory available to those who were there and who are still living and able to tell the story. Out of such conversations, it becomes clear that their work laid down some of the basis for continuing theological education that we take for granted today.

For example, Connolly Gamble Jr., the first director of Continuing Education at Union Theological Seminary in Richmond, Virginia, realized the need for a network of support and shared learning among providers. In 1967, he was elected president at the first gathering of what would become the Society for the Advancement of Continuing Education for Ministry. SACEM continues to support and encourage collegial cooperation, holding an annual meeting, circulating a regular newsletter, and maintaining a Web site on the Internet.

Gamble also instituted the "Tower Scholar Program," which brought clergy to the campus for study with professors in their area of interest, and provided an opportunity for focused learning, supported by the library, faculty, and community of the seminary. He also instituted a distance learning program, the one that began my own lifelong encounter with continuing education.

Another key early figure was Richard Yeager, a member of the staff of South Indiana Conference of the United Methodist Church, who came at continuing education from the church's side. Yeager's work was grounded in the conviction that gifted local leaders existed within the conference, and that they could be more effective than outside "gurus" in fostering learning among their peers. Using a bus, participants visited a wide variety of ministry settings, conversing both with the local church members and with the "gifted leader" who worked in that setting.

The bus also helped build a community of theological reflection on political reality. Through trips to Washington, which included a visit with the locally elected members of Congress and Senate, and a time of theological reflection hosted by Wesley Seminary in Washington, D.C., participants were encouraged to identify the connections between political and church realities at the local and national levels.

Some of the key elements of these early programs were collegiality among providers, targeted seminary programs for pastors, identification and celebration of local gifts, and contextual theological reflection. In many institutions these are still a major part of the repertoire of continuing theological education. We take them for granted, but they were, in their time, innovations in response to emerging needs and trends.

Today's Emerging Trends

Conversations with early providers demonstrate how yesterday's emerging trends led to today's "standard practice" in continuing education. Similar conversations with today's providers help us to scout out the emerging trends and promising new developments of the future.

Among the most active providers, John Savage, of LEAD Consultants in Ohio, travels throughout the United States, Canada, and Australia, working with clergy and laity. His encounters lead him to identify "an increase in diffuse anger within the church, often directed toward the pastoral leadership." He calls this "punish the pastor" syndrome, and sees the results in a significantly higher level of personal pain among more and more clergy. In response to that pain, people are seeking both opportunities to build skills and competence for dealing effectively with others, and the capacity to understand, acknowledge, and strengthen their own emotional and spiritual life. A new trend that Savage identifies is a growing number of requests to serve as a personal coach to those desiring to develop as a "whole person" in leadership.

Joyce Tucker, dean of Continuing Education at Princeton Theological Seminary, sees a trend toward shorter events, with one-day events being the preferred model. Longer events are often subject to cancellation, not because the content is off-target, but because clergy seem unable or unwilling to commit to extended programs. She also identifies a shift in the expectations of many who come to one-day events. A large majority of them do not come expecting to be lectured to on some subject. Rather, they are hoping to be in conversation with an expert—that is, a leader who is willing to bring his or her expertise into dialogue with the issues that the participants are facing in ministry. At the same time, these learners want the discussion to be focused and yet to present opportunities to get personal concerns clarified.

Robert Reber, dean of Auburn Theological Seminary in New York City, sees a number of trends emerging, both in the world of theological education, and in its engagement with the social environment. Among the most obvious signs of change is the increase in the number of women involved in leading, organizing, and supporting continuing theological education. At the early meetings of SACEM, there were very few women; currently, they constitute something like half of the active membership.

Auburn Theological Seminary received two grants from The Luce Foundation to develop a "Colleague Program for New Directors of Continuing Theological Education." Dean Reber had noticed that half the participants at the SACEM annual meetings were new to the field, so he developed a proposal for a grant to give training and support to persons new to the field. The Colleague Program has, in the estimation of several SACEM leaders, not only helped to renew the organization, but has raised the profile of continuing theological education within seminaries and is part of a growing trend toward seeing continuing education as a core activity within seminaries.

Finally, Auburn, as a result of careful reflection on its constituency and context, has developed innovative programs to support theological reflection on faith and life among such groups as lawyers, senior business leaders, managers, and health care workers. These targeted programs recognize, as did the earlier innovations such as CPE and Urban Training, that context helps shape theology, and life informs faith.

Past innovations become current practice. New trends create innovation for an unknown future. And in addressing current concerns, today's leaders will help shape tomorrow's agenda. It is to those concerns that we now turn.

Will the Program Be Needs Driven or Market Driven?

Over the year, various instruments have been developed to do needs assessment. These range all the way from one-page paper and pencil checklists, to having a question on an evaluation form asking for suggested future programs, to focus groups. In this latter format, at the Toronto School of Theology (TST), we hold a consultation every two years, to which we invite representatives from several denominations—both users of our program and judicatory officials with responsibility for continuing education. Our purpose is to review our current offerings, identify trends, and suggest possible future topics and leaders. However, there is one critical question about this process: what are we measuring—needs or just wants?

Another way of discovering needs behind the wants, is to talk with the current popular leaders. One who has frequented TST for several years is Herb O'Driscoll, Anglican preacher and author. He, like others, has noted a shift in attitude of those who come. "My topic may be on some aspect of preaching but the real agenda is framed in a question like, 'Is it still worth my while to be in ministry?' Is the real need learning or support? Can they be separated?"

At a time when there seems to be a crying need for support and nurture, many providers are paying closer attention to the bottom line and balancing the budget. It is hard to resist the temptation to play to the market. "Provide what they will pay for and attend." In any case, as providers we need to raise again the questions around basic values, vision, and mission, not only of our continuing education divisions, but also of the larger institutions of which we are a part.

Do We Lead or Follow?

What is demanded of a provider in terms of leadership in the life of the church? Several years ago, I was approached by a diocese with a request to hold a training session that would equip team members to respond to parishes that were in crises as a result of a misdemeanor of a sexual nature by either the priest or someone in leadership. We were able to provide such a program with highly qualified leadership and had teams from several different denominations. Were we leading or following?

Jack Cooper, the first director of Continuing Education at Princeton, in remarking on facing this issue of leadership, said that they decided to respond to identified needs with two-thirds of the programs, and to use one-third new programs each year. There is a call for institutions to be prophetic in their offerings, to raise issues that need to be addressed, to spot trends, and to develop adequate response.

Power and Responsibility

Ronald Cervero and Arthur Wilson, in *Planning Responsibly for Adult Education: A Guide to Negotiating Power and Interests*, raise the issue of the use of power by providers. In order to be responsible planners, we have to understand interests and power as central to our actions as adult educators (Cervero and Wilson, 1994, p. 191). Their basic thesis is that providers and planners ought to move toward a more democratic process. "Program planning practice is a social activity in which planners negotiate personal and organisational interests.... This social construction forms the core of planning that is recognisable, coherent and realisable by a variety of interested parties" (Cervero and Wilson, 1994, p. 155). Who holds the power of decision making when it comes to continuing theological education? In the past, either by intention or default, most of the decision making rested in the hands of one person or at best a small committee. Planners have the responsibility to identify all the stakeholders and the structured world of relationships around that power. In other words, who needs a place at the planning table? It is clear that more than the providers' interests are at stake.

Coping with Change and Fiscal Responsibility

As the pace of change accelerates, it is becoming more and more important to realize the implications of the very real dilemma in which providers find themselves. There is a much wider range of needs, yet participants seem to have less time to commit to learning and reflection. On the other side, institutional expectations are that more will be delivered faster and for less, than in the past. But we are dealing with the phenomenon of education and learning, and that cannot be rushed. Working with human beings means dealing with limitations and differences, for each learner brings both limitations and potential.

This dilemma plays itself out not only in the daily life of providers, but also in their future planning. The reality is that there is no easy answer to what should be provided in terms of current programming; but this does not absolve us from struggling with the questions and seeking answers that are contextual, faithful to the vision of the institution, responsive to the learning needs of the participants, and attentive to the mandate of the gospel.

Conclusion

Those early providers stood on a frontier of a developing field and created several different responses, based on the needs they perceived, and employing the resources that they believed they had to offer. Another way of naming the challenge we face today comes from the work of Ron Cervero and Arthur Wilson. "Our argument is that planners either maintain or transform the existing power relationships as well as people's expressed and real interests in negotiating to construct a program. In fact, most program planners recognize that reconstructing power relationships and interests is often as important an outcome as the program itself" (Cervero and Wilson, 1994, p. 159).

What is our real intention—maintenance or transformation? What is now required of providers? Surely it is nothing less than reframing our role. We step out on a journey, but we do so without the aid of a well-documented map. At best, we have a compass composed of our basic values about:

- adult learning and the teaching/learning process
- the learners
- all the stakeholders, personal, institutional, or societal
- democratization of the planning process
- programs that result in transformation for persons, churches, and society.

Like all compasses, this one sets us on a journey without identifying the landscape we will encounter as we travel. The principles it encourages us to weave into our practice will lead to experiments, new directions, and risk, as we embody those principles in the unpredictable world that lies ahead of us. As the world changes, continuing education for ministry will encounter new challenges and opportunities. For example, who would have predicted fifteen years ago the power of computers and communication to facilitate distance education? How do we make use of new technologies without sacrificing the dimension of "encounter" in human relationships that so enriches learning? Distance education reminds us once more that learning is what takes place within the learner in an encounter with companions and guides. Whether that encounter takes place in a real or a virtual "room," our compass invites us to see and develop opportunities for growth and transformation. The core truth, that learning is not real until it is owned and acted upon by the learner in a local setting, has not changed. But the landscape certainly has.

Transformation and growth are not, however, the exclusive concern of the churches. They are the agenda for a wide variety of serving professions and communities. The journey ahead will be enriched for all of us through rich and generous dialogue with new and sometimes unexpected partners. For instance, current research on leadership spans the disciplines of business, professional, educational, and ecclesiastical worlds. To ignore the wisdom that emerges from a business perspective is to impoverish ourselves. To insist too strenuously on the unique character of ministry is to lose the insights that come from other professions and communities. Moreover, they will provide to us, and to our partners, with new and powerful metaphors for learning from our own experience and shaping our common future. As "mission" and "stewardship" have become powerful words in business and government, we might ask ourselves what powerful images they will offer us in return. Finally, it is not simply a matter of borrowing techniques, language, and knowledge from other settings. We can no longer act as if the churches alone are the agents of the transformation that God desires. In the journey ahead, partnerships will be a sign of faithfulness.

Several years ago, in a meeting sponsored by the Association of Theological Schools in the U.S. and Canada (ATS), corporate leaders in Toronto challenged the leadership of the Toronto School of Theology to articulate the value that theological education contributes to the life of the community. "We see our work as adding value to people's lives. What value do you add?" It was a new question for us, and there was no easy or glib answer. In fact, allowing the question to stand, even as we struggled to find our response, has led us to a new awareness that theological education is part of a complex and diverse enterprise of contributing to the life of the world. Working out a response to this challenge is the real mission of every provider of continuing education for ministry.

We seek to be faithful to all of these deeply held beliefs in the presence of the Holy Spirit. We have to leave space for the interruptions, and come they will, when we seek to follow through the desert a God who is on the move.

References

Cervero, Ronald M. and Arthur L. Wilson, *Planning Responsibly for Adult Education: A Guide to Negotiating Power and Interests.* San Francisco: Jossey-Bass, 1994.

Freirichs, Robert T. "A History of the Continuing Education Movement." *Drew Gateway,* Vol. 47 No. 1 (1976–77), pp. 1-9.

Kidd, J. Roby. *Learning and Society: Readings in Canadian Adult Education.*

Toronto: Canadian Association for Adult Education, 1963. Roby Kidd, a Canadian pioneer in adult education, has edited a book filled with historical chapters on the early development of the movement in Canada. Similar historical texts could be cited for the United States. J. Roby Kidd, *Learning and Society: Readings in Canadian Adult Education* (Toronto: Canadian Association for Adult Education, 1963).

Theory and Research in Professional Continuing Education

Chapter 4

What Constitutes Effective Teaching with Adults?

D. Bruce Roberts

"So they took him and brought him before the Court of Areopagus (or to the middle of Mars Hill) and said, 'May we know what this new doctrine is that you propound? You are introducing ideas that sound strange to us, and we should like to know what they mean.'"
(Acts 17:19-20 NEB)

Standing on Mars Hill with the Parthenon crowned Acropolis towering on the right and with the ruins of the ancient Athenian marketplace below, one can get a wonderful imaginative picture of the setting for the powerful teaching moment Paul enjoyed in this passage from Acts. My thesis will be that the actions of Paul leading up to this dramatic moment help us define "teaching." Teaching is not only what happens on "Mars Hill," teaching is the activity that develops a climate of inquiry and curiosity in which persons want to learn and in which they ask, "What are these ideas? We want to know."

It is interesting to note a dictionary definition of teaching:

> Teach; teaching... **1 a**: to cause to know a subject. **b**: to cause to know how.... **2**: to guide the studies of. **3**: to impart the knowledge of.... (*Webster's New Collegiate Dictionary*, 1981)

The definition most associated with our subject is the third definition concerned with imparting knowledge; this is certainly an important aspect of the practice. However, the first meaning

This chapter appeared in *Encounter*, Vol. 59 (Winter/Spring 1998) and is used by permission.

suggested is the intriguing notion that teaching is "to cause to know." In this definition, teaching is helping a person know something, it is the process of helping another learn. One of the primary questions of a teacher, therefore, is: "What are the effective alternatives for assisting other human beings to learn?"

The elements of Paul's activity preceding his Mars Hill appearance may be suggestive. First, Paul was waiting in Athens and noticed a problem or issue he wanted to address (v. 16). We are told that he went to the synagogue and city square and argued with people and "passers-by" (vv. 17-18). So the second movement is to engage in a conversation with people which raises questions and challenges perspectives. We can assume that Paul did that in an engaging way which created curiosity and a desire for further inquiry, because he was invited to speak further (vv. 18-19). The third movement was to answer the questions more formally on Mars Hill. However, a fourth movement is suggested in the way he began:

> "People of Athens, I see that in everything that concerns religion you are uncommonly scrupulous. For as I was going round looking at the objects of your worship, I noticed among other things an altar bearing the inscription 'To an Unknown God.' What you worship but do not know—this is what I proclaim." (vv. 22-23)

The fourth movement is an attempt to engage persons from the perspective of their own experience. To teach, then, is to enter a relationship with persons in a way that helps learning. As Richard Osmer puts it:

> Teaching focuses on an increase in the student's ability to comprehend and grasp the meaning of what is being learned. The subject matter must interact with the patterns of knowing that the student already possesses, being assimilated into them and expanding them. At the deepest level, teaching is based on respect for the student, respect that takes seriously his or her personal appropriation of the subject matter being taught.[1]

Teaching is a relational activity which helps identify questions for exploration, suggests resources for alternative answers, encourages experimentation, challenges by raising questions for further learning, supports work as a peer in lifelong learning.

This interpretation of Paul's teaching in Athens is consistent with his theology. God loves all of humankind. We know this by the life and teaching of Jesus Christ and by the affirmation of Jesus Christ by God in the Resurrection. Everything we do must be done in and with love (1 Corinthians 13), and teaching in a way that invites persons into a larger and deeper conversation is a way of loving.

It is the task of teachers, therefore, to create relationships in which teaching as loving is possible. What are some ways to create a learning relationship? Let me suggest for conversation two elements for helping adults learn which I think are consistent with the Pauline model of Mars Hill: (1) shared control, and (2) provision for and support of critical and constructive thinking efforts.

Shared Control

Malcolm Knowles identifies four assumptions about adult learners in his work on adult education or "andragogy."[2] The first of the assumptions is that adults understand themselves to be independent and self-directing. Any educational enterprise aimed at adults must take into account the notion that adults will want to be respected as peers in the learning process.

The second assumption that affects the teaching of mature persons is that adults bring to any learning activity or setting a reservoir of experience and knowledge. New learning is understood and organized in terms of this accumulation, even if the new ideas mean a drastic change in the way the person understands a given problem. Involving adults in learning activities will be most powerful if it finds a way for them to relate new ideas to their own experience.

Third, persons who experience themselves to be more self-directing will be ready to learn when a question or problem arises in their own life. This assumption was corroborated by a study done by Carol B. Aslanian and Henry M. Brickell, who sought to find out why adults undertook any learning activity. They found that "eighty-three percent of the adults interviewed said that they were learning in order to cope with a life change."[3] Teachers of adults will need to find a way to tap into this strong source of motivation.

Finally, Knowles suggests that adults orient their learning toward here and now tasks and problems that they want to address. More mature persons are strongly interested in the application of new ideas and information to their life tasks and roles and will need opportunities to make individual utilization of material. Refusal to allow for this kind of idiosyncratic employment of new learning can lead to rebellion or to dropping out, depending upon the circumstance. Teaching persons with this orientation means finding ways for them to act directly upon the material and to make it their own.

Do these assumptions fit with your experience as an adult learner? They do with mine. A friend of mine observing me in an adult education course for beginning guitarists once asked, "Are you going to let the instructor teach this course?" At that moment, I realized that my frustration level was high because the course was not covering my expectations. My response was to keep asking questions—this eventually frustrated others who wanted to hear from the instructor. I think that I often observe this dynamic in continuing education programs and in my courses.

In looking over the four assumptions that Knowles and others make about the nature of adult learners and the implications for teaching, it seems that they could be summarized under the heading of "control." In other words, all four of the assumptions purport that adults learn best when they are invited at least to help control the learning setting and activities. The power of control to motivate and facilitate performance is wonderfully captured in a story told by Peters and Waterman in their study of leadership in the business world:

> Adult subjects were given some complex puzzles to solve and a proofreading chore. In the background was a loud, randomly occurring, distracting noise; to be specific, it was "a combination of two people speaking Spanish, one speaking Armenian, a mimeograph machine running, a desk calculator, a typewriter, and street noise—producing a composite, non-distinguishable roar." The subjects were split into two groups. Individuals in one

set were just told to work at the task. Individuals in the other were provided with a button to push to turn off the noise, "a modern analog of control—the off switch." The group with the off switch solved five times the number of puzzles as their cohorts and made but a tiny fraction of the number of proof-reading errors. Now for the kicker: "...none of the subjects in the off switch group ever used the switch." The mere knowledge that one can exert control made the difference.[4]

A similar dynamic was observed by Warren Bennis and Burt Nanus in their study of leadership in American companies. They observed that when persons are given some control over their work and empowered to learn and create, they "seem to get so immersed in their game of work that they forget basic needs for long periods of time!"[5]

The first hunch about teaching adults is, therefore, that the issue of control is central. When we share control (students do not even want total control, they simply want some way to influence the direction) of learning tasks and environments, most adults will be empowered to work on their most pressing agenda, and a result is that incredible energy for learning is released. Two of Cyril Houle's nine assumptions for adult education support this hunch. Houle's first assumption is that "any episode of learning occurs in a specific situation and is profoundly influenced by that fact."[6] His fourth assumption is that educational activity is always coopera-tive in two senses.

> In education the term *cooperative* is used in two major senses. In its profoundest meaning, it signifies action by both learner and educator in accordance with the dictates of nature. Learners must work in terms of their innate individualism as well as in terms of the social stimulation supplied by any learning group of which they are a part....
>
> In its second sense, the term cooperative implies voluntary interaction among individuals during learning.[7]

Effective teaching will involve learners in ways that tap into the specific situations that give rise to their motivations for learning and will invite cooperation that is deeply voluntary.

Space does not allow for a discussion of the many ways that learners can be invited to help control the direction of learning, but a few can be mentioned: (1) collaborative planning processes such as the Nominal Group Technique, (2) opportunity for learners to work on specific interests within the focus of the program or course, (3) flexible ways for students or participants to give evidence of learning which invite application of personal experience to new information, (4) evaluation procedures which invite the creation of new direction based upon the application of new learning, (5) opportunity to experiment.[8] It is important to note here that the climate for learning should be one based upon the norms of openness and experimentation. Some of the most important learning comes from trying something that does not work; there must be a climate that invites persons to risk a failure and be evaluated not on the outcome but upon the process and the learning derived from it. This idea of emphasizing processes of learning leads to the next section of this paper dealing with critical thinking.

Supporting Critical Thinking

The second hunch is that effective teaching has to do with helping students internalize a way of learning that can be applied to almost any situation. There are many adults who continue to believe that learning is a matter of memorizing what experts have written on a given subject. They have not yet relativized authority and come to the conclusion that they are also authorities who participate in the process of determining what is true through reflective experience and thought. The utilization of an open systems approach to learning and research is a complicated and complex process. The assumption is that no single factor can be utilized in determining what is true, that there are a number of considerations which must be taken into account, that context is a very real component in determining what is fact.

Stephen Brookfield calls this complex process of arbitrating between truth claims and constructing working hypotheses "critical thinking." For Brookfield, critical thinking is a primary task of adulthood.

When we become critical thinkers we develop an awareness of the assumptions under which we, and others, think and act. We learn to pay attention to the context in which our actions and ideas are generated. We become skeptical of quick-fix solutions, of single answers to problems, and of claims to universal truth. We also become open to alternative ways of looking at, and behaving in, the world.

When we think critically, we come to our judgments, choices, and decisions for ourselves, instead of letting others do this on our behalf. We refuse to relinquish the responsibility for making the choices that determine our individual and collective futures to those who presume to know what is in our own best interests. We become actively engaged in creating our personal and social worlds.[9]

For Mary Belenky and colleagues, who examined *Women's Ways of Knowing*, learning "to see that all knowledge is a construction and that truth is a matter of the context in which it is embedded..."[10] is also a task of adulthood and a way of thinking critically.

Once knowers assume the general relativity of knowledge, that their frame of reference matters and that they can construct and reconstruct frames of reference, they feel responsible for examining, questioning, and developing the systems that they will use for constructing knowledge. Question posing and problem solving become prominent methods of inquiry.... They (tend to rely) on examining basic assumptions and the conditions in which a problem is cast.[11]

Learning to become critical thinkers may be a difficult task for many persons. The shift from dependence on an external authority to participation in the construction of knowledge may be quite wrenching and bring with it a sense of loss. Sharon Parks calls the loss of truth and of established authority "the shipwreck of self, world, and 'God,' the truth of life itself betrayed."[12] William Perry, in his classic study of young adult intellectual development, describes the sense of loss in the first person:

Soon I may begin to miss those tablets in the sky. If (relativism) defines the truth for term papers, how about people?

Principalities? Powers? How about the Deity...? And if this can be true of my image of the Deity, who then will cleanse my soul? And my enemies? Are they not *wholly* in the wrong?

I apprehend all too poignantly now that in the most fateful decisions of my life I will be the only person with a first-hand view of the really relevant data, and only part of it at that. Who will save me then from that "wrong decision" I have been told not to make lest I "regret-it-all-my-life"? Will no one tell me if I am right? Can I never be sure? Am I alone?[13]

Helping students learn to become critical thinkers, therefore, involves not only familiarity with a subject matter or area of inquiry, it also involves strong human relations skills, powers of empathy, and the inclination to see pastoral work as part of the teaching task. Indeed, Stephen Brookfield lists ten strategies for facilitating critical thinking and of the ten, eight are dependent upon human relations and communications skills: affirm self worth, listen attentively, support critical thinking efforts, reflect and mirror efforts and actions, regularly evaluate progress (provide feedback), and help students create networks for support.[14]

Laurent A. Daloz, in his work on teaching and mentoring, also emphasizes the importance of the teacher-learner relationship in suggesting that good teachers "...do three fairly distinct types of things. They *support*, they *challenge*, and they *provide vision*."[15] He goes on to suggest that support and challenge must be in balance. Support for Daloz is "those acts through which the mentor affirms the validity of the student's present experience"[16] and builds trust. The important role of challenge "is to open a gap between student and environment, a gap that creates a tension in the student, calling out for closure."[17] High support and low challenge may produce a stasis; conversely, a high challenge and low support may yield a retreat by the learner. By "vision" Daloz means the dialectical process of re-examination of current ways of perceiving the world and constructing "fuller, more comprehensive...understandings"[18] that is more modeled by a teacher than taught.

Brookfield, Perry, and the team of Belenky, Clinchy, Goldberger, and Tarule all suggest that critical thinking must be publicly modeled by teachers: "Students need opportunities to watch women professors solve (and fail to solve) problems and male professors fail to solve (and succeed in solving) problems. They need models of thinking as a human, imperfect, and attainable activity."[19]

Perhaps the most important notion relative to critical thinking and its facilitation is that it is a "never-ending search for truth, which is coordinate with a never-ending quest for learning."[20] Brookfield suggests that "critical thinking is a continuous process composed of alternating phases of (1) reflecting on a problem or theme, (2) testing new solutions, strategies, or methods on the basis of that reflection, (3) reflecting on the success of these actions in particular contexts, and (4) further honing, refining, and adapting these actions according to alternative contexts."[21]

The equation of critical thinking with the relativizing of authority and the development of a methodology by which truth claims are adjudicated and appropriate alternatives for action in a given context are generated is a position that has important parallels in some of the current literature on practical theology. A survey of the work of Don S. Browning, James W. Fowler, Thomas H. Groome, James N. Poling, and Donald E. Miller, and James D. and Evelyn Whitehead suggests that there are several common steps in practical theological methodology. They are: (1) describing an issue, problem, or event, (2) attending to or contextualizing issues or problems relative to cultural information, Christian tradition, and Scripture, (3) critical analysis and comparison of various alternative answers or solutions, (4) construction of alternative interpretations and responses, and (5) deciding on a strategy for action.[22]

The point of this is that critical thinking methodology is remarkably similar. It involves the inseparable movements of reflection and action that tests the results of reflection which then moves back to reflection, revision of theory, identification of further alternatives for action to be tested. Other thinkers could be added to the list of those whose method has much in common with this basic outline of critical thinking. A partial list would include Jean Piaget, Alfred N. Whitehead, David Tracy, Edgar S. Brightman, Gordon D. Kaufman, Charles M. Wood, and Edward Farley. I dare say that for all of these thinkers, the method that they use for the pursuit of truth is at once a way of learning.

The teaching of critical thinking, therefore, involves a number of elements. Supporting students in their first steps in relativizing authority; welcoming them into the conversation of a community of inquiry, in which we are all participants by virtue of being human beings; strengthening and encouraging students in the internalization of a critical thinking methodology; reinforcing the fact that the epistemology inherent in the method of critical/constructive thinking assumes that we are all lifelong learners.

Sarah Little has developed five basic approaches to teaching which may help define kinds of teaching activity that support critical and constructive methodology in students: information processing, group interaction, indirect communication, personal development, and action/reflection.[23] Of these approaches, only the last one seems out of place. Indeed, in the introduction to the chapter dealing with action/reflection, Dr. Little admits that this particular way of teaching does not fit with the others.[24] The reason that it does not fit is because the action/reflection way of teaching that she describes is, at once, the epistemology that is assumed in our descriptions of critical thinking, and which undergirds all other methodologies for teaching and thinking. Action/reflection, as she describes it, is both an epistemology and a way of learning. Little's chapter on action/reflection describes the way persons learn by exercising some control on subject matter; the other four approaches to teaching then become alternative ways of facilitating the process of "critical thinking," "constructed knowing," or "lifelong learning."

There is no one right way to teach critical thinking or anything else. Piaget once suggested that the way to teach teachers is to have them do continuous experiments on teaching.[25] True to the epistemology assumed in this paper, let me suggest that teaching critical thinking demands experiments that involve students in activities which they help to control and in which they are asked to take some kind of relevant action on the subject matter under inquiry. There may be literally hundreds of ways to do this—most of which could be understood under four of Sarah Little's approaches: information processing, group interaction, indirect communication, and personal development.

Summary

Paul's activity in Athens, preceding and including the Mars Hill speech, provides a provocative model for teaching that is affirmed by some of the modern work on adult education. Good teaching is a relational and loving activity which (1) begins by establishing a conversation in which the student's questions and curiosities are brought to awareness, (2) challenges students to explore resources and perspectives for alternative answers to their questions, (3) lets students see how the teacher struggles with the same questions, and (4) challenges students to relate new perspectives to their own experience in constructive and critical ways.[26]

Good teaching is a process that introduces students to the questions of authority and truth, and invites them to join the teacher in a lifelong quest. This quest involves the construction of contingent and unfinished affirmations of what is true and what is appropriate to do in a given context. It is a process of constant experimentation in a community of exchange, a process that involves learning to share control and to think critically with others. As the four authors of *Common Fire* put it, "Learning is most powerful when students are given experiential opportunities to integrate new information about the world into their existing frameworks in ways that lead to fresh insights and new habits of mind."[27]

Approaching the teaching task with adults from the position of one who shares control of learning experiences and as one who invites learners into a community of conversation and inquiry is to tap into the internal motivation of persons. In *Women's Ways of Knowing*, the authors refer to the excitement and motivation for learning reminiscent of the Peters and Waterman study and the observations of Bennis and Nanus: "When truth is seen as a process of construction in which the knower participates, a passion for learning is unleashed."[28]

Finally, since teaching is relational and more art than science, those of us who want to teach effectively must be willing to be lifelong learners about teaching, modeling a reflective practice method in our profession. That means taking an experimental approach to our teaching activity, always searching for more effective ways to facilitate learning. The National Center for Creativity,

Inc. in Indianapolis has a calendar with a quotation: "There is no such thing as teaching without learning. If they don't get it, you haven't done it."[29] Helping learners "get it" is the ultimate challenge for teachers.

References

1. Richard R. Osmer, *A Teachable Spirit: Recovering the Teaching Office in the Church* (Louisville: Westminster/John Knox, 1990), p. 21.

2. Malcolm S. Knowles, *The Modern Practice of Adult Education: From Pedagogy to Andragogy* (Chicago: Associated Press, 1980), pp. 43-62.

3. Carol B. Aslanian and Henry M. Brickell, *Americans in Transition: Life Changes as Reasons for Adult Learning* (New York: College Entrance Examination Board, 1980), p. 51.

4. Thomas J. Peters and Robert H. Waterman, Jr., *In Search of Excellence: Lessons from America's Best-Run Companies* (New York: Harper & Row, 1982), p. xxiii.

5. Warren Bennis and Burt Nanus, *Leaders: The Strategies for Taking Charge* (New York: Harper & Row, 1965), p. 84.

6. Cyril Houle, *The Design of Education, Second Edition* (San Francisco: Jossey Bass, 1996), p. 41.

7. Ibid., p. 45.

8. See also Ronald M. Cervero and Arthur L. Wilson, *Planning Responsibly for Adult Education* (San Francisco: Jossey Bass, 1994) and Cyril O. Houle, *The Design of Education, Second Edition,* (San Francisco: Jossey Bass, 1996).

9. Stephen D. Brookfield, *Developing Critical Thinkers* (San Francisco: Jossey Bass, 1986), p. 139.

10. Mary Field Belenky et al. *Women's Ways of Knowing* (New York: Basic Books, 1986), p.139.

11. Ibid.

12. Ibid.

13. William G. Perry, Jr., *Forms of Intellectual and Ethical Development in the College Years* (New York: Holt, Rinehart, and Winston, 1970), p. 33.

14. Brookfield, *Developing Critical Thinkers,* pp. 72-85.

15. Laurent A. Daloz. *Effective Teaching and Mentoring: Realizing the Transformational Power of Adult Learning Experiences* (San Francisco: Jossey Bass, 1990), p. 212.

16. Ibid.

17. Ibid., p. 213.

18. Ibid., p. 230.

19. Belenky et al., *Women's Ways of Knowing,* p. 215.

20. Ibid., p. 140.

21. Brookfield, *Developing Critical Thinkers,* p. 230.

22. See Don S. Browning, *Religious Ethics and Pastoral Care* (Philadelphia: Fortress, 1983); James W. Fowler, *Faith Development and Pastoral Care*

(Philadelphia: Fortress, 1987); Thomas H. Groome, *Sharing Faith: A Comprehensive Approach to Religious Education and Pastoral Ministry* (San Francisco: Harper & Row, 1991); James N. Poling and Donald E. Miller, *Foundations for a Practical Theology of Ministry* (Nashville: Abingdon Press, 1985); and James D. and Evelyn E. Whitehead, *Method in Ministry, Revised Edition* (Kansas City, Missouri: Sheed and Ward, 1995).

23. Sarah Little, *To Set One's Heart: Belief and Teaching in the Church* (Atlanta: John Knox, 1983).

24. Ibid., p. 71.

25. Jean Piaget, *Science of Education and the Psychology of the Child*, trans. by Derek Coltman (New York: Viking Press, 1970).

26. For a provocative discussion of teaching for critical thinking, see Patricia M. King and Karen Strohm Kitchener, *Developing Reflective Judgment: Understanding and Promoting Intellectual Growth and Critical Thinking in Adolescents and Adults* (San Francisco: Jossey Bass, 1994).

27. Laurent A. Parks Daloz, Cheryl H. Keen, James P. Keen, and Sharon Daloz Parks, *Common Fire: Lives of Commitment in a Complex World* (Boston: Beacon Press, 1996), p. 221.

28. Belenky et al. *Women's Ways of Knowing*, p. 140.

29. *Creative Sparks Calendar* (Indianapolis: National Center for Creativity, 1999).

Chapter 5

Building Systems of Continuing Education for the Professions

Ronald M. Cervero

A central feature of North American societies in the late–twentieth century was the professionalization of their workforces. One estimate is that nearly 25 percent of the United States workforce claims membership in a profession (Cervero, 1988). These professionals teach our children, guide our businesses, manage and account for our money, settle our civil disputes, diagnose and treat our mental and physical ills, fight our wars, and help mediate our relationship to God. Thus, it is important to keep our eye on what is truly at stake in continuing education. The bottom line of continuing education is to improve the practice of these teachers, physicians, managers, and clergy. It is instructive to contrast this bottom line with the picture of the most frequently encountered form of continuing education:

> It is dominated by the informational update. In what is typically an intensive two or three-day short course, a single instructor lectures and lectures and lectures fairly large groups of business and professional people, who sit for long hours in an audiovisual twilight, making never-to-be-read notes at rows of narrow tables covered with green baize and appointed with fat binders and sweating pitchers of ice water. (Nowlen, 1988, p. 23)

This picture is as universally recognizable to people in any profession as it is criticized for being largely ineffective in improving the performance of these same professionals. Indeed, the familiarity of this picture would be funny if the importance of continuing education were not so great.

Historical Development of Continuing Professional Education

An incredible amount of resources, financial and human, are used to support three to six years of professionals' initial education. Until recently, however, little systematic thought was given to what happens for the following forty years of professional practice. Many leaders in the professions believed that these years of pre-service professional education, along with some refreshers, were sufficient for a lifetime of work. However, with the rapid social changes, explosion of research-based knowledge, and technological innovations, many of these leaders now understand the need to continually prepare people for forty years of professional practice through continuing education (Houle, 1980).

Beginning in the 1960s, we began to see embryonic evidence for systems of continuing education. Perhaps the first clear signal of this new view was the publication in 1962 of a conceptual scheme for the lifelong education of physicians (Dryer, 1962). The 1970s saw the beginning of what is now a widespread use of continuing education as a basis for relicensure and recertification (Cervero and Azzaretto, 1990). By the 1980s organized and comprehensive programs of continuing education were developed in engineering, accounting, law, medicine, pharmacy, veterinary medicine, social work, librarianship, architecture, nursing home administration, nursing, management, public school education, and many other professions (Cervero, 1988). During that decade, many professions developed their systems of accreditation for providers of continuing education (Kenny, 1985).

As we enter the next millennium, the picture of "a single instructor lecturing and lecturing large groups of professionals" is still easily recognizable as the predominant form of continuing education. We do not yet have a similarly recognizable picture of a system of continuing education that is effective in today's complex world. The major reason for this lack of a unifying picture of effective continuing education is that the professions are in a transitional stage, experimenting with many different purposes, forms, and institutional locations for the delivery of continuing education. These systems, such as they are, are incredibly primitive (Cervero and Azzaretto, 1990). I would characterize them as:

(1) Devoted mainly to updating practitioners about the newest developments, which are

(2) Transmitted in a didactic fashion and

(3) Offered by a pluralistic group of providers (workplaces, for-profits, associations, and universities) that

(4) Do not work together in any coordinated fashion, and

(5) Are almost entirely unconnected to the previous levels of professional education.

Relatively speaking, these systems of continuing education are in their infancy. By way of analogy, at the end of this century continuing education is in the same state of development as pre-service education was at the beginning of this century. Medical education serves a useful point of comparison. In his 1910 report on medical schools in Canada and the United States, Abraham Flexner (1910) found that only sixteen of 155 schools expected that their incoming students would have any previous college education, and he recommended closing the schools that did not. It is unlikely that anyone in 1910 would have predicted the structure of medical education today. Likewise, systems of continuing education will grow through this transitional period to achieve an equivalent coherence, size, and stature as the pre-service stage of professional education. Indeed, the leaders of most professions would probably agree that what we hardly dare prophesy today will be seen by later generations as efforts to achieve a manifest necessity (Houle, 1980, p. 302). While these systems of continuing education are in transition (Young, 1998) there are many choices that must be made.

Critical Issues for the Future of Continuing Professional Education

The task of building systems of continuing education is fundamentally more complex than what faced leaders earlier in this century as they successfully built the existing systems of pre-service professional education. First, whereas pre-service education takes place in a relatively short period of time, continuing education must help professionals for years of professional practice, which is characterized not only by constant change, but also by competing values. Second, whereas pre-service education is predominately controlled by universities and professional schools, there are multiple institutions that offer continuing education, all of which claim to be the most valid and effective provider. This section discusses three critical issues that must be addressed in building systems of continuing education.

Issue 1: Continuing Education for What? Struggle Between Updating Professionals' Knowledge and Improving Professional Practice

The most fundamental issue is, What is the problem for which continuing education is the answer? If the picture painted at the beginning of the chapter is the answer, then it is clear that the problem has been conceived as "keeping professionals up-to-date on the profession's knowledge base." In fact, keeping professionals up-to-date is as close to a unifying aim as continuing education has (Nowlen, 1988). This educational model flows from the deeply embedded view that professional practice consists of instrumental problem-solving made rigorous by the application of scientific theory and technique (Schon, 1987). This scientific knowledge is produced by theorists and researchers, and the foundation is laid in professional school, with additional building blocks added through forty years of continuing education. In a sense, continuing education becomes an extension of faculty members' lines of research. Yet most of the problems professionals face are not in the book. Schon's studies of professional practice led him to say:

> In the varied topography of professional practice, there is a high, hard ground overlooking a swamp. On the high ground, manageable problems lend themselves to solution through the application of research-based theory and technique. In the swampy lowland, messy, confusing problems defy technical solution. The irony of this situation is that the problems of the high ground tend to be relatively unimportant to individuals or society at large...while in the swamp lie the problems of greatest human concern. (Schon, 1987, p. 3)

What does it mean for education if we believe that professionals conduct most of their practice in the swamp of the real world? In response to this view, some professional schools have begun moving to more problem-centered curricula. For example, in providing the rationale for Harvard's new problem-centered, as opposed to subject-centered, medical school curriculum (one which was inspired by McMaster University), the president noted the growing change in perception of how physicians go about making their characteristic decisions of diagnosis and treatment: "Few doctors are now inclined to think of themselves as simply arriving at logically determined conclusions by applying scientifically tested truths to experimentally derived data.... Considerations of many kinds are often jumbled together to form a picture full of uncertainties, requiring the most delicate kinds of judgments and intuitions" (Bok, 1984, pp. 37-38).

Continuing education has a great advantage over other stages of professional education in seeking to promote effective practice. It occurs when professionals are most likely to be aware of a need for better ways to think about what they do. But if we are to exploit this natural advantage and move our systems beyond the update model, we need to find ways to better integrate continuing education, both in its content and educational design, into the ongoing individual and collective practice of professionals.

Issue 2: Who Benefits from Continuing Education? Struggle Between the Learning Agenda and the Political and Economic Agendas of Continuing Education

In a sense, this issue is also about the purposes of continuing education. While the first issue dealt with the various educational purposes for continuing education, this issue recognizes the reality that continuing education is about many things in addition to professionals' learning. I believe that we all recognize that continuing education can and often *does* improve professionals' knowledge and positively impacts our organizations and communities (Umble and Cervero, 1996). However, continuing education offers many additional benefits to individuals and organizations. Any director of continuing education for a professional school knows that she will be expected to generate surplus revenues to be used to support faculty members' travel, research, and instruction. Any director for a professional association knows that his programs will need to generate revenues to fund staff salaries in nonrevenue producing activities, such as lobbying, maintaining certification programs, and promoting the public image of the profession. Another example is that training programs are an important benefit that can help to retain employees, as one survey found: "Among the many benefits offered to their employees, continuing education is considered the most important after health insurance. More than 90 percent of the companies surveyed currently offer CE as an employee benefit and 97 percent plan to offer their employees this benefit by 2000" (UCEA, 1998, p. 31).

There is no reason to expect that education can, or even should be, immune from the political and economic agendas of our institutions and the wider society. To address these realities, the first question any continuing educator needs to ask is "What is the mission of my institution and where does continuing education fit in that mission?" Second, "Whose interests will be served by offering continuing education and what are those interests?" Finally, "What are the political relationships at my institution and how will they enable or constrain implementing the vision for continuing education?" This struggle between the learning and the political economic agendas will always exist. However, by answering these three questions, we will be better able to negotiate a successful resolution to this struggle.

Issue 3: Who Will Provide Continuing Education? Struggle for Turf Versus Collaborative Relationships

Most continuing education is provided through some sort of collaboration between two or more institutions. A central finding of the body of research on this topic is that any understanding of collaboration for continuing education has to recognize the larger organizational goals being pursued through the formation of such relationships. For example, a study of collaborative programs in engineering (Colgan, 1990) found that while the respondents believed that the programs were needed to keep engineers up-to-date with the new technologies, the university-corporation relationship was driven by larger institutional issues. For corporations, the benefits included access to university students as employment prospects and more direct and regular access to university faculty and research. For universities, the programs provided a mechanism to secure research contracts and faculty consulting, provided a means to secure student internships, and generated profits to subsidize other institutional functions. In a similar vein, other research (Cervero, 1984; Maclean, 1996) has found that a primary reason medical schools have extensive collaborative relationships with community hospitals is to increase the number of patient referrals to the university hospital, which results from faculty members speaking at these programs.

While there is general agreement that collaborative programming is a good, even a "politically correct," idea, the central question is always: "Who's in charge?" This governance issue is always negotiated in partnerships and the central issues typically revolve around who controls the content of the program and how will profits and losses be shared. These enduring issues are being played out in the brave new world of technology-assisted instruction. The growth of distance education has raised the questions of who owns the course material created by professors and who should benefit from the profits gained by the sale of multimedia course materials and Web-based courses? For example, in 1994 the Extension Program at UCLA signed a ten year contract with the Home Education Network. The contract granted the company exclusive rights to distribute and market video recordings of UCLA's extension courses. In 1996, the contract was amended to include on-line courses as well. In May 1998 the company changed its name to OnlineLearning.net. The central question in this case is, "Who owns the content of those courses and who will share in the profits: UCLA central administration, its Extension Program, the faculty members, or OnlineLearning.net?" (Guernsey and Young, 1998).

Collaboration is a strategy that has been used extensively and will continue to be used to develop systems of continuing education (Cervero, 1992). However, astute leaders recognize that the formation of collaborative relationships is fundamentally a political process in which costs and benefits must be clearly weighed, including those involving organizational agendas other than those connected to the continuing education program. Thus, effective partnerships will develop not from a belief that collaboration is the right thing to do, but from a definitive understanding of the goals to be achieved by the partnership, a clear recognition of the benefits to be gained by each institution, and the contribution of equivalent resources by each partner (Cervero, 1988; Collins, 1998).

A Concluding Note

The leaders of workplaces, professional associations, universities, and governments have both a tremendous opportunity and a clear responsibility to further develop the systems of continuing education for the professions. These three issues illuminate the critical choices that are before institutional leaders and individual professionals in building these systems. As with any humanly constructed system, the building of a coordinated system of continuing education for any profession is a political process. This process will be marked by fundamental struggles over the educational agenda and the competing interests of the educational agenda and the political-economic agendas of the multiple stakeholders for continuing education. As a political process, then, it is crucial that all of the stakeholders participate in a substantive way in negotiating these agendas for continuing education. For the immediate and long-term negotiation of these struggles will define whether continuing education can make a demonstrable impact on the quality of professional practice.

References

Bok, D. "Needed: A New Way to Train Doctors." *Harvard Magazine*, May-June, pp. 32-43; pp. 70-71, 1984.

Cervero, R. M. "Collaboration in University Continuing Professional Education." In H. W. Beder (ed.), *Realizing the Potential of Interorganizational Cooperation.* New Directions for Continuing Education, No. 23. San Francisco: Jossey-Bass, 1984.

Cervero, R. M. *Effective Continuing Education for Professionals.* San Francisco: Jossey-Bass, 1988.

Cervero, R. M. "Cooperation and Collaboration in the Field of Continuing Professional Education." In E. S. Hunt (ed.), *Professional Workers as Learners.* Washington, D.C.: U.S. Department of Education, 1992.

Cervero, R. M., and J. F. Azzaretto (eds.). *Visions for the Future of Continuing Professional Education*. Athens, Ga: Georgia Center for Continuing Education, The University of Georgia, 1990.

Colgan, A. H. *Continuing Professional Education: A Study of Collaborative Relationships in Engineering Universities and Corporations*. Unpublished doctoral dissertation, University of Illinois at Urbana-Champaign, 1990.

Collins, M. M. *Exploring Professional Associations' Perceptions of Institutions of Higher Education as Potential Partners*. Unpublished doctoral dissertation, The Pennsylvania State University 1998.

Dryer, B. V. "Lifetime Learning for Physicians: Principles, Practices, Proposals." *Journal of Medical Education*, No. 37 (6, Part 2, entire issue), 1962.

Flexner, A. *Medical Education in the United States and Canada*. New York: Carnegie Foundation for the Advancement of Teaching, 1910.

Guernsey, L. and J. R. Young "Who Owns On-line Courses?" *The Chronicle of Higher Education*, pp. A21-A23, June 5, 1998.

Houle, C. O. *Continuing Learning in the Professions*. San Francisco: Jossey-Bass, 1980.

Kenny, W. R. "Program Planning and Accreditation." In R. M. Cervero and C. L. Scanlan (eds.), *Problems and Prospects in Continuing Professional Education*. New Directions for Continuing Education, no. 27, San Francisco: Jossey-Bass, 1985.

Maclean, R. G. "Negotiating Between Competing Interests in Planning Continuing Medical Education." In R. M. Cervero and A. L. Wilson (eds.), *What Really Matters in Adult Education Program Planning: Lessons in Negotiating Power and Interests*. New Directions for Adult and Continuing Education, No. 69. San Francisco: Jossey-Bass, 1996.

Nowlen, P. M. *A New Approach to Continuing Education for Business and the Professions: The Performance Model*. New York: Macmillan, 1988.

Schön, D. A. *Educating the Reflective Practitioner: Toward a New Design for Teaching and Learning in the Professions*. San Francisco: Jossey-Bass, 1987.

Umble, K. E., Cervero, R. M. "Impact Studies in Continuing Education for Health Professionals: A Critique of the Research Syntheses." *Evaluation & the Health Professions, Vol. 19* (2), pp. 148-174, 1996.

University Continuing Education Association. *Lifelong Learning Trends: A Profile of Continuing Higher Education* (5th ed.), Washington, D.C. , 1998.

Young, W. H. (5th ed). *Continuing Professional Education in Transition*. Malabar, Florida: Krieger, 1998.

Chapter 6

Where and How Religious Leaders Learn

William Lord and George Brown

When clergy are asked, "What do you do for continuing education?" their answers vary. Some describe programs offered by educational institutions ranging from colleges and universities to seminaries and theological schools. Others identify workshops, seminars, or conferences sponsored by denominational agencies, megachurches, or independent organizations.

The impression left by such diverse responses makes it difficult to assess where clergy go for continuing education. This chapter seeks to explore this subject by examining three focused studies and by exploring some of the relevant research on adult learning.

The New Situation

One way to describe the current context in which clergy have to do their learning is the "in-between time." Things are changing. Well-established ways of doing things just do not seem to be working as well; new skills are needed. New expectations provide occasion for confrontations, heighten anxiety levels, and expose personal inadequacy.

We are standing on a new threshold. The new room that we are entering seems much larger than the one in which we have been accustomed to working and are now leaving. In conversation with a minister recently, he noted that, as he reflects on his ministry of just three years, he is aware that he made critical decisions often with very little information. He is conscious of how much he has learned in the interim. "Our current experience is constantly invalidating the basis that we used to inform our past action." These words are clearly from one who has a definite awareness of learning and its corollary of unlearning. There are many facets of lifelong learning within a career. We will explore some of the key elements for clergy learning below.

Research on Continuing Education

Three Studies

Three studies are the focus of this section: a 1984 study by Barbara Wheeler, Durstan McDonald, and Cameron Murchison; a 1993 study by Margaret F. Brillinger and Sharon C. Pocock, and a 1999 study by William Lord and John C. Bryan.

Barbara Wheeler, Durstan McDonald, and Cameron Murchison (1984) studied "talented" or "able" clergy. Their research was exploratory and dealt with individuals who were basically self-directed, independent learners. The researchers defined these ministers as "those clergy of outstanding ability who are widely recognized by the congregations they serve, fellow clergy, and superiors as strong leaders" (Wheeler, McDonald, and Murchison, 1984, p. 4).

The researchers focused on the educational attitudes and habits of these talented or able clergy. The group interviewed by the researchers numbered thirty-two to twenty-six men and six women (Wheeler, McDonald, and Murchison, 1984; p. 11). They came from the two major Presbyterian denominations (UPCUSA and PCUS), the Episcopal Church, the United Methodist Church, the American Baptist Convention, and the Disciples of Christ. The majority of those interviewed were in their forties or early fifties (Wheeler, McDonald, and Murchison, 1984; p. 12). These clergy did not participate in formal continuing education programs.

Margaret F. Brillinger's and Sharon C. Pocock's 1993 study also involved clergy who do not participate in formal continuing education events. The study was initiated by the Continuing Education Council of the Toronto School of Theology in order to better understand the learning needs of clergy in Ontario.

Six Christian denominations represented at the Toronto School of Theology provided the researchers with lists of names of clergy who had not participated in professional continuing education during the past year. A random sample of 45 priests and ministers was drawn from these lists.

The researchers used in-depth telephone interviews to gather data. The interviews used open-ended questions and lasted from three-quarters of an hour to two hours. Those contacted were from six different denominations: Anglican (10), Baptist (5), Lutheran (5), Presbyterian (5), Roman Catholic (10), and United Church (10). Half of those interviewed were second career clergy and the average age of participants was 46 (Brillinger and Pocock, 1993, p. 28).

Six themes emerged in the course of these interviews: control, burnout, role confusion, isolation, inconsistent/unclear denominational expectations for clergy continuing education, and inadequate seminary preparation (Brillinger and Pocock, 1993, p. 25). Control had to do with the inability of clergy to delegate responsibility and their desire for control (Brillinger and Pocock, 1993, p. 29). The authors reported physical, emotional, and mental symptoms arising from burnout and noted that few of the clergy in their study belonged to a support group that met regularly (Brillinger and Pocock, 1993, p. 30). Role confusion was reflected in the inability of many clergy to separate their professional role from their personhood (Brillinger and Pocock, 1993, p. 30). Four-fifths of those interviewed expressed a sense of isolation. The authors noted that a "...lack of accountability, regular feedback, supervision, or any kind of coaching or networking" contributed to this sense of isolation (Brillinger and Pocock, 1993, p. 31). Lack of adequate seminary preparation and lack of denominational encouragement and support for continuing education were also noted in this study (Brillinger and Pocock, 1993, pp. 30-31).

The spiritual needs of midcareer clergy were the focus of a study by William Lord and John C. Bryan (1999). The research team used a two-stage approach: an initial survey questionnaire was sent to 80 respondents, and then in-depth follow-up interviews were conducted with 45 of the respondents. The interviews, mostly face-to-face (a few of the interviews were done by telephone), lasted from one to two hours (Lord and Bryan, 1999, p. 3).

Those who participated in this study were selected from

Canadian and United States Protestant denominations. They were identified as "effective, successful, mid-career pastors who were not in crisis mode, personally or professionally" by denominational officials (Lord and Bryan, 1999, p. 3). Of the 45 respondents, there were 32 men and 13 women. Twenty-nine were Protestant clergy living in the United States (20 United Methodist, 5 Presbyterian, and 4 Lutheran) and 16 were Canadian (8 United Church, 4 Presbyterian, and 4 Anglican) clergy (Lord and Bryan, 1999, p. 15).

Some Research Findings

Clergy tend to seek learning opportunities outside their denomination (Brillinger and Pocock, 1993; Lord and Bryan, 1999, p. 32). Brillinger and Pocock identified a desire for anonymity as a reason for this tendency, especially among clergy experiencing personal crisis. The study by Lord and Bryan clearly identified the perceived absence, on the part of most clergy, of a safe place for in-depth sharing. Beyond a few close colleagues, most pastors need a space that is open, safe, and trusted, where they can engage themselves and others on significant issues, without feeling already judged or needing to protect themselves by playing a role or putting up a false front.

Clergy tend to avoid learning opportunities sponsored by judicatories (Lord and Bryan, 1999, pp. 31-32). Lord and Bryan cite the relative lack of competence of judicatories to provide quality learning opportunities as a reason for this avoidance. It may also be related to the desire for anonymity that underlies avoidance of learning opportunities sponsored or provided for clergy by their own denomination.

This may also be related to Brillinger and Pocock's comment about "inside-out" versus "outside-in" learning. David E. Hunt (1987) coined the term "inside-out" to describe the way psychologists and others could use themselves—their own knowledge and experience—as a source of expert knowledge. Hunt became dissatisfied with the prevalent top-down approach that began with theory, and then moved to practical application. A bottom-up approach, on the other hand, began with practice, and then moved on to theorizing. He encouraged psychologists to begin with their own experience rather than relying on the wisdom and knowledge of "outside" experts. Hunt wrote: "My suggestion to start Inside-out does not require that you completely reject the Outside-in, or formal psychology. It calls for Inside-out to come first, because among other things, this approach provides a valuable base from which to consider Outside-in information" (Hunt, 1987; p. 2).

Most judicatory-sponsored learning opportunities seem to utilize outside-in approaches to learning. That is, they feature an outside expert and the presentation of a predetermined body of knowledge. This approach tends to ignore or discount the experience and practical knowledge of those who participate in judicatory-sponsored continuing education events. Clergy who are perceived to be more able or competent prefer independent study over formal learning opportunities (Wheeler, McDonald, and Murchison, 1984). Brillinger and Pocock also noted the importance of providing consultation for self-directed learning. It is suggested in the Wheeler, McDonald, and Murchison report that most clergy do not fit the profile of the self-confident, self-disciplined clergy in that study.

The New Situation in Learning

Skills and Technical Learning

New theories and information are constantly emerging from the research being pursued in theological colleges and seminaries. Areas of particular interest include theology, Bible, and congregational studies. Frequently, there are well-known names associated with a field of study, such as Walter Brueggemann, Marcus Borg, or Phyllis Tribble in biblical studies. For years, Fred Craddock has been seen as the dean of preaching in North America, and emerging names are Barbara Brown Taylor and Paul Scott Wilson. The Alban Institute, with its research, workshops, and publications, has been seen as being in the forefront of congregational studies. Individuals flock to learn from those who are viewed as experts not only in conveying developments on the academic front, but who are excellent communicators as well. There is still a need for a solid and clear journal article or book, and a well-delivered lecture, whether in person, on a video, or on audiotape. However, it is clear that information alone cannot deliver all that is needed in the current context of change.

Learning Procedures and Processes

There is a growing interest in procedural knowledge. In times of transitions one needs to know not only the "what" but also the "how to." Our recent experience, at least at the Toronto School of Theology, is that there is a sustained interest in "how to" topics like handling conflict, introducing small group structures into the life of a faith community, and preaching more effectively. So also one can identify names often associated with topics like those just listed. However, as with the content area above, a wider understanding of learning is needed.

Learning from Experience

Donald Schön was the first to begin using the phrase, "the wise practitioner." This was his vision of what it means to be a lifelong learner within a profession. His thesis was that one enters into a profession by learning a framework and detailed information and theories, what he called, "technical rationality." These are the truths that are communicated as problem-solving processes and the answers to clear problems, usually arising from research, but, upon entry into the working world of the professional, the neophyte finds that there are few clear problems and mostly complicated messes. So the practitioner begins to learn from his or her experience by developing a repertoire made up of images, metaphors, rules of thumb, stories and 911 strategies. However, this assumes a different understanding of learning. The person needs something very basic which is a realization that his or her experience is, in fact, a vital source for learning.

Ronald Cervero has written extensively on the dimension of learning from practice, and on one occasion offered the following three propositions for the improvement of continuing education within the professions.

These are:

- The goal of professional practice is wise action;
- Knowledge acquired from practice is necessary to achieve this goal;
- A model of learning from practice should be the centerpiece of systems of continuing education for the professions (Cervero, 1992, p. 92).

For many professionals there is a need to explore what they understand about the learning process.

Learning How to Learn

Although there are many similarities in the ways people learn, each one learns somewhat differently. Learning is an idiosyncratic activity. David Kolb's Learning Style Inventory has been helping individuals identify their preferred learning style for many years. He basically identified two components that are critical to learning. The first dimension has to do with the way in which we prefer to take in new material, that is either by direct experience through the senses or through symbol and concept. It is true that all of us use both modalities but we have a preference. So also with the second dimension, which refers to the way that we deal with the new information. Some move into a reflective mode and probe the breadth and depth of the experience, whereas others want to move immediately to working pragmatically with it, in terms of how to use this in a future situation.

Looking Ahead

Implications for Continuing Education

A number of characteristics for a continuing education program for clergy emerge from these three studies. The exploratory research by Wheeler, McDonald, and Murchison (1984) suggests that continuing education for clergy who are "talented" and "able" should:

- have a fresh, cutting edge theological or secular topic as its focus,
- be intellectual rather than practical in character,

- be by invitation,
- be sponsored by a trusted institution, and
- use group inquiry and other participatory education approaches and methodologies.

The 1993 study conducted by Brillinger and Pocock of clergy who had not participated in continuing professional education during the past year suggests that continuing education should:

- feature "inside-out learning,"
- have ecumenical or nondenominational sponsorship,
- counter clergy's sense of isolation by providing access to information networks to counter feelings of isolation,
- offer consultation for self-directed learners,
- be a collaborative effort among continuing education systems and providers, and
- encourage participation by clergy-laity teams.

More recent research on the spiritual development needs of mid-career clergy by Lord and Bryan (1999) suggests that continuing education opportunities should address the need for:

- role clarity and integration,
- recognition and affirmation,
- a dependable place or person for spiritual direction,
- a community of learning, trust, and affirmation, and
- expert knowledge about spiritual disciplines and skilled experience.

Future Directions for Research

There is a substantial body of literature on participation in adult learning. But this literature does not include continuing professional education for clergy. A great deal has yet to be learned about the participation and nonparticipation in continuing professional education by clergy. The studies reported in this chapter represent but a modest effort in this direction.

While the studies examined in this chapter offer useful information and helpful advice for those who provide continuing education for church leaders, the picture is not complete. Additional information is needed to provide a more comprehensive understanding and better direction. For example, while the older study by Wheeler, McDonald, and Murchison identified important characteristics and learning needs of talented and able clergy, relatively little is known about the "average" pastor or priest. While the Brillinger and Pocock study provides helpful information about Canadian clergy who do not engage in continuing education, more knowledge is needed about clergy who do engage in formal continuing education.

Donald Schön once asserted that one learns artistry by "carefully studying the performance of unusually competent performers" (Schön, 1987, p. 13). It could also be said that one learns about participants in continuing professional education by studying the religious professional counterpart of Allen Tough's "high learners." As Schön looked to "unusually competent performers" to discover an epistemology of practice, so researchers might discover insights about where and how church leaders learn by studying those church leaders who are highly engaged in continuing professional education. Research on clergy who participate to a high degree in both self-directed, nonformal learning, *and* in formal continuing education programs could yield fruitful data. Following on the observation by Brillinger and Pocock that participation by clergy-lay teams from congregations can be beneficial (1993; p. 34), it would also be useful if such research would include nonordained church leaders, including both professional church staff and lay members serving as leaders in congregations.

While the Association of Theological Schools' annual *Facts Book* yields information about Doctor of Ministry education that is relevant to one form of continuing professional education, it is difficult to identify a similar clearinghouse or source for information about other forms of continuing professional education offered by schools, megachurches, independent organizations and agencies, and so forth. The Society for the Advancement of Continuing Education for Ministry (SACEM) and the Association of Continuing Christian Education Schools and Seminaries (ACCESS) are the only professional organizations where one might look for such data about church leaders, and they do not have the means for gathering such a wide range of information from such a diverse range of sources.

The gathering of additional useful data will require a collaborative effort by continuing education providers, denominational agencies responsible for clergy support and development, and professional organizations such as SACEM and ACCESS. Given the scope of such research, foundation support in terms of grants will likely be needed in order to stimulate study along the lines indicated here.

Toward a Wholistic Approach to Learning

What is the basic metaphor which we use to understand ministry? The concepts embedded within our deep belief system, whether we hold these consciously or unconsciously, do determine how we relate to others and how we do ministry in the world, and our effect upon learning. If we reflect for a moment on a medical field, using it as a metaphor, is our basic orientation that of a surgeon or a physician who "fixes" problems and focuses on cures or is our focus on wholistic care with an underlying belief in the innate capacity of the human body to heal itself? The former or mechanistic model leads one to be about learning as it relates primarily to problem identification, discernment of solutions and processes of saving and repairing. However, the wholistic model invites one to view ministry from a systems perspective, where life is viewed in all of its complexity and interaction and no one solution can achieve the desired results. A different kind of learning is required if we are to function in a way other than as a rescuer and a fixer. However, it is not a matter of either/or, but rather of seeing the whole picture.

Jackson W. Carroll in his book *As One with Authority* has identified three core tasks for ministerial leadership:

(1) The interpreter of meaning, that is, through preaching, teaching, and counseling, the pastor assists both individuals and the congregation to understand their life in the context of the story of the good news of the gospel.

(2) Community formation and building: individuals are always in relationships and this task is to develop communities in which persons can experience the love of peers as well as the love of God.

(3) Empowering public ministry: enabling individuals and the faith community to live out its belief in the world. However, the clergy learner is not just a practitioner searching for a better method or even greater personal insight, although both of these are important (Carroll, 1991; p. 99).

However, we must place this alongside the need to be a person of faith as well, and therefore, attending to the dynamics of our own relationship with the Divine. To integrate both task and personal learning will require offering many learners both permission and a structure. The structure will need to address at least the following areas:

(1) Who am I in ministry? What informs my understanding? This will involve an unpacking of my own deep beliefs, formative stories and metaphors. To do this requires a safe space with expert professional support to face and express aspects of ones deepest reality.

(2) What do I need now at this stage in my ministry? Is it more information, further knowledge, skill development, motivation, peer support, personal growth, supervision or faith development?

(3) To what ministry focus am I being invited? This involves a clear assessment of my gifts, talents, and abilities as well as the needs for ministry of the context in which I am working. What is the fit?

(4) What is my vision for the future? Can I look beyond the end of my career or the end of my life, and identify the legacy that I want to leave? Can I take the perspective that there is a future for the church of which I will not be a part? What can I do now that will make a difference?

An area in Muskoka, Ontario, Canada, along the shores of Muldrew Lake, was devastated by a major forest fire shortly after the turn of this century. A professor of agriculture encouraged his students to come up to that area and plant trees each summer. Today the area is richly forested—the legacy of Professor Potter and his students. We have shade today because of his vision yesterday.

Conclusion

J. Bradley Wigger in his book *The Texture of Mystery: An Interdisciplinary Inquiry into Perception and Learning* has written the following about the process of learning. He has delineated a five-step dynamic. It begins with (a) a blur or unclarity, then (b) to attentive searching, and (c) clarity or understanding leads to (d) joy and (e) new possibilities, new ways to communicate, and deeper relationships (Wigger, 1998, p. 200).

> In this movement from blur to new possibilities is what James Loder would call a "transformational grammar," setting her in a new, deeper and more complex relationship with her environment. As Gibson describes transformation, there is a "stretching without tearing" the form of the relationship. (Wigger, 1998; p. 200)

Earlier he had identified both the experience of joy and the challenge that can come from learning:

> The joy of learning includes, but involves even more than, the "aha" of discovery. It refreshes our posture in the world. We have sensitivities that did not exist, or we have the capacity to explore more fully the life before us and within us and around us. Learning thus enlivens the ability to attend to reality as such. (Wigger, 1998, p. 177)

To live is to learn. To live is to be a lifelong learner.

References

Brillinger, Margaret F. and Sharon C. Pocock. "Learning Needs of Clergy Who Have Not Participated in Continuing Education Events for Clergy." *Canadian Journal of University Continuing Education*, Vol. XIX, No. 2 (Fall 1993), pp. 25-35.

Carroll, Jackson W. *As One with Authority: Reflective Leadership in Ministry.* Louisville: Westminster/John Knox Press, 1991.

Cervero, Ronald. "Professional Practice, Learning, and Continuing Education: An Integrated Perspective." *International Journal of Lifelong Education*, Vol. II, No. 2 (April-June, 1992), pp. 91-101.

Hunt, David E. *Beginning with Ourselves: In Practice, Theory, and Human Affairs.* Cambridge, Mass.: Brookline Books, 1987.

Lord, William and John C. Bryan. *Project on the Spiritual Development Needs of*

Mid-Career Clergy. Toronto: Toronto School of Theology, 1999. (Unpublished report is available through the Society for Advancement of Continuing Education for Ministry or the Toronto School of Theology.)

Schön, Donald. *Educating the Reflective Practitioner.* San Francisco: Jossey-Bass, 1987.

Tough, Allen. *The Adult's Learning Projects: A Fresh Approach to Theory and Practice in Adult Learning,* No. 1, *Research in Education.* Toronto: Ontario Institute for Studies in Education, 1971.

Wheeler, Barbara, Durstan McDonald, and Cameron Murchison, "The Educational Preferences and Practices of Talented Ministers: Report on an Exploratory Study," 1984. (unpublished report)

Wigger, J. Bradley, *The Texture of Mystery: An Interdisciplinary Inquiry into Perception and Learning.* Lewisburg and London: Bucknell University Press and Associated University Presses, 1998.

Learning from Practices

Chapter 7

Motivated Learning and Practice: A Peer Group Model

D. Bruce Roberts

Innovation Needed!

"Mainline" Protestant churches are experiencing a serious decline in the membership of once vital congregations. Many observers of this situation agree with Loren Mead, congregational consultant and founder and past president of the Alban Institute:

> that the storm buffeting the churches is very serious indeed. Much more serious than we have admitted to ourselves, and much more serious than our leaders have yet comprehended. The problems are not minor, calling for adjustments or corrections. They are problems that go to the roots of our institutions themselves. What I am describing here is not something we fix. It is a state of existence in which we must learn to live even as we seek new directions for faithful response.... The storm is so serious ...that it marks the end of "business as usual" for the churches and marks a need for us to begin again building church from the ground up. (Mead, 1994, p. ix)

Mead suggests that church leaders at all levels need to face the reality of the storm and mobilize all available resources toward transforming congregations: He wants to see "the structures that surround congregations—the judicatories, the national structures, the seminaries, and educational institutions—building skills in new ways, ready to help transform congregations from what they are to what they must be as centers of apostolic ministry" (Mead, 1994, p. 119).

What are the appropriate responses needed in this situation?

Edwin Friedman, in a video *Reinventing Leadership,* suggests that what is needed in situations of uncertainty and high anxiety is exploration (Friedman, 1996 video). Leadership is needed which will be willing to risk exploring new structures, new ministries, new music, even new articulations of the ancient faith. Theological education at all levels, basic and continuing, is challenged to find ways of stimulating leadership which will foster innovations in congregations in order to learn and discover what will effectively convey the gospel message in our time.

A primary question for theological educators is how to deliver theological education in a way that addresses the need for innovation in congregational leadership. The need for innovation only arises in situations in which it is not clear what action to take in a given context. The decline of the old-line denominations requires new approaches to congregational leadership and ministry. It is not clear that there is any one answer; it is not clear that national or regional judicatories or, particularly seminaries, have answers to the problem. Much of what we have been doing for the past several decades (if not centuries) is not working now.

I strongly suspect that if we want to address our current problems, we will need to learn how to learn. We will need to foster a climate of openness, in order to sponsor innovations and experiments that will help us learn what kind of action, and what kind of leadership can be effective in restoring vitality to sagging and boring churches. In effect, we will need to learn how to prepare leaders for ministries who do not "know" as much as "know how to learn" through their own practice in a specific context.

Continuing theological education is in a strong position to initiate experiments aimed at developing innovations in congregations. Pastors as well as judicatory leaders at all levels are looking for answers, and in some cases have funds that could be expended to help address the pain inherent in the situation. This article will suggest ways of thinking about adult education, models for adult learning, and a particular model of peer group learning that encourages the kind of innovation and experimentation needed.

Perspectives on Adult Learning and Continuing Education for the Professions

In an article on continuing professional education, Ronald M. Cervero proposes that the goal of professional practice in any field is "wise action," and that although formal knowledge gained in traditional academic settings is important, "knowledge acquired from practice is necessary to achieve [the goal of wise action]" (Cervero, 1992, pp. 92-98). Based upon the importance of knowledge gained from practice, Cervero goes on to propose that "a model of learning from practice should become the centerpiece of systems of continuing education for the professions.... It is important ... to involve groups of practitioners and a context of practice," because "learning advances through collaborative social interaction and the social construction of knowledge within a community of practitioners and a context of practice" (Cervero, 1992, pp. 98-99).

There is ample theoretical support for Cervero's proposals from a number of sources, only a few of which will be used here. Jean Piaget, the Swiss genius, made a lifetime study of the way individuals learned to know and his ideas have come to form the basis of many movements in adult education. Piaget suggested that a characteristic of humankind is that we organize our perceptions of reality in an attempt to understand. Of course, these organizations are always inadequate, because they are limited by our particular levels of perspective, experience, and maturation. As we live with a particular cognitive organization, what Piaget called an "equilibration," we attempt to make that organization explain everything; we "assimilate" all data into it until there are so many questions and inconsistencies that we are forced to revise our understanding. Piaget called that reorganization of our worldview, "accommodation," which leads in turn to a new balance or "equilibration."

Piaget understands cognitive development to be the movement through stages of progressively more adequate organizations of our perceptions in interaction with our world. The highest adult level or "equilibration" is the recognition that we are always working at assimilating data into our current worldview with the understanding that eventually we will have to accommodate, to develop a new equilibration or understanding. Adult knowing is a lifelong process of continuing to revise (accommodate) our current understanding (equilibration) into a more adequate and coherent way of organizing our perceptions. (See Piaget, 1954, p. 354 and 1967, p. 103)

Peter Senge and his associates have given the phenomenon Piaget called cognitive organizations (or equilibrations) a different name. Senge has identified five disciplines for creating a "learning organization" one of which is the process of identifying "mental models":

> Mental models are the images, assumptions, and stories that we carry in our minds of ourselves, other people, institutions, and every aspect of the world. Like a pane of glass framing and subtly distorting our vision, mental models determine what we see. Human beings cannot navigate through the complex environments of our world without cognitive "mental maps"; and all of these mental maps, by definition, are flawed in some way. (Senge, et al. 1994, p. 235)

These flaws in our current "mental maps" create conflicts between our internal mental organization of the world and the external structures of reality. These conflicts make it necessary for all human beings to be lifelong learners; old ways of understanding become inadequate, and we are forced to change (accommodate) in order to solve new problems or account for new information (a new equilibration).

What are the implications for professional education from this way of understanding human learning? In the *Science of Education and the Psychology of the Child*, Piaget raises questions about education, makes some suggestions for change, and talks about teacher (adult) education. He raised three fundamental questions: (1) What is the aim of teaching? (2) What should we teach? (3) How should we teach? (Piaget, 1970, p. 12).

In answering the first question, Piaget suggests that the primary goal of education is the facilitation of mature reflective thought through the interaction of a maturing student with the physical and social environment. What we all need most to learn is how to learn, how to be self-directing and independent. Much of what is taught will be out of date in a short time, but creative, inventive, critical minds will always be needed. For Piaget, the task of teaching is to facilitate creativity, "to form the intelligence rather than to stock the memory, to produce intellectual explorers rather than mere erudition." (See Pulaski, 1974, p. 200)

Since, for Piaget, learning grows at all levels through action, the training of teachers and other professionals must take on an action-reflection orientation. He advocated preparing teachers by involving them in research projects on how children learn, done under the supervision of a trained research assistant. This is the kind of professional education now being advocated by Cervero and others. Since adults learn through a dialectical interaction of their current understandings or mental models with the reality in situations of living or practice, it is important to set up professional continuing education in a way that engages that interactive process.

Piaget's understanding of the way adults learn is corroborated in the work of Patricia King, Karen Kitchener, and Parker Palmer.* In a study of how persons develop critical thinking, intelligence, and reflective judgment, Patricia M. King and Karen Strohm Kitchener reach conclusions similar to Piaget. Persons at the highest levels of what they call "reflective judgment" are lifelong learners:

> Knowledge is the outcome of a process of reasonable inquiry in which solutions to... problems are constructed. The adequacy of those solutions is evaluated in terms of what is most reasonable or probable according to the current evidence, and it is reevaluated when relevant new evidence, perspectives, or tools of inquiry become available. (King and Kitchener, 1994, p. 15)

Parker Palmer, in his book *The Courage to Teach*, echoes Piaget in suggesting we are able to learn and develop more adequate conceptions of reality only in intentional social interaction he calls "communities of truth." The hallmark of such a community is

---

*No attempt is made here to be inclusive of all theoretical sources that corroborate Piaget's approach to adult learning. Only a few sources have been selected.

"that *reality is* a web of communal relationships, and that we can know reality only by being in a community with it" (Palmer, 1998, p. 90). For Palmer and Piaget, the most mature form of knowing involves *"an eternal conversation about things that matter, conducted with passion and discipline*...as the passionate and disciplined process of inquiry and dialogue itself, as the dynamic conversation of a community that keeps testing old conclusions and coming into new ones" (Palmer, 1998, p. 104).

Piaget, Palmer, King and Kitchener, and Senge all understand adult learning to be a complex process that involves willingness to have our current worldviews challenged in a communal process in which we attempt to understand a particular subject or context. For Palmer, it is a process that involves

> sharing observations and interpretations, correcting and complementing each other, torn by conflict in this moment and joined by consensus in the next. The community of truth, far from being linear, and static and hierarchical, is circular, interactive, and dynamic.
>
> At its best, the community of truth advances our knowledge through conflict, not competition. Competition is a secretive, zero-sum game played by individuals for private gain; conflict is open and sometimes raucous but always communal, a public encounter in which it is possible for everyone to win by learning and growing....Conflict is the dynamic by which we test ideas in the open, in a communal effort to stretch each other and make better sense of the world. (Palmer, 1998, p. 103)

There is ample theoretical support for the contention that professional education, both basic and continuing, is most effective when it involves actual practice as a basis for learning, reflection, and evaluation of other information and knowledge. It is in living and working that we experience the dissonance of old ways of thinking that no longer are adequate, that no longer solve problems but that raise more questions. It remains now for us to examine some of the models of adult education that have been developed which embody the theoretical insights cited above.

Processes for Thinking-in-Action Adult Learning

There are many examples of the kind of learning in practice that are consistent with the above perspectives; most of them have been called by different names.

In the early part of the twentieth century, the Methodist Episcopal Church South developed a program for training Sunday school teachers that evolved into what was called "Laboratory Schools" by the Methodist Church after 1939. The training involved teachers and other leaders in processes of (1) diagnosing learning needs; (2) setting learning goals; (3) planning; (4) selecting resources for teaching or leading; (5) practicing the teaching or leading on an appropriate age level group; and (6) seeking feedback and evaluating the results. By the decade of the 1950s the "Laboratory School" was a primary instrument of leadership development, and produced several generations of persons who were excited about "laboratory" learning and who passed that excitement on to members of congregations.

Malcolm Knowles published *The Modern Practice of Adult Education: Andragogy Versus Pedagogy* (Association Press, 1970) which proposed a process for adult education with essentially the same steps as the Methodist Laboratory Schools of half a century earlier. Knowles called his process for adult learning, "andragogy," involving seven steps: (1) establishment of a climate conducive to adult learning; (2) creation of . . . a structure for participative planning; (3) diagnosis of needs for learning; (4) formulation of directions of learning (objectives); (5) development of a design of activities; (6) operation of the activities; and (7) rediagnosis of need for learning (evaluation) (Knowles, 1980, p. 59). Note that the final step involves returning to the diagnosis of needs for learning involving a continuous lifelong cycle of learning.

A movement concurrent with Knowles's work (and with which he was familiar) was developed by social scientists and came to be known as "The Laboratory Method." Leland Bradford, Jack Gibb, and Kenneth Benne, in *T-Group Theory and Laboratory Method: Innovation in Re-education* (1961) report work by social scientists to find understandings of the way change takes place in individuals and in all kinds of human institutions. Bethel, Maine, became the center for many experiments and innovations in education for change. As Bradford, Gibb, and Benne express it:

> A laboratory curriculum is designed to help some unit of human organization assess its needs for change and to support that unit in inventing and testing ways in which changes may be achieved. The focal unit may be a single individual or a team of individuals. In either case, the desired direction of learning and change is toward a more integrative and adaptive interconnection of values, concepts, feelings, perceptions, strategies, and skills. (Bradford, et al. p. 18)
>
> For the learners, every day in a laboratory is full of episodes of relearning, of reorganization of previous learnings, of confrontations of old patterns with new possibilities. The achievement of each learning objective ordinarily involves examination of the relationships between old and new experiences, between old and new learnings, and the arduous process of achieving some viable choice or synthesis between the old and the new. (Bradford, et al. 1964, p. 19)

A laboratory curriculum reflects the idea that adult learning involves the process of what, in Piaget's terms, is "equilibration," for King and Kitchener is "reflective judgment," and for Palmer is the "community of truth."

The laboratory style of learning has been used by Clinical Pastoral Education (CPE) and by theological field education. While CPE used a kind of laboratory method primarily in hospital settings, field education used parish settings for laboratory style learning. In the latter years of the 1960s, theological educators, partly in response to an exasperated constituency of local congregations that wanted better prepared leaders, moved from requiring theological students to have "Field Work" to having an experience of "Field Education." While "Field Work" involved assigning students to work in a congregation or other appropriate work environment, "Field Education" worked at integrating the practice of ministry in a particular context with courses taken concurrently in the theological curriculum utilizing a trained facilitator called a "Supervisor" (using the CPE terminology).

Field Education, as a way of learning through the practice of ministry, anticipated work by Donald A. Schön, *The Reflective Practitioner: How Professionals Think in Action* (Basic Books, 1983) and by Ronald M. Cervero, *Effective Continuing Education for Professionals* (1988). The basic idea for Cervero is to help "learners become researchers of their own practice" (Cervero, 1988, p. 56)— essentially the same purpose as theological field education. The process of Theological Field Education involves a trained and experienced "Supervisor" who leads a process of helping students identify learning needs, set learning objectives, identify and do appropriate work in ministry, and then reflect on what is being learned. Reflection on the practice of ministry includes several emphases including theological perspectives in the situation, social analysis, personal emotional states, and perception of inter- personal dynamics. Students are asked to work in peer groups with a supervisor and to ask each other evaluative questions: What alternatives are there if you could do this work over again? What theological perspectives are present in the situation (including one's own)? What are the alternative next steps? Of the alterna- tives, which will you try in the near future? This style of reflection encourages experimentation and creative work in the practice of ministry.

More recently, new perspectives for adult education have grown out of the literature on organizational systems theory. Peter Senge, in *The Fifth Discipline: The Art and Practice of the Learning Organization*, advocates for the creation of "learning organiza- tions" which will integrate five disciplines: personal mastery, men- tal models, shared vision, team learning, and systems thinking. The discipline which captures most fully the kind of learning processes we are attempting to articulate here is that of "team learning."

> The discipline of team learning starts with "dialogue," the capac- ity of members of a team to suspend assumptions and enter into a genuine "thinking together."
> The discipline of dialogue also involves learning how to rec- ognize the patterns of interaction in teams that undermine learn- ing. The patterns of defensiveness are often deeply engrained in how a team operates. If unrecognized, they undermine learning.

If recognized and surfaced creatively, they can actually accelerate learning.

Team learning is vital because teams, not individuals, are the fundamental learning unit in modern organizations. This [is] where "the rubber meets the road"; unless teams can learn, the organization cannot learn. (Senge, 1990, p. 10).

Senge distinguishes two key skills in the discipline of team learning: dialogue and discussion. Dialogue is that procedure in which participants on a team listen to each other carefully and note the dissonance in themselves without reacting; it is an exercise in hearing others and in observing our own mental models and assumptions. By contrast, discussion is the presentation and defending of specific views and the movement toward a decision (Senge, 1990, p. 237). Although both dialogue and discussion are necessary to team learning, most of us utilize "discussion" in advocating for a position without the examination of our assumptions that comes in "dialogue."

Dialogue is necessary, because no one perspective is adequate; we need a diversity of perspectives to help develop competent solutions to a given problem. In this respect, Senge is consistent with cognitive developmental theory.

Another contemporary source of thinking about adult learning is Ronald A. Heifetz writing in *Leadership Without Easy Answers* (1994). Heifetz distinguishes between "technical" and "adaptive" work. Technical work is primarily aimed at routine problems for which there is an available technical solution. Adaptive work "demands innovation and learning" (Heifetz, 1994, p. 8).

Adaptive work consists of the learning required to address conflicts in the values people hold, or to diminish the gap between the values people stand for and the reality they face. Adaptive work requires a change in values, beliefs, or behavior. The exposure and orchestration of conflict—internal contradictions—within individuals and constituencies provide the leverage for mobilizing people to learn in new ways. (Heifetz, 1994, p. 22)

The Heifetz strategy for stimulating learning is primarily one of facilitative leadership, leadership that facilitates or even provokes the learning needed in a group or institution. That is, Heifetz does not want to provide easy answers; rather, he advocates helping groups identify the adaptive challenges in their institutions and then to create a climate for identifying alternative solutions by asking questions of people involved and by encouraging groups to take responsibility for experimentation that involves learning in a particular context.

This strategy is similar to Piaget's ideas that people learn best when they experience the dissonance of their own internal disequilibrium, and to Senge's notions about dialogue. For Senge there are three basic conditions for learning in dialogue:

(1) ... "suspend" ... assumptions, literally to hold them "as if suspended before us";

(2) ... regard one another as colleagues;

(3) there must be a "facilitator" who "holds the context" of dialogue (Senge, 1990, p. 243).

To suspend assumptions is tension producing; that is, we must know what we are assuming while staying open to testing our current understanding (mental model) against other perspectives. The disease of that tension is exactly why we must, in Senge's words, "regard each other as colleagues," and in Palmer's words, "create a community of truth" in order to produce what Knowles identifies as a "climate for learning." Senge argues that dialogue is a difficult discipline and that groups need a skilled process facilitator to help create and hold the climate of community conversation that leads to the deepest kind of learning (Senge, 1990, p. 246).

There are several common characteristics in all of these approaches to adult education and learning.

(1) Persons are most motivated and energized to learn when they are working at finding answers to internal questions and at discovering more adequate ways of thinking and working (Piaget, Senge, Knowles, King, and Kitchener).

(2) Adult learners need a climate of openness (Knowles), a "community of truth" (Palmer), a supportive and challenging team for learning (Senge and Cervero), and a facilitator to hold the process (Senge and Heifetz as well as experience from CPE and theological field education).

(3) Great energy is released for learning when adults are involved in determining what they want to learn, in planning learning activities, and in evaluation as a process of deciding what to learn next (Knowles, the Methodist Laboratory Schools, laboratory method, Cervero).

Let us now turn to a model of professional continuing education that demonstrates these characteristics.

A Model of Peer Group Learning: Methodist Educational Leave Society (MELS)

In 1985, the Dixon Foundation in Birmingham, Alabama, began experimenting with the creation of clergy peer groups aimed at improving preaching in the North Alabama Conference of the United Methodist Church. Edwin M. Dixon started the project after finding a peer group program for business leaders extremely helpful to him personally. Mr. Dixon, a longtime and loyal United Methodist layperson, recruited a United Methodist pastor, the Reverend Burrell B. Hughes, to help establish a peer group program. The Dixon Foundation had been doing work in clergy continuing education prior to the peer group experiment in which individual pastors would be funded for a "leave," hence the name, the Methodist Educational Leave Society (MELS). Eventually, the peer group program replaced the funding of individual study leaves because of the perception that what happened in peer groups was far more powerful. Early in 1996, the FCP Faculty (Facilitator/Convener/Process Person) of the Methodist Educational Leave Society asked Dean Robert E. Reber to design an evaluation process for MELS to determine whether the program had been effective over ten years and to develop recommendations for the future. Bob Reber subsequently invited me to help with the evaluation.

In the spring of 1996, approximately 130 pastors had participated in MELS over the ten years of its existence (not all of whom were in peer groups). We sent all of them surveys and had 97 of them returned, 67 of these from peer group participants. In addition, we interviewed 114 people individually or in groups ranging in size from three to ten; the groups were representative: four MELS peer groups; eight Pastor Parish Relations Committees; four spouse groups; judicatory officials; a peer group of "Spirit Women"; and the MELS Board. In addition, we read the annual reports of six peer groups and reviewed two partial histories and a Doctor of Ministry thesis on MELS.

The usual MELS pattern was for peer groups to gather themselves together (they were self-selecting) into groups of six to eight pastors. Peer groups were assigned a "facilitator" who would assist the group in deciding what they wanted to learn, in developing plans for the learning, creating and submitting a proposal to the MELS Board, executing the plans, making applications of learnings in individual ministry practice, and evaluating at every step. Most of the groups ranged from 3 to 6 years in duration and met between 10 and 15 days per year, so there was a planned and sustained search for appropriate resources, experimentation in practice, and accountability in a lively community of conversation. The role of the facilitator was an important aspect of the program; FCP's were responsible for holding the process, for conflict management, and for asking critical questions at every point.

From what we heard in the interviews and read in the surveys, there is little doubt that the peer group process improved preaching in general as well as helped to create new energy in pastoral leadership. One spouse said of her husband, "When he got involved (in MELS) it was like someone built a fire under him!" (Reber and Roberts, 1996, p. 31). A participant summed up many other perspectives saying, "I believe that MELS has been the most transformative educational experience of my life. Through my MELS experience, I have been forced to reexamine the foundations of myself, my ministry, and my future." Some of the judicatory level leaders were convinced that MELS had improved the preaching in the whole North Alabama Conference, and one person reported that lay committees were now making participation in MELS one of the criteria in reviewing possible pastoral appointments to their churches.

The basis for this kind of transformational learning may lie in the nature of adult learning surveyed earlier. When we asked

MELS participants what had been most effective for their learning, there were two primary responses. First we heard, "my favorite and best instructors were the other folks in my group. We taught each other by interaction, honesty, critique, and love. They were by far my best teachers, the true experts (Reber and Roberts, 1996, p. 29). Second, participants mentioned about six resource persons in preaching who were considered to be excellent teachers primarily because of their style of teaching: "collegial, interactive, challenging, enthusiastic, upbeat, and passionate" (Reber and Roberts, 1996, p. 30). In his best-selling book, *Principle Centered Leadership*, Stephen R. Covey says that learning can create tremendous energy when it includes the following steps: (1) determine what learning is needed; (2) expand on what has been learned adding your own ideas; (3) find, review, and capture the essence of relevant material; (4) teach the material, sharing what has been learned, (5) apply the learnings in the context as an experiment; and (6) evaluate the results for further learning (Covey, 1991, p. 71). The MELS peer group process embodied all of Covey's elements and did, indeed, create energy in both the participants and in the congregations they served.

The MELS peer group program embodied all of the characteristics noted in the material reviewed from adult education and the models cited above. A facilitator helped create a "community of truth" in which pastors were invited to identify what learning was needed. The peer groups became, in effect, learning teams, which explored "mental models" with each other, supported experiments in the practice of ministry, and helped each other evaluate what was learned. The results of persons working together in such learning communities was high energy and motivation that led to willingness to risk innovations and explorations—exactly the kind of leadership needed for the church in our time.

References

Bradford, Leland P., Jack R. Gibb, Kenneth R. Benne. *T-Group Theory and Laboratory Method: Innovation in Re-education*. New York: John Wiley & Sons, 1961.

Cervero, Ronald M. *Effective Continuing Education for Professionals*. San Francisco: Jossey-Bass, 1988.

Cevero, Ronald M. "Professional Practice, Learning, and Continuing

Education: An Integrated Perspective," *International Journal of Lifelong Education*, Vol. 11, No. 2 (April-June 1992), pp. 92-98.

Covey, Stephen R. *Principle Centered Leadership*. Simon & Schuster, 1991.

Edwin Friedman, *Video Reinventing Leadership*. New York: Guilford Publications, 1996.

Heifetz, Ronald A. *Leadership Without Easy Answers*. Cambridge, Mass.: Belknap Press, 1994.

Knowles, Malcolm S. *The Modern Practice of Adult Education: From Pedagogy to Androgogy* (rev. ed.). Chicago: Association Press, 1980.

King, Patricia M. and Karen Strohm Kitchener *Developing Reflective Judgment*. San Francisco: Jossey-Bass, 1994.

Mead, Loren B. *Transforming Congregations for the Future*. Washington, D.C.: Alban Institute, 1994.

Palmer, Parker. *The Courage to Teach*, San Francisco: Jossey-Bass, 1998.

Piaget, Jean. *The Construction of Reality in the Child* (trans. Margaret Cook), New York: Basic Books, 1954.

———— *Six Psychological Studies* (trans. Anita Tenzer) New York: Vintage Books, 1967.

————. *Science of Education and the Psychology of the Child* (trans. Dereck Coltman), New York: Viking Press, 1970.

Pulaski, Mary A. S. *Understanding Piaget*. New York: Harper & Row, 1974.

Reber, Robert E. and D. Bruce Roberts "Study of the Methodist Educational Leave Society," Birmingham, Ala: The Dixon Foundation, 1996.

Senge, Peter M. *The Fifth Discipline: The Art and Practice of the Learning Organization*. New York: Doubleday Currency, 1990.

Senge, Peter, Charlotte Roberts, Richard B. Ross, Bryan J. Smith, and Art Kleiner, *The Fifth Discipline Fieldbook*. New York: Doubleday Currency, 1994.

Chapter 8

Linking Faith and Work: Continuing Education for Professionals

Robert E. Reber

For several years, Auburn Theological Seminary has worked with groups of Jewish and Christian attorneys and judges on issues of religious faith and the practice of law; health care professionals on discovering the unity of mind, body, and spirit; middle managers and chief executive officers on issues of corporate leadership and values in American society; and new directors of continuing education at seminaries and conference and retreat centers.

Auburn is an atypical seminary. Like other theological schools, our primary focus is on strengthening religious leadership, but we no longer grant degrees. Instead, we educate laity and clergy in a great variety of settings. Our programs take place both on the campus that we share with Union Theological Seminary in New York City and off campus at different sites around the country. A major priority for us is working with members of local congregations in those areas where they spend the most time and energy: the workplace, family life, and the larger community.

Getting Started

In our work with any of the professional groups, we began slowly and deliberately to identify persons within particular professions that might meet with us for exploratory conversations. Pastors and rabbis put us into contact with persons in their congregations who seemed to be open to and interested in how their religious faith and values relate to their work and the larger society in which they find themselves. Generally speaking, we never went "cold" to anyone. Through others, Auburn's educational interests and staff were initially introduced to professional men and women.

A specific example of what I am talking about is our beginning work with attorneys. In an informal conversation, a rabbi who is on Auburn's Board of Directors and I decided to ask two attorneys whom we knew—one Jewish, one Christian—about developing programs that would focus on issues arising from what it means to be a Jew or a Christian and a lawyer. We had a hunch that the two would respond favorably and that the interreligious dimension would make it even more appealing. We made it clear that a careful planning process would be set up to involve attorneys with us in making decisions about the purposes, design, leadership, schedule and venue for any possible program.

The response of the two attorneys was overwhelmingly positive. We asked them to be co-chairs and to help us identify other attorneys who might agree to be part of a planning committee. Twenty men and women met with us for an exploratory meeting where people became acquainted and learned more about Auburn. Over the next six months, we developed a three-part program on "Faith and the Practice of Law." The larger committee of twenty agreed to having a subcommittee of six work out details and then test them with the larger group. In total, there were five meetings—three of the larger group and two of the smaller one. The planning process was a highly significant educational experience. Participants got to know one another better, explored the territory of religious faith and law, and gained considerable ownership of the program.

This same kind of planning process was replicated in working with health care professionals, middle managers, CEOs, and directors of continuing education. We identified, with the help of others, who might be interested; had an exploratory meeting to share information and get acquainted; asked who else might be interested; and called together a larger group to test interest in the proposed programs and to be a part of a planning team over a six- to twelve-month period. During the initial steps, it was very important that participants be asked to come to only one meeting and that those in attendance would decide whether they wished to be involved further. Also, I had to be very clear about Auburn's interests and why we would want to engage them in developing an educational program. Laity are a bit wary of theological schools and centers that have paid little attention to them, especially when it comes to focusing on their professional lives and workplace issues.

Examples of Programs Developed and Carried Out

Let me give examples of programs developed and carried out by the different professional groups, and then address what has been learned that may be helpful to those who are responsible for continuing theological education for laity and clergy.

The programs for lawyers have involved more than four hundred over the last six years and now include judges. Increasingly, men and women, young and old, in different areas of practice, have served on planning committees and participated in programs. The Stein Center for Law and Ethics at Fordham University Law School and the Finkelstein Institute of the Jewish Theological Seminary have joined in as partners. Muslim attorneys are now coming to programs and taking part in the planning. In addition to the annual three-part series for local attorneys and judges, there has been a major conference, "The Relevance of Religion to a Lawyer's Work" involving attorneys across the country. More recently, there has been a conference, "Rediscovering the Role of Religion in the Lives of Lawyers and Those They Represent" which included teams from local communities across North America that are made up of attorneys, religious leaders and educators, and professors of law and ethics. One of the goals has been to help get programs going in local and regional areas. The papers presented at both conferences resulted in special publications of the *Fordham Law Review*.

Among the topics of different programs have been "Faith and the Practice of Law: An Overview," "Law and Religion Today: Challenges in Faith and Practice," "Keeping Faith and Your Legal Practice," "Conflicts Between Religious Beliefs and the Lawyer's Role," "Faith/Religious Perspectives and the Work of Judges," "With God in My Briefcase: Putting Your Religious Values to Work," and "Quinlan to Cruzan: Forging a Consensus on End of Life Decisions."

The programs for health care professionals have involved physicians, nurses, clergy, psychologists, mental health care workers, psychoanalysts, psychotherapists, counselors, social workers, medical and seminary students, chaplains, and practitioners of wholistic medicine. The overall theme has been "Discovering the Oneness: Mind, Body, and Spirit." Programs have been varied and based on different formats: large conferences, weekly seminars, and public lectures. Partners with Auburn in the planning and sponsorship have been the Blanton-Peale Institutes of Religion and Health; C. G. Jung Foundation of New York; Interweave Center for Wholistic Living; Programs in Religion and Psychiatry at Union Seminary; Center for Contemporary Spirituality at Fordham University; Department of Religion at Rutgers University; The Temple of Understanding; and The Psychotherapy and Spirituality Institute.

The topics of particular programs have included "Oneness and Soul: What Can Science Say?" "Experiencing Oneness of Body, Mind and Spirit," "Prayer and Healing," "Music and Meditation," "Principles of Wholistic Medicine," "Mysticism and Matter: Levels of Consciousness in the Spiritual Journey," "Traditional Christian Salvation and Psychosomatic Medicine," "Sacred Dialogue in Healing," "Meditating for Health and Wholeness in the Workplace" and "Integrating Spiritual Direction with Individual Psychotherapy."

Working with chief executive officers (CEOs) of major corporations on issues of corporate leadership and values in American Society has been an exciting and challenging venture. Both Christians and Jews have been involved from the profit and not-for-profit sectors. The first program was on "Ethics and Corporate Leadership in America," and others have been the "Ethics of Executive Compensation," "Human Rights, Religious Values, and International Trade" and "Market Pressures, Accounting Principles and Ethical Failures."

The programs are planned by a small group of CEOs and take place in different corporate headquarters. Participation is by invitation and limited to sixteen to twenty CEOs. The standard format includes a meal (usually breakfast or dinner), a half-hour presentation, and a good hour and a half of off-the-record discussion.

Recently, a vision statement was adopted by the planning committee. The purposes of the Chief Executive Officer Seminars on How Religious Values Impact Us are: to discuss a range of religious/ethical issues that CEOs face; probe religious/ethical values that may inform our decisions; explore the impact these issues have on corporations and the larger society; and participate in discussions that are mutually beneficial with peers.

The group has also developed guidelines to ensure that seminars contribute to the accomplishment of this vision. The following stipulations guide planners:

- only CEOs of major institutions in the New York City area are to be invited;
- each event should involve no more than 15 to 20 participants;
- participants should represent diverse constituencies with respect to religious affiliation, both profit and not-for-profit sectors, gender and the like;
- all conversations are to be considered off the record and confidential;
- presenters should be leaders in their field; and
- study papers for background reading are to be provided in advance.

In addition to the CEOs, Auburn has now established a program that involves a broader cross-section of corporate managers. Again, with the help of corporate officers, a small group of Jews and Christians was invited to sit down with staff of Auburn to talk about the interests and needs for such a program on religious/ethical values and corporate life. There were two exploratory meetings before deciding on a four-part program series for the first year. This group decided to alternate holding the programs in a synagogue and a church on Monday evenings from 6:00 to 8:30, with a buffet supper, presentation, and discussion. The titles of the programs are "Being Practically Faithful in the Workplace," "Being Faithfully Visible in the Workplace," "Being Spiritually Disciplined in the Workplace," and "Being Just and Faithful in the Workplace."

The Colleague Program for New Directors of Continuing Theological Education emerged out of discussions among directors active in the Society for the Advancement of Continuing Education for Ministry (SACEM). Auburn Seminary convened a group of directors to consider the need for a training program and it was recommended that one be launched. Begun in 1995, the Colleague Program is funded by The Henry Luce Foundation, Inc. Designed for small groups of no more than twelve newly appointed directors of continuing education in seminaries and independent centers in the U.S. and Canada, colleagues meet four times over an 18-month period for three-day gatherings. Since most participants began their jobs with little or no experience in continuing education, the Colleague Program creates opportunities for them to learn from one another and from seasoned professionals about a field that has been neglected in many theological institutions and centers.

What Has Been Learned?

What has been learned from working with these diverse professional and occupational groups? Here are some general recommendations for other continuing theological educators who would like to get involved in similar ventures.

- People are eager to explore the relationship between their faith and their daily lives; the church or synagogue does not usually offer the time and space to do this. We are called to live primarily outside the walls of these institutions. The more we see how our faith relates and speaks to our whole lives, the more we will become committed as people of faith and as stewards of all creation.

- Time and energy must be given to planning educational programs with people. Ultimately, we want people to own and take responsibility for their own lives and the life of faith. When a program fails because of a lack of response, it is almost always because people representing the group to be served were not involved in planning the why, what, how, who, when, and where.

- In working with professionals, or any particular group, it is important to begin by asking them as members of congregations or of a particular religious faith. This has been a key factor in our work. The common denominator of religious commitment has been a critical basis for getting together. That does not mean that there is always clarity about what we mean or understand religious faith to be, but it is a primary factor that draws people. In fact, our interfaith advisory committee at Auburn said that knowing that these would be interreligious was particularly appealing.

- Tap into the growing body of articles and books in the field of religion, law, medicine, business, and ethics. In the last ten years, numerous books and articles have been written on faith and the workplace, spirituality and daily life, a wholistic approach to living, and so forth.

- Develop programs that have some sustained educational thrust over time and that allow for a lot of give and take among participants and leaders. You may have to begin with a one-shot program, but one good experience can pave the way for many more.

- Recruit participants through letters of invitation signed by members of the planning committee who suggested them. One person inviting another with similar background or interests to join him or her in the program is a powerful appeal and gives the program immediate credibility in the eyes of the invitee.

- Network with other individuals, institutions, and community organizations. When an idea for a program, or work with a particular professional group come up, ask who else might you work with. None of us can afford to go it alone. We need each other in order to demonstrate real collaboration in a world often fragmented and divided. As I indicated earlier, we may not know who is best situated to help us with a particular goal but, most likely, somebody we know does!

- Money is not the issue. Once a key group is involved in planning and deciding with you, they are almost always willing to give or help you get the funding that is needed. This has been my experience for more than twenty-five years. The real challenges are our imaginations, and our willingness to take risks and to engage in new ventures.

One of the quotes shared with one of our professional groups has become a rallying point of inquiry as we move ahead to explore the connections between faith and our work and daily life. It was written by Martin Buber:

> We shall accomplish nothing at all if we divide our world and our life into two domains: one in which God's command is paramount, the other governed exclusively by the laws of economics, politics, and the "simple self-assertion" of the group. . . . Stopping one's ears so as not to hear the voice from above is breaking the connection between the existence and the meaning of existence. (Buber, 1966, p. 34)

Professionals and laypeople in our congregations are eager to explore "the connection" and we need to provide opportunities for them to do so.

Reference

Buber, M. *The Way of Response*, ed. N. N. Glatzer. New York: Schocken Books, 1966.

Chapter 9

Why Would Laypeople Want Theological Education, Anyway?

Sally Simmel

The soul of education is ... a lifelong cultivation of the wisdom each of us possesses and can share to benefit others.
—Parker Palmer

In this new world, this global village we inhabit, growing ever more complicated and accessible through science and technology, we think daily about the meaning and purpose of our lives. We are mindful of the decisions that need to be made to make sense of the world and our place in it. We can all tell stories of significant life experiences and the role we feel God is playing in them. A child is born, a child dies. A job is terminated; a new one is begun. We fall in love; we encounter something in nature that stirs us beyond anything we have known before. A parent dies and the loss lasts a very long time. We feel yearnings in our very soul for something yet unknown. We witness an incredible sunset or experience an amazing piece of art or poetry. We wonder about God's role in the universe and our role with God in the ongoing creation of the world. It is to this world that we introduce the question of why and how to provide theological education for laity.

Who Are These People of God?—The Laity

A funny thing happened on the way to the kingdom.
The church, the people of God, became the church, the institution.
—Verna Dozier

Laity are those members of the church whom God has called to *be* the church outside the walls of the church. In unison, they might say, "We write the laws of our lands and invent new technologies to serve humanity. We know how to clone animals and humans and measure germs on Mars. We rear and educate children. We run corporations, governments, and health care systems. We build roads and homes. We write and produce movies and TV shows. In those endeavors, we seek to practice our faith. We need the wisdom of faith through deeper theological reflection to help discern the 'how' and 'why' of it all."

They might also say in unison that they are not theologians. For the most part, that means that they are not trained in theology, for preaching, teaching, and Word and sacrament ministry. That is a particular call. "Doing theology" does not merely mean studying tradition, doctrine, and scripture, so that we *know* about those things. Theology balances fact and theory with the lived experience of God each of us has. All experience has meaning and provides insight for the journey. To stay either in the academic mode or the experiential mode would deny the wholeness of each person, God, and the universe.

The people of God begin to speak to God, to recognize there is a God, even without fully understanding, at a very early age: "Now I lay me down to sleep, I pray the Lord...."

Theological Education for What?

To prepare for the writing of this article, I sent surveys to more than three hundred laypersons of several denominations, cultures, ages, and geography. The survey was simply to obtain some insights into questions, such as:

- With what meaning-of-life questions are you currently wrestling?
- What kind of information, support, or challenges would assist you in clarifying your questions?
- If you were just starting on a new path in terms of your work or family, what kinds of faith-based education, reflection, or sharing would be helpful to you?

- How would you define theological education?
- Where and when have you experienced theological education?
- What has helped—or would help you—integrate such education into your daily life?
- What would be the most convenient way for you to get or do theological education and reflection for your daily life?

The response was encouraging in both quality and quantity. Research indicates a 5 percent response is necessary for reliable results. We had a 15 percent response. The respondents ranged in age from twenty-five to seventy-seven, with each decade in between represented. They live in Canada and from coast to coast in the United States. They are American Baptist, Presbyterian, Lutheran, United Church of Christ, United Methodist, and Roman Catholic. There was an even distribution of male and female, and about a 2 percent representation of persons of color. I thank them all for sharing their stories, their issues, and their hopes for opportunities to reflect theologically on the lives God has called them to. All of that is scattered throughout this chapter.

Laypeople of all ages and cultures are searching for meaning and purpose. The church risks losing them if the only theological reflection available to them is the congregation/parish church school. A forty-three-year-old from the East Coast of the U.S. sums up some of the longing for meaning in life when she asks, "What is this deep longing I feel in spite of success and happiness? What is God's purpose for me? How do I know when God is speaking to me?" And from another person, "How do I do the integrative work of my life?"

Even in their mature years, people wonder about meaning and purpose, as they remain vital, but begin, as one sixty-something puts it, "to deal with end of life decisions for parents and in-laws. How, as Christians, do we make choices for ourselves and our loved ones?" Some issues in the third stage of life are about new relationships with children and grandchildren, with meaningful retirement, or new directions for the vital years yet to come. Other issues are connected to new technologies that are frightening and often not understood by clergy or laity who are not working in the fields of science and technology. How do we bring the science and faith perspectives together in ways that assist Christians in making decisions?

According to the survey, mature Christians appear to be doing more of what we call "inner" work. The stress of earlier years, of demanding jobs, making ends meet, raising families, and just staying on top of things, gives way to some space for moving from external demands to the inner work of letting go, making new choices, staying faithful, and contemplating God's work in and through them. It is full time for many, and theological reflection would provide time for sharing, and engaging in activities that deepen their relationship with the sacred. This is true for some people of every generation.

The Knower

I pray to have a wise heart.
—Thomas Merton

In *To Know As We Are Known: Education as a Spiritual Journey*, Parker Palmer designates a person on a journey of spirituality and education a "knower." The term "knower" gives special meaning to the passage in 1 Corinthians 13:12: "For now we see in a mirror, dimly, but then we will see face to face. Now I know only in part; then I will know fully, even as I have been fully known."

That sense of knowing and being known stretches our understanding of the objectives of education. Theological education helps us move from being the "learner"—always a bit of a second-class position—to being a "knower." Not once and for all, or of all things, but of much and more as we continue the journey.

The knower, in this case the layperson discerning how to live faithfully *in the world*, has a worldview different from those who are called to work *in the church* as institution. For them, the church is not the center of the universe, and the majority of the people they encounter are not of the same faith group or denomination as they. As they go about their daily work, in relationships, in neighborhoods, and in the larger community, they increasingly engage with people of little faith, no faith, and other faiths. Their lives are enriched by what they come to know from friends, coworkers, and acquaintances who are Hindu, Muslim, Buddhist, Jewish, or some combination of traditions.

Recently, I met a Zen priest who was also a member of a Quaker meeting. His regard for Buddha and Christ were not separable. In our pluralistic society, we need to invite people of all faiths into the conversation that educates.

In the places of the world where Christians find themselves, many of the church's dualisms do not hold up. If God created *all* of the world, how can something be sacred and something else be secular? Everything and everyone (good or evil) has a place in creation, whether we like it or not.

Reflection and Conversation as Education

The invitation to theological reflection should not be taken lightly for while full of promise, it requires much of those who accept.
                                                                —Killen and DeBeer

Breaking the mold of presenting education in a traditional/ classroom/lecture model may not be easy in some places, but it will be necessary if laypeople are to be included in the theological offerings of schools, seminaries, and independent centers.

Parker Palmer suggests that we need an alternative theory about the nature of knowing, not based on methods and models, but on a transforming relationship between knower and knowledge. It means going back to recover a time when humans depended on emotion, intuition, and faith for their knowing, blending the reason, logic, and analysis of modern times. It allows sound fact and theory to spring from a truer passion and work toward a truer end.

Survey respondents would support that kind of blending. They seem disinterested in fact and theory as an easy way to answer life's dilemmas. They spoke of theological education in language that is familiar to us, but which is often difficult to support and nurture. That is the challenge before us. How do we provide the spaces, and the places, and the times for greater "knowing" that fits the yearnings of laypeople in our time? A few responses to the question: How would *you* define theological education? contain some insights:

- "Continuing growth in understanding of God's call in my life."
- "Should relate how our faith can be more fully expressed in the kind of life we live."
- "Serious exploration which examines (from a faith-based perspective) tradition and issues of contemporary life."
- "Very practical. Something like, reflecting on what God's doing in the world/my world/your world."
- "Learning the stories, examples of Jesus' treatment of issues. Sometimes I'm not sure they (ministers) know the questions."
- "Some academic content about my faith, but mostly living in relationship with Jesus."
- "Study and meditation on the significant questions of life."
- "Research and study of faith and religious material, along with stories of how individuals act out their beliefs."
- "Gaining new insights into how Christian faith impacts daily living and decision making."
- "Preparation and support for one's faith journey."
- "Education that helps me think about my/our relationship with God. Teach us how to move into the future with God and prepare us to effectively live out our faith."
- "Hearing from those who have studied various religious schools of thought and hearing what they have to say about how to live life with meaning, and to please God."
- "Too often, it seems that we get caught up in the study of the history of religious thinkers and acts and miss the experience of God, which I believe is essential to theological education."
- "An attempt to provide answers to questions about the origins and reasons for human existence on earth. It raises questions that are not readily answered and challenges seekers to ponder such questions as why we are here (or why not), helping them understand humans' need to adopt faith positions."
- "Pushes seekers to examine the consistency between their religious teaching or faith positions and their daily behavior. . . .".
- "A process of learning about God and how God relates to the

world. The process needs to include real experiences, not just intellectual, hypothetical situations."

- "Study and reflection on the nature of God, our purpose in the world, relationships with God, Jesus, our neighbors, and religious beliefs and practices."
- "Our lives in action, where we live, with our own questions —always questions."
- "Learning which brings us to a closer relationship with God."

The respondents would add to the teaching of fact and theory, the element of reality, and experience as a critical component of theological education for the whole of life. Not just knowing *about* faith and religion, but knowing how to apply it to *living*. Continuing education centers, seminaries, schools, and institutions that are interested in including laypeople in their processes and programs, might want to consider ways of thinking and organizing to consider these real-life educational desires.

If You Build It, Will They Come?

The purpose of knowledge is not to control, but to love.
—Bertrand Russell

If you build it, they will probably not come—at least, not at first. The average layperson who understands herself/himself on a spiritual journey, seeking a deeper relationship with God, has typically found less organized or structured ways to walk that walk.

Because of the clericalism of centuries of organized religion, laypeople have learned their lessons well—they come second, behind clergy. Clergy are provided theological education, which is then "given" to the people. This system has dishonored the "lived" experience of all people, lay and clergy, individually, and in community. As we move to a cosmic civilization, we can no longer afford to allow the purpose of education, as Palmer would point out, to be "to control those who have less knowledge, but come from a source of compassion." Clergy must continue to have the theological education that prepares them for their particular calling, just as lawyers, doctors, plumbers, secretaries, and computer operators must have the education they need to prepare them for their calls. Beyond that, there needs to be communal "knowing," face to face, together for the journey.

Laypeople have also been led to believe that they need to "get it right" before they share their faith stories. Getting it right could be interpreted as another form of systemic clericalism. It takes us back to times when the priest/pastor had access to the faith and acted as intercessor. None of us will ever get it "right," lay or clergy. We can only keep sharing our insights, our knowing, our truth, and keep moving, keep checking in, in a spirit of mutuality and accountability to one another and the faith. We check in and explore more deeply. We go out and live as faithfully as possible. We come back to the faith for more wisdom, in order to go back out and act again. And, so it goes—all the days of our lives.

Several of those who replied to the survey would treasure theological education at the seminary level or the postseminary level at continuing education and retreat centers. The Education for Ministry project, offered by the Seminary of the University of the South, Sewanee, Tennessee is an example of a long-term process of theological education and reflection that combines theory and reality, giving equal weight to each.

Men and women in all the generations represented in the survey would take advantage of continuing education, along with clergy, that would allow more and more reflection and conversation-type "knowing" to take place in the congregation, involving both lay and clergy persons, exploring God's activity in the world, and their role as cocreators with God in sustaining a just world.

Others, especially those in their forties and fifties, would be eager to participate in particular issue- or occupation-based groups that might be designated "vocational theology" groups, and in which a common language is shared among the participants. I met with a group in the high-tech industry not long ago, and was amazed that they were applying their belief systems to such important issues as the ownership of intellectual property. The same yearning for connections between faith and work can be found in dozens of occupational fields, as people meet together in homes and workplaces, because they find little understanding or support within their communities of faith. One forty-four-year-old man spoke of dealing with the midlife work of "integration...of faith and work...of sacred and secular. The world I live in seems to be very fragmented; at times, my faith community seems to add to the sense of fragmentation." Such people explore their spirituality as a way of looking at how God is active in the situations in which they are involved. People in all occupations, in all life situations (including students, the retired, and unemployed) in every level of work and economic situation, have both joyful and tough issues to face on a day-to-day basis. Insights, stories, and examples from scripture, tradition, and doctrine that have direct application are invaluable.

In an informal interview with a professional grant writer and consultant, I alluded to the idea of theological education for all interested laypeople. She asked, "Would a plumber want to go to seminary?" I wondered. The completed survey of a forty-one-year-old shoemaker gave me a partial answer. He was one of only a few people who had formal theological training, in Mennonite and Roman Catholic settings. "Spiritual formation has always been the most helpful education for me. The major theme seems to be that God reveals himself through people that we come in contact with throughout our days."

I interviewed a thirty-something woman who feels genuinely called to teaching as a religious vocation, as well as a professional career. I was impressed by her commitment to that call, as she embarks on a part-time course of study in a theological school, while continuing to teach high school full time.

During the last two years, I have been engaged in a continuing education program in spiritual formation. In class, we have heard lectures on, among other things, Native American spirituality, Julian of Norwich, Thomas Merton, and Jung. I now know the important dates in Merton's life, what he was doing when, and what kinds of influences shaped his life and thinking. But, I also know the "soul" struggles that brought him to a deeper knowledge of his own existence as connected to the entire universe. He shared a lot of the searching that goes on today among all people.

Program members could identify and connect with both the life and teachings of Merton. Alongside the facts and the theory, we shared stories of our spiritual mothers and fathers, whoever they were, and at whatever juncture in our lives they appeared—a gift of God to teach us about God and about life. Given a chance to tell the stories, we were amazed at what we had come to know, and from whom. One woman told of getting most of her knowledge about the Christian faith from books. She reached back to realize that her love of books came from the mother she had resisted for so many years. That led to more realizations about her mother's curiosity and courage, and threw light on some of our own experiences with parents, siblings, and friends. From whence cometh the knowing? From angels God has sent along the way to teach what we need to know at that point in our lives.

Models and Methods

Knowing is a profoundly communal act...since the self is inherently communal in nature.

—Parker Palmer

Keeping all of this in mind, methods and models are still needed for the education/reflection process. It is impossible to advertise something that has no form or purpose. "Y'all come and hang out" just doesn't do it. Instead, it is necessary to structure experiences in order that participants can be oriented to unfamiliar models, concepts, and ways of teaching.

There are many books on theological reflection, new and classical, that incorporate what some might call theological education. In designing retreats a couple of years ago, I became aware of *The Art of Theological Reflection* by Patricia O'Connell Killen and John DeBeer. The text is thorough in describing why there is a need for theological reflection, and how to do that well with individuals and groups.

Killen and DeBeer include the following models, along with content and process. All could be used in a retreat or continuing education context.

1. Beginning with a Life Situation (you get the picture)
2. Beginning with the Tradition I (piece of the Christian heritage)
3. Beginning with the Tradition II (a story from scripture)
4. Beginning with Cultural Text I (literature, art, social conflict, and so forth)
5. Beginning with Cultural Text II (from cultural situation to tradition and experience)
6. Beginning with a Theme (birth, creativity, relationship, transition)
7. Beginning with Personal Positions (assessing in light of our best understanding of our religious heritage, lived narrative and wisdom from the culture)
8. Beginning with Religious Experiences (encounters, interactions with life)
9. Reading Another's Theological Text (books, articles, in dialogue)

Everything you ever needed to know about putting together a full process, even a series of events on theological reflection and conversation, is contained in the pages of this book.

My survey respondents described the most convenient ways for them to engage in theological education and reflection in these terms:

- Conversation with networks related to my occupation
- Short courses in neighborhoods
- Conversations with good Christian friends and family
- Open exchange with others in their faith experience
- Conversations on-line.
- Bible study and retreats
- Reading
- College and seminary courses (weekends and evenings)

All Christians need a time and a place to think about their experiences, to make meaning from them, to find truth in them and, to take their beliefs into the world where they do their primary ministry, and where God is already present and active.

Conclusions: Challenges and Directions

The continuing theological education needs of laity are varied, according to their situations in life, work, family, and community. That is no surprise. Most pastors and other people in church-related vocations appear to want "how to" education (how to do worship, or stewardship, or evangelism programs, for example). Laity get that kind of training from their clergy and other leaders, of course, and, in addition, desire solid theological and biblical content which help them achieve "crossover" from Sunday life to Monday life. What is surprising is that, at least in my survey, there was no measurable difference in the needs expressed by members of various denominations.

This may be good news *and* bad news. Unlike the more predictable and compact list of theological needs of church professionals, the possibilities for educational programming for laity are awesome. All of life and faith is out there to be "chewed" on. That makes developing educational opportunities tricky. However, accepting the challenge means multiplying the number of persons who are equipped for ministry in the world and in the church. People in church-related occupations may also be grateful for such offerings. Many will appreciate a shift in emphasis for their own particular ministries. Surveys would quickly indicate continuing interest.

Continuing educators can enter the lay market in any number of places, slowly, and then incrementally increasing or reframing offerings, testing, and checking with the audiences. I offer four strategies that will help you get started.

1. Involve laity in solid theological education (along with clergy in many instances) where presenters and teachers pay special attention to the application of their material to real-life situations. That will require a shift in teaching style for some presenters.

2. Create reflection groups of persons in similar occupations. Use a small group approach. Systems of small groups provide information, support, accountability, and deep engagement in the issues of work and the marketplace. Such groups are very difficult to form in individual congregations, since often there is usually not a sufficient number of people working in the same field. If

done ecumenically, it strengthens relationships and better represents the day-to-day workplace connections of most Christians.

3. Extend these groups to online conversations where possible. The Internet allows people to relate in real time and cyber time from anywhere participants find themselves working. Ethical and moral situations in which people find themselves on any given day can be discussed from a distance with trusted friends. A combination of face-to-face and online time probably appeals to many. The group can decide that for itself. Continuing educators need to be open to this type of format.

4. Face squarely the challenges that this new group of participants will bring to traditional areas of your curriculum. For example, preaching events are popular for clergy. With laity, we can think about how pastors preach so the Word can be heard. How do laity hear the preaching and then re-word it for themselves? Who is responsible for the translating? Can we do that together? How? Clergy and laity could participate in evening, one day, and weekend events.

There is no end to the corners of life which would benefit from theological reflection and education. Our faith should reach every aspect of work and family life, global economics, politics, and religion in a post-Christian world. Millions of laity are eager for the opportunity to expand their horizons, to think differently, to live differently. Learning happens in all of life and through all of life.

Why would laypeople want theological education, anyway? For life, of course.

References

Killen, Patricia O'Connell and John DeBeer. *The Art of Theological Reflection.* New York: Crossroad, 1997.

Palmer, Parker. *To Know as We Are Known.* San Francisco: Harper, 1993.

Vaill, Peter B. *Learning as a Way of Being.* San Francisco: Jossey-Bass, 1996.

Chapter 10

Bending Over Backward to Train Special Students

Marvin T. Morgan

A Continuing Revolution in Zion

I grew up on a farm in North Carolina. Work on the farm often required that my father, six brothers, two sisters, and I do work that involved bending over for long periods of time. We pulled corn by hand, working in teams. One team of four persons would break off the ears of corn and place them in small piles between the cornrows. In a ten-acre field, they would make several hundred piles of corn, with more than fifty ears of corn in each pile. Because the piles were located between the cornrows, the ears on the bottom were always down in a trench six to eight inches deep. Those of us who collected rather than pulled the corn would spend hour after hour bending over to pick up the ears of corn that the pickers had stacked throughout the field. After bending over for many long hours, our backs ached profoundly, and we received the midday and evening periods of rest with great joy.

We also picked cotton, which requires a lot of back bending. We had no mechanical picker; we picked cotton the old-fashioned way. We picked with our hands. Each year, we raised several acres of cotton. When I was a child, I can remember thinking that the acres of cotton on our farm would have multiplied to a number no person could count, if God had not shown mercy by providing a large grove of trees at the edge of the farm. I will always believe that the grove of trees, and it alone, convinced my father that it was time to stop planting. To harvest the cotton, our entire family spent hour after hour, day after day, bending over the short cotton stalks, picking the cotton, one boll at a time. Strapped over our shoulders were cloth sacks that we dragged along the ground from one end of the field to the other. As we worked in this bent over, stooped position, our backs ached indescribably. In fact, it was not unusual to need the helping hand of another person just to stand upright at the end of the cotton row.

The backaches of those harvest seasons rushed back to me when my mother gave me some parental advice. After patiently listening to my lament over having failed to finish a particular task, she said, "Marvin, in order to achieve some of life's most important goals, you have to bend over backwards." In turn, her words reminded me of Langston Hughes's poem, "Mother to Son":

> Well, son, I'll tell you:
> Life for me ain't been no crystal stair.
> It's had tacks in it,
> And splinters,
> and boards torn up,
> and places with no carpet on the floor—
> Bare....
> Don't you set down on the steps,
> 'Cause you finds it's kinder hard...

Although I did not fully understand the long-range implications of my mother's advice, there is one thing of which I am quite certain. Because of my experiences in the cornfields and cotton fields of North Carolina, I know that bending over requires considerable effort. Therefore, bending over backward surely must require extraordinary effort, a high level of commitment, and a degree of tenacity that is far beyond the norm.

Why Call This a Revolution?

Dr. Charles Shelby Rooks, former associate director and later executive director of the Fund for Theological Education (here-inafter referred to as the Fund, or the FTE) published a book, in 1990 *Revolution in Zion: Reshaping African American Ministry, 1960–1974.* He writes that, following his "call" to the position of associate director of the FTE in September 1960, an event that he experienced as divinely ordained, he "set out to organize a revolution" (Rooks, 1990, p. 14). He referred not to just any revolution, but rather to a "revolution in Zion," a revolution in the African American church (p. 6). His was to be a "religious revolution" that would result in the infusion of new, well-trained, leaders in African American churches, who would be committed to bringing about social justice in those churches, and in the lives of church participants and their families.

Using the Fund for Theological Education as his "base of operations or staging area" (p. 15) he assumed primary responsibility for the development of leadership for Protestant churches in the United States and Canada (p. 14). This was a noble endeavor.

The Fund, organized in 1954 "to strengthen Protestant churches and theological seminaries, by recruiting prospective ministers from among the most talented college graduates of the time," had already become recognized as a key contributor to leadership development for Protestant churches in the six years preceding Shelby Rooks's arrival (p. 15).

Nevertheless, Dr. Rooks's tenure with the Fund spans a period when revolutionary ferment was everywhere in the nation and was having an impact upon most major institutions of that period. The FTE was no exception. Although he was concerned about leadership development for all Protestant churches, it is easy to understand why Dr. Rooks chose as his primary focus, the recruitment of the most able African American college students for the profession of Christian ministry. The identification and provision of financial resources to "support their graduate theological education" was a visible sign of his high level commitment to this endeavor (p. 14). It was his hope that this new pool of well-trained church leaders "would enable African American churches to develop their potential for changing the conditions under which their members and the people in their communities lived" (p. 14).

Several FTE programs were implemented. One program, the Trial Year in Seminary, provided full scholarships to more than sixty students per year, as they studied theology and reflected upon possible careers in ministry. Another was the Rockefeller Doctoral Program that succeeded in producing what appeared to be an overabundance of "doctors in religion." However, these were not African American doctoral scholars. To meet this unique need, the Doctoral Scholarship for Black North Americans program was established. This program was designed to enable the Fund, and indirectly the churches, colleges, and seminaries, to "compete with other occupations for the most promising college graduates of that era" (p. 24). Finally, this same goal was further achieved through the Protestant Fellowship Program (PFP). It is to this program that Dr. Rooks was "called" to serve as staff person, in 1960 (p. 34). The primary purposes of the PFP were threefold:

> (1) to support the education of thirty-five to forty persons per year who were committed to Christian ministry—it was hoped as pastors of local churches; (2) to engage in research about ministry in African American churches and; (3) to stimulate and organize a broad range of activities that would strengthen the mission and ministries of those churches (p. 24).

With this broad range of initiatives, Dr. Rooks set out to lead a "revolution in Zion."

Between 1960 and 1988, the number of African American seminary students increased from 387 to 3,379; the number of African American faculty serving at predominantly white institutions increased from 6 to 186, and the number of African American doctoral students increased from 18 to 89 (pp. 174-76). Today, many of these same FTE program participants are making major contributions to Black religion as faculty members, college and university presidents, writers, researchers, and pastors (p. 23).

The lists of names and accomplishments read like volumes of "who's who" in world religions. In many ways, Dr. Rooks and the FTE "leaned over backward" to identify and train new leaders for the Black church. What they have succeeded in doing and what is evident even until this day, is nothing short of a revolution that has changed, for the better, the influence of African American religious leaders throughout the world.

Notwithstanding their many accomplishments, there is one line Dr. Rooks wrote regarding the need for continued student recruitment, that may prove to be his most prophetic expression. He wrote, "the revolution will never be complete" (p. 174). He could not have been more correct. Like most revolutions, there are, within the revolution in Zion, other bases of operation or staging areas, with different sets of players, whose stories have not yet, been told. The following is an attempt, somewhat comparatively, to tell, as Paul Harvey would say, "the rest of the story!"

A New Stage, but the Same Zion

Eleven years after Shelby Rooks left the FTE, inspiration for further revolutionary action in Zion came to Dr. James H. Costen, immediate past president of the Interdenominational Theological Center (ITC) in Atlanta, Georgia. ITC is the largest and strongest predominantly African American theological seminary in the United States. Jim Costen's sojourn, first at Johnson C. Smith Theological Seminary (JCSTS) and later at ITC, began as he studied for the Bachelor of Divinity degree, the degree now known as the Master of Divinity degree, which he received with highest honors, in 1956. His professional career at these institutions spans a twenty-eight-year period, 1969–1997. He was the dean of JCSTS following its move from the Johnson C. Smith University campus in Charlotte, North Carolina to the ITC campus in Atlanta. He served with distinction in this position for fourteen years. Then, in 1983, he was named president of ITC. During his fourteen-year tenure as president of ITC, Dr. Costen developed a legacy worthy to become the standard by which the work of all future education administrators may be measured (see Marsh, 1996–1997). His tenure represents the most prosperous years in the history of that unique institution. While many of his accomplishments are unique, our primary concern here is with his support of continuing education.

Dr. Costen would be one of the first education administrators to agree that "the best and the brightest" students are "special" and should be encouraged to pursue graduate theological studies. He would also agree that such special students are better able to reach their highest potential when education administrators, judicatory leaders, and directors of major foundations put forth extraordinary effort and, yes, "bend over backwards" to help with their professional preparation. However, Dr. Costen also asked,

145

rhetorically, "can not effective strategies that are applied at the highest levels of professional preparation, with appropriate contextual modifications, be equally effective when applied at other levels, even remedial levels?" And so to the question, should graduate theological schools and foundations provide special assistance to the best and the brightest students while failing to do the same for others who have not yet received high honors? he answered a resounding "no!"

There is a sentence of scripture in Matthew's Gospel, referring to the matter of tithing in the practice of Hebraic Law, that addresses the human tendency to do good in one area of life, while neglecting to do good in another: "... these ought ye to have done, and not to leave the other undone" (Matthew 23:23 KJV). The FTE should have done precisely what was done for the best and brightest students of that era. However, Jim Costen had the wisdom, foresight, and personal sensitivity to recognize that there was another group of special learners that were urgently in need of continuing education for ministry. These were pastors and lay leaders who did "not qualify to enter a graduate professional school" (Costen, 1984, p. 1). These special learners were "already established, accepted, and respected leaders in their communities" (p. 1). Many of them were "gifted, highly articulate preachers in their pulpits but were often extremely limited" in their other pastoral skills (pp. 1, 2).

Dr. Costen was convinced that a continuing education program at ITC could help these pastors and other church leaders to provide the high quality leadership capable of addressing the social, economic, moral, and spiritual needs of contemporary society. This need for more professionally trained African American clergy was not a new phenomenon. However, because of the increasing demands being placed upon clergy and lay leaders, to get on with the business of "equipping the saints," there was a sense of urgency to remedy this shortage and to begin the task immediately. Dr. Costen sought to meet these and other needs of the African American churches through the development of the continuing education and life longlearning program at ITC.

As revolutionary ferment again roiled the waters surrounding Zion, Jim Costen was clearly captain of the ship. It was equally apparent that his cocaptain and primary point person, for matters related to continuing education, was Dr. Mance C. Jackson, associate professor of Church Administration and Leadership Education at ITC and not surprisingly, a product of the FTE's Protestant Fellowship Program. Dr. Jackson, an ordained clergyperson, pastor, and presiding elder in the Christian Methodist Episcopal Church, also served as part-time director of continuing education. He shared, and implemented Dr. Costen's vision for the future of continuing education at ITC. Doctors Jackson and Costen were in close collaboration every step of the way, as they worked to firmly establish continuing education and lifelong learning as one of the priorities of the seminary.

All conditions seemed ripe for continuing revolutionary activity in Zion. It is estimated that, in the early 1980s, more than 80 percent of the pastors serving the approximately sixty-five thousand African American congregations in the United States lacked professional theological education. A minimum of two thousand ministers were needed each year to fill vacant pulpits, in addition to the scores of persons needed to fill nonparish related ministry positions. However, the average annual number of African American seminarians graduating from theological schools in the United States was three hundred and fifty. Having no other seminary trained clergy to fill the additional sixteen hundred and fifty pulpits each year, congregations looked within their own ranks to find those persons who had acknowledged receiving a "call" to the vocation of ministry. Who would step forward to provide professional theological training to these non-college-trained pastors and church leaders? If not the ITC, then who? If not in the 1980s, then when?

There were many other factors that seemed to indicate a need to devote special attention to continuing education and lifelong learning at the ITC. Drs. Costen and Jackson recognized that the very low level of alumni support, being received at that time, was a reflection of the high level of frustration alumni were experiencing over critical leadership development issues within their local churches.

Understandably, the first few years of the Costen presidency had been devoted to the demanding tasks of fund-raising and staff and faculty development, in support of the basic degree programs of the seminary. Dollars for the support of theological education were limited, and the competition with the seminaries of historic, prestigious universities and highly influential mainline denominations was fierce. While the ITC directed most of its resources to strengthening its basic degree programs, little, if any, resources remained to respond to alumni requests for continuing education opportunities.

The requests were many and quite varied in scope. There were local pastors whose judicatories required that they complete a minimum number of hours of continuing education each year. They could, and often did, register for courses at other institutions. However, they expressed a desire to return to their alma mater, the ITC, for what they perceived to be more relevant continuing studies. These same pastors and others served local churches where laypersons volunteered for a myriad of leadership positions. Many new skills were needed, as laypeople volunteered to serve as directors of Christian education, superintendents of church schools, youth directors, church school teachers, and so forth. The pastors looked to the ITC for help in training and equipping these volunteers.

Finally, there were public issues such as aging, domestic and world hunger, increasing crime rates, the peace movement, and the nuclear arms race. Others were concerned about substance abuse, racism, sexism, homophobia, human rights, medical and legal ethics, economic development with justice, peace with justice, toxic waste disposal, prayer in public schools, and public versus private schools, and so forth. This host of issues confronting congregations needed to be addressed from religious perspectives. Pastors were being challenged to become what the current ITC president, Dr. Robert M. Franklin, calls, "public theologians" and they were ill equipped to do so (see Franklin, 1987, pp. 122-24). Seminars, institutes, workshops, lecture series, and minicourses would be excellent ways to train these pastors, so that they could, in turn, train their congregations to deal with these many public issues. Responding to these many needs was essential, if ITC was to maintain the allegiances and confidences so carefully developed while these alumni were enrolled in degree programs.

To fulfill effectively this broad range of training needs, ITC would need a comprehensive, multifaceted continuing education and lifelong learning program. The goals and objectives for the program would need to be stated, in such a convincing way, that the staff of a major foundation would be totally assured of its positive impact and long-term benefit to our beloved Zion. Doctors Costen and Jackson were equal to the task.

They proposed a fourfold agenda for the continuing education and lifelong learning programs:

Three-Year Program of Continuing Education for Ministers (Including Military Chaplains) with Seminary Degrees

First, the program would support the graduates of ITC's degree programs with ongoing classes. A survey was conducted among ITC alumni to determine the topics they wished to have covered in continuing education events. In response to the survey, the decision was made to offer two continuing education institutes or modules per year, over a three-year period. These would consist of a three-day seminar each fall and a one-week-long seminar each summer. These were to be held on the ITC campus. The proposed topics for the fall sessions were Biblical Studies (year 1), Systematic Theology (year 2), and Church History (year 3). The instructors were to be members of the ITC faculty, faculty persons from other institutions, and guest lecturers. The summer sessions were to focus upon the participants' ministry style and techniques as applied when working with different segments of the congregation. The proposed themes were Senior Citizens (Year 1), Young Adults (year 2) and Youth (year 3).

Three-Year Program of Lifelong Learning for Ministers Without Seminary Degrees

This program was based on the assumption that non-college-trained clergy have essentially the same professional training needs as those who are qualified to enter graduated degree programs. At the same time, it was understood that these participants might lack certain basic liberal arts competencies. The intent was to offer, at convenient hours (evenings and Saturdays), some of the same courses that were being offered in the seminary's Masters degree programs. Students were to meet on Tuesday evenings, Thursday evenings, and on Saturdays and were to take courses such as Introductions to Old and New Testament, Systematic Theology, Church History, and so forth. These courses were to be taught by members of the ITC faculty or by qualified guest lecturers. Following the completion of twelve ten-hour courses (a duration of about three years,) the participant would be issued a certificate of completion. One continuing education unit would be granted for each course.

Three-Year Program of Lifelong Learning for Church Lay Workers Through a Lay School of Theology

Third, instruction for lay leaders was needed. Recognizing the broad range of ministries, within and beyond the local church, which are provided by laypersons, the need for special training opportunities would appear to be obvious. Nevertheless, very few continuing education courses were available, at that time, that were designed to equip laypersons for the broad range of ministries in which they were engaged. The ITC's proposed Lay School of Theology was intended to be a three year course of study, that would parallel that of the program for ministers without seminary degrees. Some of the courses were designed to prepare participants for ministries traditionally rendered by the laity. However, there were other lay ministries that required the same theological competencies as those services provided by the clergy. The proposed program was also designed to help enable laypersons to more clearly articulate their faith, lead worship services, and provide spiritual guidance. Lay participants would receive a certificate of completion, after finishing twelve ten-hour courses. One continuing education unit would be granted for each course.

Short-term Learning Experiences for Ministers, Laypersons, and Special Interest Constituencies

Finally, a variety of special events might be sponsored. The ITC is located within the rich academic environment of the Atlanta

University Center, only a few miles from the center of Metropolitan Atlanta. It is uniquely situated to address the many public policy issues that affect the African American church and community. The proposed seminars, workshops, and short-term intensive courses were intended to facilitate ongoing dialogue among theologians, physicians, ethicists, psychologists, psychiatrists, politicians, and the various segments of the business community. Continuing education sessions were designed for one-hour luncheons, half-day "intensives," daylong "intensives," and weekend retreats. Anticipated participants were to consist of persons from various professions, public housing tenants, unemployed and underemployed persons, welfare recipients, and families of incarcerated persons. These events were intended to enhance contact and interaction between the seminary and the community.

Martin Paul Trimble, Program Officer and later, Religion/ Program Associate with the Pew Charitable Trusts located in Philadelphia, Pennsylvania became a critical supporter of the program. The program, as initially proposed, was too broad to be successfully coordinated by a part-time director. After consulting with Mr. Trimble and receiving some helpful advice, they requested and received, in 1987, a modest planning grant from the Pew Charitable Trusts, which provided valuable time for the completion of data gathering and careful refinement of the original proposal.

Utilizing the data gathered from surveys, consultations with judicatory leaders, college and university presidents and members of a very gifted central advisory committee, ITC implemented a program that focused on the second and third agenda items outlined above—educating clergy who had not received graduate training, and educating laypeople. These two branches of the program have been since 1991 jointly known as the Certificate in Theology program. Although some participants are college graduates, an earned college degree is not a prerequisite to enroll in the program. Refinement of the program required two years of intense development work, and involved some false starts, some trial and error, some moderate successes and, certainly, some failures. However, Drs. Costen and Jackson were determined to persevere and Martin Trimble was equally determined to be generous with his patience.

In the spring of 1990, with a $300,000 grant from the Pew Charitable Trusts to be received over three years, ITC gained renewed capabilities and much needed reassurances, to further the revolution in Zion. On more than one occasion, during this protracted planning process, Martin Paul Trimble played key roles in helping to assure the eventual acquisition of funding.

Unfortunately, despite the now strengthened basis of support, ITC faculty began to express some concerns regarding the very limited amount of time they could commit to teaching remedial courses, over and beyond their regular course loads. The evening hours, weekend schedules, and modest stipends dampened their enthusiasm for traveling great distances to teach certificate level courses. Therefore, twelve members of the faculty were asked to deliver lectures before a video camera, and discuss essentially the same material they covered in their graduate level classes. For each course, twelve forty-five-minute lectures were recorded. These videotaped lectures could then be delivered to seminary trained local instructors who were hired to teach courses at extension study sites. The instructors were asked to acquaint themselves with the content of each course and then to show major portions of the videotaped materials to those persons attending the weekly class sessions. The local instructors then served as discussion facilitators and provided many of the other services for students that would ordinarily have been provided by ITC faculty.

This redesigned Certificate in Theology program was based on some key assumptions regarding the ways learning occurs. It was hoped that learning and significant sharing of information would take place in at least three ways. First, through the videos, the students would be introduced to the latest thinking and ideas of the ITC's distinguished faculty, without having to travel to the Atlanta campus. Second, seminary trained local instructors would be available to clarify the content of the videos and lead class discussions. And, third, by participating in numerous classroom discussions, these students would learn valuable lessons from each other, because of their many years of service within local churches and communities.

The initial extension study sites were established at Edward

Waters College in Jacksonville, Florida, and at Stillman College in Tuscaloosa, Alabama. College campuses were chosen because of the ready-made resources and in hopes that some of the certificate students would enroll in some undergraduate courses. However, this synergy did not materialize. Therefore, when ITC received requests to establish extension study sites in cities and small towns, where the seminary had not cultivated any close relationships with local colleges, ITC administrators felt free to modify their approach.

Beginning in 1991, classes were no longer limited to college campuses. Study sites were established in the educational wings of local churches, community centers, public schools, Baptist association assembly halls, and so forth. Wherever the minimum of twenty students could be recruited, competent seminary trained local instructors and coordinators hired and adequate class meeting space found, ITC moved quickly to establish new extension study sites. During the period 1992–1999, the program grew from forty-five students meeting in three cities to more than six hundred students meeting in forty-two cities. Study sites were established throughout the United States and also in Canada, Bermuda, and the Bahamas. To date, six hundred eighty-eight students have earned the Certificate in Theology at the ITC. Of this number, approximately twenty students, with Bachelors degrees, have enrolled in one of the Masters level programs at the ITC. Many of these former certificate students have distinguished themselves as exceptional degree program participants.

Not unlike the students who were helped by the FTE's Protestant Fellowship Program, many of the students who earned the Certificate in Theology are now serving in local churches where they are making outstanding contributions to the quality of life in and beyond Zion. Positive changes have been made in the ways they do ministry. They now serve with increased competence and renewed confidence in their own abilities, and are thereby better able, with the help of God, to offer hope to others. They greatly appreciate the seminary's willingness to meet them "where they were" so they could move to higher levels.

When they arrive at their classes, these students are bent over with fatigue, having already worked eight hours in secular jobs. Nevertheless, they meet for three to six hours weekly. They meet in Tupelo and Marks, Mississippi; in Grambling, Louisiana; in Hamilton, Ontario, Canada; and in the Hamilton Township of Bermuda. Wherever they meet, they do so at the end of long, hard days. When they come to the end of the program, perhaps they realize what the staff and official boards of the FTE and ITC already know—that "in order to achieve some of life's most important goals, you have to bend over backwards."

A Challenge to All Seminaries and Theological Centers

The FTE stood alone as it recruited the best and brightest students and encouraged them to pursue ministry-related careers in the 1960s and early 1970s. Similarly, the ITC has enjoyed very little company among mainline ATS member schools, as it has provided certificate level courses to predominantly African American constituents in local, national, and international settings. Providing training for nontraditional theological students is demanding, even backbreaking, work when done by only a few, but would be far less demanding and infinitely more productive if done by many.

For better or worse, ours is a market-driven society that rewards those who respond positively to the market. There is a great demand for theological training among clergypersons and other church leaders who have not yet been able to pursue formal college and/or seminary training. Throughout the history of Christendom, untrained men and women have been inspired, called, commissioned and/or ordained to do ministry. They are going to minister to others, rightly or wrongly, whether seminaries help to equip them, or not. They are going to seek training in unaccredited Bible colleges, in denominational academies, and often at the feet of untrained instructors, unless the seminaries respond to their critical training needs.

The challenge for every seminary is to interpret its mandate to provide theological education as all-inclusive. Seminaries must continue to train those persons who have already earned college degrees. Our admission standards for graduate level theological studies are clear and appropriate. Nevertheless, there are other prospective students, who are calling upon the seminaries to show greater flexibility in the types of courses offered, in the times and places courses are offered, in the media through which they are delivered. A willingness to be flexible in these and other areas may enable seminaries to bend over backward in efforts to more effectively serve those students who do not fit traditional models. By accepting the challenge to train all students, the gifted and the remedial, all accredited theological seminaries may become part of a new, more inclusive staging area for the ongoing revolution in Zion.

References

Costen, James H. "A Proposal for the Creation and Development of a Continuing Education and Lifelong Learning Program at the Interdenominational Theological Center." Presented to The Pew Charitable Trusts, Philadelphia, Pennsylvania in May 1984 (all quotations used with permission).

Franklin, Robert M. *Another Day's Journey: Black Churches Confronting the American Crisis.* Minneapolis: Augsburg Fortress, 1997.

Hughes, Langston. "Mother to Son" in *Collected Poems of Langston Hughes.* New York: Random House, 1995.

Marsh, Clinton M. *"The President's Legacy"* in *The Journal of the Interdenominational Theological Center* 24 (Fall and Spring 1996–97), pp. 113-29.

Rooks, Charles Shelby. *Revolution in Zion: Reshaping African American Ministry, 1960–1974* (New York: The Pilgrim Press, 1990).

Chapter 11

Educating Religious Leadership for a Multireligious Society

Robert E. Reber

The religious landscape of America is rapidly changing! The religious pluralism of the world is increasingly at our doorstep. No longer are Buddhists only in Japan or China, Muslims in Egypt or Indonesia, or Hindus in India and Thailand. Adherents of these faiths and more now reside in many different communities across North America. What is new is not the number of traditions, but their proximity. There are numerous cities and towns where one can find churches, synagogues, mosques, and temples within easy walking distance of each other. We are living in an ever-growing multireligious environment, whether in New York City, Hartford, Washington, D.C., Atlanta, Toledo, Indianapolis, Chicago, St. Louis, Cedar Rapids, Houston, Denver, San Francisco, or Los Angeles.

Christians, accustomed to dominating the religious sphere in the United States, respond in a variety of ways to this new reality of religious pluralism. Some withdraw, even move away. Others ignore it. Others increase their efforts to convert non-Christians. Some are threatened by religious pluralism while others are intrigued and open to learning more about this new reality. Issues of identity come to the fore for every religious tradition as it lives alongside different traditions. Each faces the question of what it means to live as a religion within a family of religions.

Living and working in one of the most multireligious areas in this country has raised directly for me the issue of what is my responsibility as a continuing theological educator in a historic Presbyterian institution that is committed to developing religious leadership for the future of the church and American society. For many, confronting the reality of religious pluralism is not a strongly felt need or interest. To move into an arena pretty well ignored by many continuing and adult education enterprises is full of risks and promises. The territory is rather uncharted, in terms of developing educational programs for both clergy and laity. There is considerable history of Jews and Christians working together, but little to go on when you seek to engage Buddhists, Hindus, Muslims, Jains, Sikhs, and Baha'is.

My first effort in multifaith programming was almost eight years ago when we invited a team of educators from the Multi-Faith Centre in Birmingham, England, to come to lead a workshop here, over a seven-day period, on Multi-faith Dialogue in a Multicultural Society. The team included laypeople from the Buddhist, Hindu, Jewish, Muslim, Sikh, and Christian communities. They had been working together for several years to bring about knowledge and understanding that fosters multifaith and intercultural relationships and contributes to the quality of life in local settings. It was an extraordinary occasion that left us dizzy with ideas, exhilarated by their relationships and stories, and challenged to take seriously our own society and particular community settings.

During the intervening years, Auburn Seminary has involved representatives of twelve different faith traditions in planning and carrying out programs that have included visitations to different religious centers; partnering with others in holding multifaith festivals of ritual, music, dance, fellowship, and education; sponsoring programs for women of faith on death, healing and the afterlife, raising children in today's world, women mystics of different traditions, and feminine images of the divine; developing a yearlong series on spirituality and the different religious traditions; holding public lectures by scholars from different traditions; and planning an ongoing program called "Building Bridges: Understanding Our Neighbors' Faiths." To give you an idea of what is involved in developing an interreligious educational program, let me describe this last one in more detail.

Under the sponsorship of the Multi-Faith Forum of Long Island, Auburn Seminary, and the Long Island Council of Churches, I chaired the Education Committee for the past three years that developed the Building Bridges program. Members from each of the following traditions have been active members: Baha'i, Brahmas Kumaris, Buddhism, Christianity, Hinduism, Islam, Jainism, Judaism, and Sikhism. In the beginning we spent considerable time getting better acquainted and exploring what kind of educational programs might be needed on Long Island. We talked to religious leaders, educators, and members of different religious communities, and reviewed regularly our ideas with the representatives of twelve different faith traditions who make up the Long Island Multi-Faith Forum, and the members of the Interreligious Task Force of Auburn Seminary. As an Education Committee, we identified four main objectives of the "Building Bridges: Understanding Our Neighbors' Faiths" program:

- Educate communities about religious diversity in their world;
- Encourage neighbors to reach out to one another in friendship and respect;
- Expand horizons of knowledge about beliefs and customs of our neighbors;
- Explore ways to make our communities more just and peaceful for all peoples.

We wanted the program to be flexible in terms of length, and to occur in a variety of settings, such as religious communities, congregations, high schools and colleges, civic groups, hospitals, professional organizations, senior citizen centers, and so forth. We thought that it was important that the programs be interactive, use different teaching methods, and offer ongoing possibilities for people of different faith traditions to work together, to better understand each other, and to address issues that could make for a qualitative difference in the lives of their local communities.

We came up with a program that would have four key components: a twenty minute audiovisual that gives an overview of how multireligious Long Island is; a panel presentation by representatives from different faith traditions; an open question and discussion period; and a booklet on each faith tradition that includes follow-up contacts and bibliographic suggestions. All of this proved to be a big undertaking, and required obtaining modest grants to underwrite the production of materials.

The first thing that we tackled was developing a four-page folio on each of the twelve faith traditions represented on the Long Island Multi-Faith Forum. In addition to the nine already mentioned in the membership of the Education Committee, we included Native American Spirituality, Unitarian Universalism, and Yoga Spirituality. Lucinda Allen Mosher, a longtime student of world religions and a graduate student at General Theological Seminary, volunteered her time as writer and editor. She began by asking committee members what would be important to include in the folio. Members came up with key symbols, origins, sacred writings, key beliefs and practices, holidays, organization, social action, and Long Island contacts for more information and local leadership in particular traditions. She interviewed different religious leaders, read materials that they suggested, and drew on her own rich background in the study of world religions in drafting the different folios. Each step along the way, members of a specific religious tradition reviewed the materials and made suggestions. Then the document was presented to the entire Education Committee for review and vote. Finally, the twelve different four-page folios were reviewed and voted upon by the Long Island Multi-Faith Forum. This process was time consuming, but absolutely critical for coming up with documents that were both affirmed and owned by each particular religious group, and understood and affirmed by the twelve traditions in the Multi-Faith Forum. These have now been printed by the Long Island Multi-Faith Forum as "An Introduction to Your Neighbors' Religions."

The next major task was the development of an audio-visual presentation. The Education Committee met with Michael Fairchild, a well-known photographer and frequent contributor to *National Geographic,* in order to explore what was needed to show and tell people how the religious landscape had, in fact, changed on Long Island. Over a period of two months, Michael took pictures of the places of worship, rituals, and community activities of all twelve religious traditions. A script was developed with the input and critique of Multi-Faith Forum members, and they helped to obtain a broad selection of recorded music and chanting that could be used. The end product is a spectacular kaleidoscopic view of the religious and cultural diversity of Long Island.

Staging live panel presentations on "what it has meant for me to live out my faith on Long Island" required training people to be open, interactive, spontaneous, and free in a public setting, rather than simply giving a minilecture about what a Buddhist, Hindu, Jain, Sikh, Christian, or Jew believes. We generated a long list of possible questions for moderators of panels to use to get the discussion going, including:

- What is a big challenge you face in raising your children in your faith tradition?
- What kind of misunderstandings have you encountered about your faith from others on Long Island?
- What does your religious tradition say about other religious traditions?
- In what ways might communities on Long Island affirm publicly that religious pluralism is a reality and is to be valued?

The training sessions were designed to be practice sessions for potential panelists and moderators, and to be fun! The process involved an orientation to the Building Bridges program, listing suggestions of dos and don'ts for panelists, getting volunteers of at least four different traditions to be on a panel, having an actual panel discussion, letting the audience address questions to the panel, and then getting feedback on how it went from panelists and the audience. More than fifty persons from the twelve traditions have participated in these training sessions. The Education Committee has kept notes on who did well and when various people are available. All of us have learned a lot about each other's faith and some of our deepest concerns and hopes.

Panel members are all volunteers. Most are laypersons living, working, and raising families on Long Island. All treasure their own communities while cherishing American society and its values, which protect and affirm religious diversity. All are well informed about their own religious tradition and eager to share its values and customs with others. All are genuinely interested in learning about other religious traditions and building bridges of understanding.

Only recently has the "Building Bridges: Understanding Our Neighbors' Faiths" been publicly launched. The brochure about the program has been widely distributed and requests have begun to come in. So far, it has been an exciting and challenging venture for all of us. The entire planning, designing, and training process took over three years and has been an incredible educational journey. We have learned a lot. Below I identify seven key learnings that may be helpful to anyone in adult, continuing, professional, or religious education who develops programs that address questions and concerns emerging from our ever-growing religiously and culturally pluralist society. For these learnings, I am indebted to persons from many different religious backgrounds with whom I have worked during the past seven years in planning and carrying out numerous inter-religious, educational programs.

1. Be clear about why you want to engage the multireligious community in developing educational programs.

Most of these communities are still in minority positions, and members will want to know why you are interested in working with them. As a member of a dominant religious community, I believe that I am called by God to help build human community that seeks to relieve suffering and cares for the planet. I need their help in bringing about a better understanding of their traditions in my own community, and in building a just and peaceful society for all people who value religious and cultural pluralism. I am firmly convinced that plurality in a positive sense means becoming a community of communities, a concept receiving considerable attention in the World Council of Churches. There are many other reasons that can be added. The point is to be clear about why any of us are doing what we are doing!

2. Take time and care to find out what religious groups are in your community.

This is not an easy task. Many religious groups are not organized in the ways that Christians and Jews are. There is often neither an overarching organizational structure nor a directory or listing of all the religious traditions in a particular area. On Long Island, we looked in the telephone directory, contacted school systems, drove around neighborhoods, went to media outlets, and called the Center for the Study of World Religions at Harvard University. This center, through the Pluralism Project, has developed a database that includes many communities across the United States and lists of the different religious groups that exist within them. Increasingly, there are interfaith organizations that have membership lists and can be very helpful in identifying groups.

3. More often than not, there will not be an expressed interest or felt need for interfaith educational programs.

It does not work for program directors to just set up programs and hope that somebody comes. We have to create a climate, build expectations, and develop a constituency base. We have to involve others in an educational partnership with us. Many immigrant religious communities have continued to be strangers in this land, because members of the dominant group have not reached out to welcome or get to know them. Those of us in the dominant community need to take the first step. I remember the surprise and delight of a Jain family when I went to their home to introduce myself and indicate something of my interest in their religion and culture. I discovered later that they had been in this country for twenty years and no Christian had ever come to their home except to try to convert them!

4. Building mutual trust is a challenge for all of us.

Do not ever assume that trust is there. Considerable patience, understanding, time, and caring are required. Trust is not built overnight or in one event. We have to get to know each other by sharing our religious convictions, why our faith is important to us, what fears we have, and what we hope for ourselves and the world in which we live. This says a lot to us about the kind of educational programs that are needed. Is there space for sharing and interaction between and among participants so that trust may emerge?

5. Part of our task is to become mediating centers.

As educational institutions we can provide a place where persons of vastly different religious traditions may come to understand and experience the multi-faith and multicultural society that is growing every day. Allen E. Richardson in *Strangers in This Land: Pluralism and the Response to Diversity in the United States* says that we need ... "mediating institutions that provide middle ground between public and private life, between values of homogeneity and diversity. . . . Mediating institutions deal with the question of identity by maintaining a balance between competing ideologies of pluralism and assimilation. They affirm the value of ethnicity and at the same time offer a vehicle for helping members of tightly knit ethnic communities to overcome their apprehension of the experience of public life" (Richardson, 1988, p. 202). To be a mediating center is an extraordinary demand of our educational enterprises, but a very critical and important one. If we are committed to adult and continuing education that makes a qualitative difference in the lives of individuals and their communities, should we not take up the challenge that Richardson offers?

6. The planning process is crucial and demanding.

In planning educational programs with representatives of the constituency to be served during the past twenty-five years, there is none more exacting than in the interfaith domain. It is a rocky road and full of hazards. Who represents whom is a tough question to answer. Those of us who are Christian need to remember that there is considerable diversity within any particular faith tradition, just as there is in our own. Whenever possible, care must be given to have broad representation from within as well as among the different traditions. For example, in New York City the Muslim community is very complex and diverse, and is made up of people from the African American and Anglo communities, the Middle East, Africa, Asia, the Caribbean, and Eastern Europe. There are Sunnis, Shiites, Sufis. Whom we invite into the planning process will affect the focus and outcome of educational programs that we offer. Planning is not just what we do to make education happen, but is a part of the educational process itself and can have a powerful impact on those involved.

7. We must give primary attention to the involvement of laymen and laywomen in different religious communities.

To a large extent, interreligious dialogue and programming in this country has been in the hands of paid professional religionists. We desperately need to expand the base of involvement to include the vast number of people in the different religious traditions who have not been invited into the multifaith educational arena and who have enormous influence in private and public life, whether at home, at work, in the larger society, or their own particular faith community. In my experience, I have found that we must insist on this. Otherwise, our educational programs will have little impact within and among these communities. Every step along the way, we should commit ourselves to involving laity as well as religious professionals in our work as program planners and educators. Particular attention must be given to involving women, who constitute the majority of the faithful in most traditions, and yet are often excluded from interfaith dialogue. Ursula King points out this appalling truth.

> Such narrowness is evident with regard to the marginalization, invisibility and exclusion of women, for wherever interreligious dialogue has developed, women seem to have little part in it, at least at the official level. Proof is found in every single book on interfaith dialogue, religious pluralism, the theology of religions, or the "wider ecumenism" of global inter-religious encounter. (King, 1998, p. 42)

For Christianity in the United States, this is a new historical moment, in which we can now recognize an increasingly multi-religious society. Many of us would not have dreamed of having a Muslim, Buddhist, or Hindu living in our neighborhoods a generation ago. However, the first mosque in this country was built sixty-five years ago in Cedar Rapids, Iowa, and now the Muslim faith is growing faster than Christianity and is expected to be the majority faith worldwide in this century. Perhaps even more important for us today than the opportunity of knowing about different religions is the possibility of encountering persons of different faiths. What W. C. Smith wrote almost forty years ago has even more validity today.

> The religious life of [humankind] from now on, if it is to be lived at all, will be lived in a context of religious pluralism.... This is true for all of us: not only for [humankind] in general on an abstract level, but for you and me as individual persons. No longer are people of other persuasions peripheral or distant, the idle curiosities of travellers' tales. The more alert we are, and the more involved in life, the more we are finding that they are our neighbours, or colleagues, our competitors, our fellows, Confucians and Hindus, Buddhists and Muslims are with us not only in the United Nations, but down the street. Increasingly, not only is our civilization's destiny affected by their actions, but we drink coffee with them personally. (Smith, 1963, p. 11)

We are no longer in a position to plead ignorance, to content ourselves with caricatures of persons of other religious traditions than our own, or to avoid engaging our religiously plural world. It is our responsibility as educators to develop programs that celebrate religious pluralism, foster understanding, respect difference, and promote justice and peace for all peoples. The goal is not to make us one, not to engage in syncretism, but "to generate a strong social fabric through the interweaving of commitments" (Eck, 1991, p. 195) which will move in the direction of a community of communities.

References

Eck, Diana. *Encountering God: A Spiritual Journey from Bozeman to Benaras.* Boston: Beacon Press,1991.

King, Ursula. "Feminism: The Missing Dimension in the Dialogue of Religions," in *Pluralism and the Religions: The Theological and Political Dimensions.* London: Cassell, 1998.

Richardson, Allen E. *Strangers in This Land: Pluralism and the Response to Diversity in the United States.* New York: Pilgrim Press, 1988.

Smith, W. C. *The Faith of Other Men.* New York: Harper & Row, 1963.

Chapter 12

Continuing Education by Extension

Rodney Parrott

Continuing education at extension sites provides an important service to the churches. In a recent count (ATS *Bulletin* 42/4, pp. 131-35), there were 229 seminaries in the United States and Canada associated with the Association of Theological Schools. It would be easy to suggest that all of these exist by divine pleasure, but most have resulted from the accidents of history and reflect the realities of denominational strength (numbers, dollars, and leadership). There are, of course, some notable exceptions, such as the major ecumenical seminaries, but for the most part, the seminaries began life as children of particular denominations.

The consequence is that the location of seminaries reflects the predominant population and resource demographics of particular churches. They also, at the present, reflect the urbanization of American culture, and, almost exclusively, are located in major urban centers (populations of 500,000 or more) where population density has been sufficient to provide for their continued existence. Fewer than a dozen are located away from such centers. Some of the urban centers where seminaries are clustered include Los Angeles, Chicago, New York, Boston, Berkeley/San Francisco, Atlanta, Toronto, Philadelphia, Edmonton, Washington, D.C., Vancouver, and Richmond. The ATS directory lists no affiliated seminaries in sixteen U.S. states and three Canadian provinces (or territories).

Without taking sides in a debate over urbanization, or engaging in a (perhaps justified) criticism of the rules by which the deployment of the church's ministries is governed, one can note that extension education is an attempt by established organizations (seminaries, institutes, or independent centers) to provide resources to pastors and other church professionals who minister in places where those resources are not otherwise available locally. They are an acknowledgment that every pastor needs to refresh her or his outlook and skills on a regular basis, and that institutions with available resources have an obligation to use them not only on their primary campuses, but also beyond. In other words, extension education is more than a matter of distance—or at least of distance understood primarily in *geographical* terms. Often (erroneously) described in terms of *outreach*, extension education is about connecting and sharing, about an equitable and sufficient distribution of resources within church systems. But even more profoundly, it is about how we are the church together. There are some critical issues at stake in this area, to which we will return later. In the meantime, we simply underline the importance of providing continuing education to the church by extension and turn to some factors to be considered in the development or enhancement of this area of ministry.

Models

Models for continuing education by extension include short-term clergy seminars with seminary faculty leadership; summer institutes with seminary administration and a mixed faculty of regular and visiting professors; and regular courses hosted by a local pastor, who invites colleagues and a facilitator to her or his church. Examples of these sorts of programs abound. The Disciples Seminary Foundation in Claremont, California, has sponsored an ecumenical seminar in Montana every fall for more than ten years. Iliff Theological Seminary, Brite Divinity School, and the Alban Institute have sponsored summer institutes in attractive vacation locations for at least as long. Princeton Theological Seminary, perhaps one of the largest seminary continuing education programs, features a number of events away from the campus throughout the year. In many cases, a course or seminar is located in a church facility, and a notation indicates that it is made possible by an endowment honoring a pastor or other church leader. Princeton also works in conjunction with Ghost Ranch (New Mexico) to provide summer educational and vacation opportunities.

Having noted this variety, we should perhaps be more specific about the definition of our subject. Simply put, continuing education by extension is any version of a program operated by an institution at a location other than its base location. All of the above programs fit more or less comfortably within that definition. However, it is useful to draw a distinction between what might be called "vacation" continuing education and true extension continuing education programs. In the case of the former, persons from one (or more) location(s), often both instructors and students, travel to another location for the event. In the latter, the educational resources are transported to the location where the students reside. Our emphasis in what follows is more on this second type.

Staff

Extension programs operate with a variety of staff configurations. Some programs are coordinated by a full-time staff person on the home campus who works with local pastor-coordinators at various sites in the seminary's larger territory. Others make management of the program one portfolio for an administrator, who may have several other responsibilities. Still others may operate at the initiative of interested faculty members, usually in the area of the arts of ministry. Yet others may involve a summer migration of administrative and instructional staff from the main campus to a commercial or nonprofit site in an attractive resort location. No matter which model is involved, it is important to provide adequate staff time and effort to the program. A successful program requires careful attention to a host of detailed arrangements.

Courses and Curriculum

When it comes to curriculum, there are at least two, perhaps three distinctly different models available. At the more formal and structured end of the spectrum, one can find successful programs, which have at their core a curriculum designed for participants seeking the Doctor of Ministry degree. The majority of students in courses will be actively pursuing the degree, but others may be there because they find particular course offerings attractive.

There are both positive and negative aspects to such programs. On the positive side, the primary benefit is money. The larger tuition fees paid by Doctor of Ministry students simply make more resources available to cover the costs of instruction and administration. It does not particularly matter whether the resources are paid directly to adjunct or visiting professors, or are indirectly expended by providing credit to regular faculty against their contracted teaching load.

A second advantage is commitment or ownership. Students who have matriculated in the degree program often take their work more seriously than persons who have simply elected to undertake a specific course. This is not always true; many disciplined and self-directed pastors take their continuing education commitments seriously. But, the commitment to a *program* extends beyond the individual course, and relieves the seminary of some of the need to constantly promote its offerings.

Disadvantages of the Doctor of Ministry-based program are that its courses and seminars must meet particular requirements for content (subject) and length. Typically, that means a one-to-three semester hour course, with multiple sessions, and subjects that fit into the traditional seminary curriculum. While most Doctor of Ministry curricula allow more specialization than the Ministry Division, there are still expectations of balance. Students will take *required* courses they might not otherwise have chosen. They also will find faculty limited to those approved by the seminary's faculty, sometimes eliminating otherwise well-qualified and gifted teachers or practitioners.

The primary alternative to the Doctor of Ministry-based programs are those which focus on noncredit or CEU offerings. These are, for some of the reasons listed above, more difficult to maintain, but they provide some opportunities not available to those involved with Doctor of Ministry programs. The program can include short courses or seminars, as well as longer ones; faculty can include larger numbers of practitioners and consultants; and the range of subjects can be both narrower and wider.

Hybrid programs may be more the norm, however. If an

extension site has a strong charter to meet the educational needs of a given area, it may be host to both credit and noncredit offerings. If an on-site staff person is involved, offerings may even include conferences or ongoing working groups. Such programs, however, are much more fluid than Doctor of Ministry-based ones, and tend to have a shorter lifetime. An extension center may be able to do both; a particular extension site is less likely to do so.

Partners

In the interest of extending both the denominational reach and life span of extension programs, some seminaries have entered into partnerships with denominational or ecumenical judicatories. In return primarily for public relations support, a program may be linked to an association of churches or ecumenical council, or to a particular arm of a denomination's national or regional structure. For a number of years, San Francisco Theological Seminary has partnered with Ecumenical Ministries of Oregon to hold regular classes in Portland, Oregon. Another example is the Red River Preaching Conference, which brings together two seminaries (Brite Divinity School in Fort Worth and Phillips Theological Seminary in Tulsa) and two Disciples of Christ regions (Oklahoma and the Southwest [Texas, New Mexico]). Held biennially at a resort on the Oklahoma/Texas border, the event typically brings together several hundred pastors for the better part of a week.

There are several concerns connected with such partnerships. One is the question of accountability and quality control. The partners need to be clear about how decisions about program direction and content will be made. Since seminaries are also accountable to accrediting associations and the like, they must be especially careful, particularly if the shared program involves courses for academic credit.

A second concern, more relevant to the judicatory than to the seminary, is whether the partnership expresses a bias in favor of a particular educational program. The issue is especially clear when more than one seminary services a given area with extension programs. The wise judicatory executive or board will be careful to examine the potential for such trouble before committing to partnership.

The possibility of multiple partners, including multiple seminaries, is a challenge few take on for long. Not only must one deal with different denominational or judicatory expectations, one adds the task of meeting each seminary's institutional goals.

The Local Coordinator

Unless the seminary or college has full-time extension education staff (see above), it will likely need—and use—a local coordinator for its courses. Such a person often is an alumnus/ae of the institution, or has strong ties to it. He or she is frequently the pastor of a congregation whose facilities are adequate to house the courses themselves. And the coordinator may be enrolled in the seminary's Doctor of Ministry program.

If there is a considerable distance between the main campus and extension location, or the seminary has a series of extension sites, the local coordinator functions as the primary "field personnel" for the program in the area. Responsibilities include not only the practical matters of local hospitality for instructors and students (classroom, instructional equipment, snacks, lodging, and so forth), but some correspondence (occasional and regular) with students and seminary staff, especially as the latter seek to decide the subject of future offerings.

The local coordinator, if enrolled in a Doctor of Ministry program, for instance, usually participates in each course free of charge. If the program is not for credit, the same may be true, or he or she may receive some discount in the cost of seminary courses at the main campus. Other types of remuneration might include some sort of personal recognition at seminary or denominational events.

Core Groups

Particularly in Doctor of Ministry continuing education, a critical component is the core clergy group or colloquium. Comprised of usually about a dozen students, this group is convened on a regular basis (usually monthly) so that members can report learnings, exchange ideas, and process material assigned by the instructor. Faculty members meet from time to time with the group, or it may be convened by someone selected by the program's administrator. Aside from those times when a faculty member is present, much of the content of the group meeting comes from the group members themselves, relying on each member's ability to take responsibility for his or her own learning.

In a noncredit extension program, a core group may also develop at a given site. Its members will be the self-selected continuing participants in the program, persons who are committed to and generate a "program" of studies even though there is no official curriculum. Leadership in this group may be shared among a small number of members, usually two, who are catalysts and cheerleaders for the program.

Facilities/Centers

As noted above, extension continuing education takes place in a variety of settings. Perhaps the most common is the local congregation. If the extension program is substantial, the seminary may lease space from a congregation for an office, as well as for instruction. In such a case, the office space is usually reserved solely for the extension program, while the classroom space may continue to be used by the congregation. Long-term use agreements spell out the details of schedule, equipment, and compensation.

Relationship to the Home Campus

Extension programs that focus on the Doctor of Ministry degree usually involve a component that must be completed at the main campus. Frequently, that means the student must undertake a concentrated period of study, either at the beginning or end of his or her program. Arrangements for that study, unlike participation in local colloquia, is usually coordinated directly between the student and the seminary, since course projections are made with a view to the needs of persons from a number of extension sites.

Faculty

Not every faculty member is interested in education by extension. Even in Doctor of Ministry-based programs where teaching an extension program usually results in an adjustment in one's on-campus class load, there are faculty members who successfully resist the lure, cajoling, and arm-twisting of the Academic Dean. Recruitment of faculty for noncredit programs, unless they are able to offer outstanding stipends or provide other attractions (such as a recreational location), is an even more difficult task. Having said that, there are still many faculty members who respond positively when given the opportunity to share their work with pastors and other church professionals whose experience has sharpened their perceptions and helped them to formulate critical questions.

Especially in noncredit extension programs that cater to an ecumenical audience, the administrator will face the challenge of meeting the high expectations of prospective participants, especially when it comes to assembling a program with a consistent, ongoing clientele. In such cases, participants may think first of a prominent, well-published scholar, rather than of the seminary's resident faculty in the field. Sponsorship of a series of well-received courses by the seminary faculty, interspersed with occasional appearances by their more prominent colleagues, is a key in the development of the trust that undergirds a strong program.

Libraries and Bookstores

If seminaries are located on the basis of demographics and market population, bookstores with resources for the working pastor are even more so. Consequently, many pastors find themselves at some distance from a good source of books. Most seminary libraries maintain a vigorous program of interlibrary loans, at least for the benefit of faculty, and informed and self-disciplined pastors often may access such resources through participating regional or local libraries. However, an extension program that transports faculty resources from the seminary's main campus to areas at some distance from it may also be a useful link in distributing printed resources. By making available for purchase books authored or recommended by course instructors, the program can help every participant secure materials relevant to his or her present interest, often at some discount from retail prices.

The key is for program coordinators and administrative staff to coordinate with the teaching faculty, securing a recommended reading list several months in advance of the course. Most seminary bookstores will secure books for the course on the same basis as for regular on-campus courses, and can ship them to the extension site at minimal cost. Or, administrative personnel who travel to the site can carry a small package with them. The resulting enrichment is worth the relatively small investment of time and energy.

Costs

This is not the place to discuss in detail the financial structure of extension continuing education. However, some general comments may be useful in outlining its typical shape. As one would expect, the primary difference between campus-based programs and extension programs involve the added costs for transportation. Faculty must travel to the extension site either from the home campus or elsewhere. If the faculty involved are visiting faculty, the cost differential between the course on campus and the extension course may not be great, since the faculty must travel in any case. If the faculty are the regular seminary faculty, the travel to the extension site adds new costs.

An additional cost is the expense of transporting the administrative personnel to the extension site for planning and/or management. For that reason many programs are linked to the church relations office of the seminary and administrative activity is dovetailed for efficiency. A negative consequence of such a connection is that the true costs of the continuing education program are not always evident, with the result that tuition levels are kept artificially low. A program lacking endowment income or an administrative linkage then finds that what it would need to charge in order to be financially sound is out of line with what potential participants are accustomed to paying. In this regard, one can safely say that the tuition structure for the whole of the continuing education field needs to be reviewed.

Finally...

There are other practical factors that affect every extension continuing education program. In this concluding section, I list the salient ones. What is most important is that resources are delivered to those in the church who do not live near seminaries. The issue is more than the primary and secondary location of theological resources, and more than the distribution of resources across geographical space; rather, the development of these programs raises questions about the nature of the church itself and what it means to be in ministry in a given place.

Put another way, the question is one of contextualization: how can extension courses or programs take seriously the participants' locus of ministry? Extension educational events bring the wider world of faith and scholarship to participants, by definition. That is one of the purposes of transporting instructional resources to various sites. But what happens when the resources arrive on site? How are they integrated with the experiences, knowledge, and wisdom of the participants? How are the gifts of the latter taken into account? How is the learning made incarnate? As surely as there are differences in available resources, there are differences in circumstances, settings, and understandings between the seminary (or institute or center) and the extension site. Consequently, extension continuing education must involve adaptation and transformation. Those who would seek to employ it—whether administrative staff or faculty—must be willing to do the study and planning necessary to plant and nurture it.

I end with three observations based on my experience in the field. The first is that extension continuing education remains a tenuous and fragile enterprise. Because it is so systemic, it is vulnerable to the constant variety of changes that occur throughout the church: the advancement, retirement, or other relocation of personnel (including participating pastors!), fluctuating budget allocations, and so forth. Anyone working with extension continuing education must be flexible, willing to work with change. My second observation, and my ecumenical bias emerges at this point, is that however well some seminary and denominational programs may serve their constituencies by extension, gaping holes in coverage remain. Entrepreneurial institutes take up some of the slack, and not a few pastors have learned how to secure resources beyond those provided by their denominations. Most programs remain stubbornly denominationally focused, and do not look beyond members of the sponsoring denomination. As a result, less is attempted than actually could be done, and precious resources that are deployed do not serve as many as they could. Finally, continuing education by extension delivers an important service to the churches. Comparative studies remain to be done, but they would no doubt reveal the presence of stronger, more stable, and more effective ministries where pastors are involved in extension continuing education than where it is not available to them. While those who manage such programs or seek to establish them would do well to consider the various practical suggestions outlined earlier in this chapter, they can begin by celebrating what the church's seminaries, institutes, and centers already do. Their efforts truly build up the church and its ministry.

Reference

Association of Theological Schools *Bulletin* 42/4 (academic year 97/98), chapter 12, pp. 131-35.

Development, Management, and Promotion of Programs

Chapter 13

The Politics of Moving Continuing Education to the Center of the Institutional Mission

Donald C. Guthrie and Ronald M. Cervero

At a time when the necessity for lifelong learning has been recognized throughout society, there is a significant opportunity to negotiate a more central role for continuing theological education within the broader enterprise of theological education. It has become axiomatic to believe that lifelong learning is a necessity because of the mind-numbing scope and pace of change in our culture. However, there is more to continuing theological education than keeping up with the latest content, technique, or motivational innovation. Continuing theological education, like all educational endeavors, is about people. Moving continuing theological education to the center of the institution's mission, therefore, is about people. Real people with real interests, real power, real experiences, and real perspectives. It's about how these real people do the best they can to teach others about God, train practitioners to reconcile those who are unable or unwilling to be reconciled, and advance the message of faith, hope, and love in which they believe. Continuing theological educators should take the lead within their theological institutions to promote such a person-centered perspective among their colleagues and leaders.

As continuing theological educators promote such a perspective, they will quickly find that some will wholeheartedly endorse its implementation across the institution's spectrum of services. These stakeholders will enthusiastically support this person-centered movement because they embrace change rather than fear it. Others, however, will be less excited about this movement. These stakeholders will seek to maintain the status quo of the institution, perhaps because the uncertainty inherent in change is threatening to them. Either way, problem-solving, persuading, bartering, and negotiating will be necessary as continuing theological educators engage their colleagues and leaders about the centrality of continuing theological education to the institution's mission.

If these communication strategies (for example, persuading, negotiating) will be at the core of what continuing theological educators employ as they promote their vision and model their agenda, they would do well to increase their understanding of such strategies and of the political process in general. The political process, after all, is just as real as the people who engage in it. Indeed, the political negotiation in which the continuing theological educators engage within their institutions is the same political process they should draw attention to in the continuing education programs they develop.

Continuing theological education is necessary because wise action requires that informed practitioners understand how the ever-evolving relationships among educational stakeholders determine the content that is usually the focus of educational efforts. Distributing content, however, represents only part of continuing education's equation. If continuing educators hope to truly help those for whom their programs are intended, they must engage in political advocacy, not just to advance their own interests, but so that the interests of those whom they seek to serve are represented. This is particularly true if the clients are those who live at the margins of society and therefore do not enjoy positions of power or have relationships with those who do. Continuing *theological* educators are in a strategic position to serve those that tend to be marginalized and others who minister to them, and thus demonstrate they have heeded God's mandate to identify with the alien and stranger.

This chapter discusses how continuing theological educators can increase their political awareness and negotiation skills. Through an analysis of two case studies, we will describe how to develop these skills in continuing theological education planning contexts by (1) naming the political context for continuing theological education; (2) identifying potential stakeholders within the church, seminary, conference center, and other educational settings; (3) discussing the interests of and the political relationships among these stakeholders; and (4) suggesting potential negotiation strategies, so that continuing theological educators may observe this process within their own and other related institutional contexts.

Seeing the Political Context for Continuing Education

Continuing theological educators do not typically work in situations characterized by symmetrical power relations within which all interests are equally important and negotiation proceeds on a consensual basis. Rather, the most common situations are marked by asymmetrical power relations, which both threaten and offer opportunities for their continuing education program. In response to these realities, continuing theological educators need to see that their work is a form of political action. Because of this, it is important that continuing theological educators can read the political relationships in their social and organizational contexts in order to understand how they constrain and enable their work.

Power Relations Frame the Contexts for Continuing Education

Our starting point is that continuing education practice, like any other human activity, must be located in a set of social dynamics. As we have seen, this work nearly always involves working with other people, so we have to think about it in terms of "the enduring social relationships" (Isaac, p. 51) that support or constrain educators' working relations and actions. The fundamental enduring social relationship that structures the context in which planners routinely work is power: who has it and what do they do with it.

Giddens argues that power, which is the socially structured capacity to act and not just a matter of personal attribute, is a central feature of these relationships. He says that "action only exists when an agent has the capability of intervening, or refraining from intervening, in a series of events so as to be able to influence their course" (Giddens, p. 256). While action is the result of human intention, the ability to act is structurally distributed. Thus, power is the capacity to act, which is distributed to individuals by virtue of the organizational and social positions that they occupy (Isaac).

Interests Produce Continuing Education Programs

Interests, which direct the actions of all people, are complex sets of "predispositions, embracing goals, values, desires, expectations, and other orientations and expectations that lead a person to act in one direction or another" (Morgan, p. 41). Interests, then, are the motivations and purposes that lead people to act in certain ways when confronted with situations in which they must make a judgment about what to do or say. Quite simply, people's interests directly produce continuing education programs. We believe that, more fundamentally, educational programs are causally related to the exercise of power in relation to people's interests, which always matter in determining program purposes, content, and formats. That education programs are causally related to these interests is not a superfluous claim, for we must ask: If programs do not depend on people's interests, upon what do they depend? Perhaps more important, if programs were not causally related to people's interests, why would it matter which educational programs were constructed?

Negotiation Defines the Practice of Continuing Education

In order to make the direct connection between the continuing educator and the organizational context, we argue that negotiation is the central form of action that they undertake. Continuing educators always negotiate in two dimensions simultaneously. First, and most obviously, their actions construct an educational program. For this, we draw upon the conventional usage of negotiation, which is defined in Webster's *New World Dictionary* (1976) as "to confer, bargain, or discuss with a view to reaching agreement" with others.

Within this conventional usage, educators not only bring their own interests to the process of negotiation, but they must constantly negotiate between others' interests to construct the educational program. Second, and at a more fundamental and encompassing level, educators also negotiate about the interests and power relations themselves. People's interests and power relations are not static, but are being continually acted upon by the negotiation practices themselves. Continuing theological educators' actions, while directed toward constructing educational programs, are also always reconstructing the power relations and interests of everyone involved (or not involved) in the planning process.

Matching Negotiation Strategy to Organizational Context

Figure 1 offers a conceptual scheme that delineates four different ways that power relations and interests structure the situations in which continuing theological educators carry out their work (Cervero & Wilson, 1994; 1996; 1998). It presents a template for how continuing educators should read situations resulting from particular configurations of power relations and interests.

Figure 1

Negotiation Strategies in Continuing Education Practice

Interests	Power Relations	
	Symmetrical	Asymmetrical
Consensual	(1) Problem Solve	(2) Network
Conflictual	(3) Bargain	(4) Counteract

Its four-cell design is created by crossing the type of power relations in which continuing educators act (from symmetrical to asymmetrical) and the relations among legitimate actors in the organizational context (from consensual to conflictual). In terms of power relations, some may be symmetrical, in that the continuing theological educator's capacity to act is equivalent to other relevant actors, while others may be relatively asymmetrical, in that his or her capacity to act is not equivalent to other relevant actors. In the figure's second dimension, the people who have a legitimate stake in the continuing education program may have interests that are largely the same (consensual) or different (conflictual). The distinction is important because when people have conflicting interests, those with the greatest amount of power will often exercise it to achieve their interests.

In the face of the four different situations laid out in the figure, different negotiation strategies will be necessary: problem solving (Cell 1), networking (Cell 2), bargaining (Cell 3), and counteracting (Cell 4). The major point of this figure is to recognize that it is not possible or responsible to act the same in all situations, because what would protect democratic planning in one situation may actually prevent it in another. Of course, the figure cannot be a complete mapping of all situations that educators face in practice, since situations do not typically fall neatly into one cell or another. Rather, it is meant as a framework to focus attention on what really matters as educators nurture a substantively democratic planning process.

In Cell 1, in which there is little or no conflict or differences in power among those planning the program, *problem solving,* is the most appropriate strategy. Discussions and dialogues among the interested parties can be conducted in an open atmosphere of trust, with everyone seeking to arrive at optimal solutions to issues about the purposes, content, audience, and format for a program.

Cell 2 is more complicated, because the setting is differentiated in terms of a division of labor, in which power is distributed asymmetrically, although everyone involved is cooperative and shares a similar set of interests related to the program. In these kinds of situations, the most appropriate strategy is to *network* among all the parties that have information and authority to construct the program. Networking means knowing who has what information relevant to the program, who has a legitimate stake in the outcome, and how to involve them in the relevant parts of the planning.

Although the power relations among which planners must act

are relatively symmetrical in Cell 3, different actors have competing interests and are willing to use their leverage to further those interests. In these settings, planners must use their position of power in the overall strategy of *bargaining* among the competing interests. Short-term compromise becomes the typical negotiating strategy and can be a responsible approach as long as all affected parties are legitimately represented.

In the situations covered by Cell 4, there are competing interests held by people working among asymmetrical power relations that are rooted in organizational and social structures. Strategies that are most likely to address inequalities of power are related to political and community organizing, which require educators to *counteract* the effects of established interests. This may take a variety of forms from providing information to affected groups to more active interventions.

Although the figure suggests a most appropriate strategy for each cell, continuing theological educators need to draw on the entire repertoire of strategies across the situations. These strategies should be seen as cumulative in that each one, while most appropriate in its own context, can be called upon at more complex levels, as well.

Case Studies

The following case studies illustrate how continuing theological educators could account for the stakeholder interests and power relationships during a program planning process so that they might choose appropriate negotiation strategies. Each brief scenario is followed by a discussion of how the continuing theological educator might negotiate through the process depending on how the stakeholder interests and power relationships are interpreted. A seminary provides the context for the first case, and the central character is the Associate Dean. The second case involves a conference center director and a judicatory representative.

The Associate Dean and the Foundation Grant

Suppose that a seminary's president decides to pursue a large grant from a major foundation that will enable the seminary significantly to expand its continuing education program. The president assigns the responsibility of assembling the proposal research and writing team to the Dean. The Dean invites several administrators, faculty members, and local church representatives to a meeting to explain the opportunity and to select a chairperson for the project. The Dean invites suggestions from the group about who should serve as chairperson, but suggests that the Associate Dean is most qualified and experienced. Everyone agrees with the Dean's suggestion. The Associate Dean assumes responsibility for the supervision of the project although the Dean asks for regular updates on the project's progress from the Associate Dean.

How should the Associate Dean proceed as she steers the project? How does she identify who has an interest in the project and what those interests are? How does she weigh the relative merit and importance of the interests? How does she assess the power relationships among the interested parties? Notice in this scenario that the interests among the principal planners appear to be consensual, and that the power relations among the principal planners appear to be asymmetrical. If this were generally true, the suggested strategy for the Associate Dean would be to network (Cell 2) with team members and others who may be able to provide helpful information or special skills during the planning process.

The Associate Dean's networking could take the form of casual conversations, emails, letters, telephone calls, or meetings. Since she can assume the support of the Dean and the President, the Associate Dean can use this representative power as she networks to persuade those with greater power to support the project and provide information or skills during the planning process. Having the support of superiors and communicating that support to others in strategic ways will help the Associate Dean make the best use of those who can help her most within the organization, who might otherwise see the project as being low priority for the institution.

However, what if there was great interpersonal conflict among the principal planners or significant differences in perspective about the project's legitimacy? For instance, what if everyone agreed with the Dean's suggestion about the Associate Dean's leadership, because to disagree with the Dean's perspective meant certain professional difficulty for the administrators and faculty members on the team? What if the president is the only one who thinks the project is worth everyone's time and energy, but to disagree with him is tantamount to professional suicide for the administrators and faculty members? What if one of the seminary's large donors pushed the project on the president, so that the president is not free to disagree and reject the project, even though he knows it will consume large amounts of his overworked staff's time?

If any of the elements of this scenario were true, we could conclude that the interests among the principal planners would be conflictual and the power relations asymmetrical. Therefore, the Associate Dean may want to consider how to counteract (Cell 4) the power and interests of those involved so that a more democratic planning process would occur. We are not suggesting the Associate Dean engage in unethical actions to subvert authority or merely negotiate her own interests during the planning process. She, like other continuing theological educators, must operate within the constraints of her theological convictions when applying the delicate counteracting strategy. She must consider what are the potential personal and institutional costs if she decides to counteract, for instance, the overbearing desires of the donor so that the broader interests of the seminary are served. To what extent will she go to protect her job or maintain her convictions? As she deliberates such potentially explosive matters, in whom can she confide as she weighs the options?

The Conference Director and the Judicatory Representative

Suppose a conference center director receives a call from a prominent local pastor who represents the regional judicatory. The pastor would like to meet with the conference director to discuss how the center might create and deliver a series of continuing education workshops for newly ordained pastors in the judicatory. The judicatory has experienced a recent influx of new pastors, who are fresh out of seminary and possess little parish experience. The series is to cover planning church budgets, leading stewardship campaigns, assimilating new members, and maintaining family unity in the midst of ministry. The pastor mentions that while the judicatory has the ability to pay a significant sum to the conference center for the workshops, it does not possess the personnel to help develop the plan. The Center needs the money. The judicatory needs the training.

It appears that this scenario provides the conference director with an opportunity to problem solve (Cell 1) with the pastor, because they share, as the principal planners, a relatively equal capacity to act and consensual interests. The conference director and the pastor could begin by assessing what the new pastors already know. This could be done by written surveys, face-to-face or phone interviews, focus groups, or some combination of these and other data gathering methods. Next, the planners could identify and prioritize the purposes, goals, and hoped-for outcomes of the program. They could then move to select the most appropriate methods and resources they will employ for the workshops. Finally, they could design or identify evaluative tools so that the effectiveness of the training could be determined.

What if, however, the interests of the two planners were decidedly at odds while their capacities to act remained relatively equal (Cell 3)? In this scenario, although the professional interests of the pastor and the conference director intersect, their personal desires for the partnership's outcomes remain in conflict. Prior to the meeting with the conference director, the pastor had successfully persuaded the judicatory to adopt his training plan for the new pastors which includes the topics he thinks are most needed. The conference director does not necessarily disagree that the chosen topics would be helpful to new pastors. He does, however, believe that the pastor has overemphasized the pragmatic areas of ministry and overlooked the spiritual areas. For example, the conference director prefers including more topics which cover establishing personal and corporate spiritual disciplines in ministry; cultivating healthy work and rest patterns; and nurturing the spiritual development of the pastor's family.

Are the planners consigned to disagree silently about the content of the workshops as they simultaneously smile and wince at each other during the planning meetings? Or, should they voice their workshop preferences and the rationales behind them to one another, and agree to disagree? According to the suggested strategy in Cell 3 (bargaining) the planners could voice their interests; provide evidence for inclusion of their preferred workshop topic; and seek to arrive at a mutually agreeable solution that encompasses the interests of both legitimate perspectives. This outcome is ultimately more satisfying, because the participants will enjoy the benefit of the series' negotiated content and the continuing theological educators can build on this success for future mutually productive endeavors.

Notice how in each scenario, the same story, when interpreted from the perspective of differing power and interests, suggests very different negotiation strategies. We doubt that many scenarios exist where employing one negotiation strategy will produce the most desirable outcome. Scenarios with clear-cut problems and strategies that produce pure solutions do not exist in a fallen world. However, as continuing theological educators consider the interests and power relations of program stakeholders, identify those interests, and discern which negotiation strategies to employ during the planning process, they can more accurately account for the interests of all stakeholders, because they recognize the planning process in the context of political reality.

Conclusion

We believe that this approach to planning requires the continuing theological educator to move beyond merely employing techniques and move toward cultivating a way of seeing the planning process as a context full of power relations and interests. Accordingly, we advocate that the continuing theological educator continually assesses stakeholder interests, power relations, and negotiation strategies. If wise action is the goal and method of continuing theological educators, recognizing the political context of the planning process will enhance the possibility that such action is realized. Such recognition begins by asking wise questions. The following list summarizes the key questions continuing theological educators should address when assessing any program planning process.

Planning Process Questions for Continuing Theological Educators

1. Who has an interest in the program, issue, or meeting?
2. What are the interests? How do they relate to one another?
3. What is the relative merit and importance of each interest?
4. What are the power relationships among the interested parties, including yourself?
5. Which negotiation strategies would be most appropriate, given the interests and power relationships among the stakeholders?
6. How do your theological and ethical convictions inform your choices and decisions?

Addressing these questions will direct continuing theological educators toward the heart of continuing education—people. Keeping people at the heart of continuing theological education promotes the mission of the educator's institution, addresses the needs of the institution's constituents, and promotes the institution's mission of service derived from its service of God.

References

Cervero, R. M., and A. L. Wilson. *Planning Responsibly for Adult Education: A Guide to Negotiating Power Interests.* San Francisco: Jossey-Bass, 1994.

——— *What Really Matters in Adult Education Program Planning: Lessons Negotiating Power and Interests. New Directions for Adult and Continuing Education,* No. 69. San Francisco: Jossey-Bass, 1996.

——— "Working the Planning Table: The Political Practice of Adult Education." *Studies in Continuing Education,* No. 20, pp. 5-21, 1998.

Isaac, J. C. *Power and Marxist Theory: A Realist View.* Ithaca, N.Y.: Cornell University Press, 1987.

Giddens, A. *Central Problems in Social Theory: Action, Structure, and Contradiction in Social Analysis.* Berkeley: University of California Press, 1979.

Morgan, G. *Images of Organization.* Beverly Hills: Sage, 1986.

Chapter 14

Program Planning, Development, and Evaluation

Cynthia Crowner

When invited to write this chapter, I asked myself first, *For whom am I writing?* because that would inform what I have to say. I have imagined someone who may have come from congregational ministry, or someone who is on a seminary faculty who has just been made responsible for the development of a continuing adult education program for a seminary or retreat center. In addition, she may have no previous experience designing continuing theological education programs. Ah, someone like myself just five years ago. What advice would I impart now from my own experience?

Start with Your Mission Statement

Does your program have a mission statement? Ideally, the mission statement for your continuing theological education program defines some basic parameters for your work: the constituency you hope to serve (denominational or ecumenical, clergy or laity), the core values of your program, and its geographic scope. Any specifics you can glean from that mission statement will help you define your work—and limit your own ambitious reach. A warning one of my board members shared with me after my second year as a continuing education programmer may help you as it helped me: "Let's not attempt to be all things to all people." Rest assured, with all the seminaries, conference and retreat centers out there doing creative continuing education, if you are not doing a certain type of program, someone else undoubtedly is. All programs do not need to replicate each other. That would be a competitive disaster and overwhelming to a programmer. Pay attention to the focus of your institution and attempt to be true to its unique mission.

If your institution does not have a mission statement, great! You are now in a position to help shape the particular emphasis and values of your program by helping the institution define the mission for its continuing education program. You can shape it in ways that mesh with your own theological and missional vision. Just be sure to bring your board or planning committee into the process so they feel a sense of ownership. They may alter what you'd like to create, but if you are able to maintain a piece of your own vision while honoring their ideas, you will have their support as stakeholders, as they allow you to pursue your own goals as well.

Having said that...

During a program for new directors of continuing theological education programs at Auburn Seminary several years ago, I was exposed to the Mission vs. Market grid, a handy model that gave a vocabulary to a dynamic I had been discovering in my own experience of planning.

Let me illustrate this dynamic for you. Let's say that you have inherited a mission statement, or better still, you have helped your institution to develop or review a mission statement to which you feel committed. In addition, out of that shared sense of your institution's directions, you have planned programs to respond to those mission priorities. However, after putting your best thinking and planning into this effort to make those priorities real, you discover that not all the programs you plan succeed. People just do not sign up in sufficient numbers to sustain these programs. In other words, your mission did not find a market. What do you do?

- You can explore new ways to reach the constituents who are most likely to want your programs. (The business world calls this "target marketing.")
- You can find partner institutions with similar commitments that will help recruit participants for those programs. Examples of partners are congregations, institutes, seminaries, and denominational judicatories.

- You can be content with a small, intimate turnout by letting these programs be subsidized by programs that really draw a crowd but to which you are less committed mission-wise or pedagogically. (The market-responsive event can support the mission-inspired event.)

Lets look at an example. You and your board have decided that you want to resource aging congregations by offering a series of programs on older adult ministry. You contract with someone who has just written the latest book on this topic to offer a program that will help congregations respond creatively to this challenge.

But after much planning and good publicity, only ten people sign up for the first workshop while you had hoped for twenty just to make the event pay for itself. Does this mean you abandon the emphasis?

Not necessarily. You could check in with your denomination's program office that deals with older adult ministries and ask them to cosponsor the next event, with a promise to help advertise the event in their publications. You could contact your judicatory office and ask them for a list of congregations with aging populations in your region. Then call the pastors of those congregations and invite the participation of the pastor and one to two lay leaders. You might even ask them to become part of a planning team for the event. This would bring them into the planning process and help them clarify what they need to learn about their own special challenges in ministry with older adults. The planning process could actually be more educational for them than the final event (and after all, continuing education is the goal).

Finally, you may want to stray slightly from your primary mission goals or your pedagogical convictions, and invite a lively and renowned speaker to your institution whom you know will draw a big crowd. It may not be your mission priority, but it will serve the needs of the market. (Ideally, you can invite big name speakers who do address your mission priorities!) The income from that shorter but more lucrative event could subsidize your smaller gatherings, which are more intentional, thorough, and supportive for participants. There is certainly nothing wrong with the big name lecturer, as these occasions do encourage and motivate the listeners. But one has to wonder about how deep such an educational encounter is, how lasting the effect of such a speech as compared with a more in-depth two-to-three-day training event, in a community of peer learners with a common goal. In any case, you do have the option of offering both sorts of programs with this symbiotic relationship in mind.

To chase only big name presenters is unwise, in my opinion, as you may sacrifice the smaller, more in-depth opportunities for transformational learning.

Unfortunately, if no one shows up for any of your mission priority programs even after recruiting, partnering, and reaching out to new constituents, you may need to review your mission statement yet again.

A Caution

I receive many proposals every month from people who would love to present a continuing education event at my institution. It is a rare case when I actually contract with such leaders. It would be easy to fill our calendar with leaders from this source. But then the tail is wagging the dog. You are the nose of that dog, if you will, keeping your nose to the ground to sniff out what the needs are of your constituency and determining how those expressed needs jibe with your institution's goals.

You need to be the one to initiate contact with leaders who will fulfill your vision of the programs your institution needs to offer. So, assume your leadership role and stay focused. And, wish these enterprising presenters well.

The Grid

In my own planning process, I use a grid that flows right out of our mission statement. Let me share this with you by way of illustration.

Program and Pedagogical Objectives

You are likely to experience success more frequently in your planning work, if you can define clearly your learning objectives for each program. What will make for an effective continuing education experience for each program you offer? We know, as educators, that people learn in a variety of ways—some people are deeply intuitive while others are analytical, some hunger for practical answers for what appear to be practical problems, others need a deeper theological encounter with the assumptions that may lie beneath that same problem. Some people learn best through direct experience—of practicing what is being taught, on the spot.

Not every leader or teacher of a program will be able to meet all these diverse learning styles. However, many can be encouraged to diversify their pedagogical approach to respond to these diverse styles.

At an event at my institution, a professor finished his theology lecture by confessing, "Though I don't understand this, I am told that I should allow you some small group discussion time, so you can react aloud to what I have presented. After twenty minutes in the small group we can convene in our plenary again for a group discussion." This confes-

Program Grid

As I plan our annual program, there are certain balances I strive to maintain within the framework of our Mission Statement. Our mission statement is:

Kirkridge is a **retreat** and **study** center, rooted in **Christ**, close to the **earth**, where people from **diverse** backgrounds find community and experience the transforming power of the Spirit for **personal wholeness, reconciliation, and justice** in the world.

The words in bold provide a key to our program emphases. For example, I try to schedule **retreat** events with a heavy emphasis on prayer, silence or other contemplative disciplines and I schedule events that are more **study** oriented—theological explorations, training events, etc.

While we are **rooted in Christ**, we also welcome **diversity** of background, so most events appeal to people of the Christian faith, but I also invite leaders from other faith backgrounds to present programs to which Christians and others are equally welcome and in which they will feel comfortable.

Diversity also means keeping an eye on issues of age, race, gender, sexual orientation, physical ability, and denominational identities. This concern includes finding a balance among the faculty I invite to present as well as establishing program offerings that will meet the needs of these diverse groups.

Personal wholeness means we provide events where healing from trauma or psychological or spiritual wounds is emphasized. **Reconciliation and justice** events tend to emphasize political or social themes. **Close to the earth** means we include events that honor God's creation and delve into the meaning of earth stewardship.

I also must keep in balance the tension between trying to be true to this overall mission, honoring all of its parts and those who have loved certain streams of our programs in the past, and our need to bring in the money to keep the operation going. Some types of events are more popular and produce more income, while others are deliberately small. We do not wish to sacrifice too much of any part of our mission in order to chase the market. So we live within this tension. In my trade, this is called the mission vs. market grid.

Another practical balance I attend to—scheduling. I always plan several mid-week programs each semester with the understanding that generally clergy can only attend midweek programs while most laity prefer weekends. I also attempt to maintain a balance between the big name presenters and those who may have excellent offerings but may not be as well known. There is a strong push factor in limiting these lesser known presenters as their track record in drawing people here is not great. Sad but true.

sion was good. It alerted the participants that this lecturer would be happy to be center stage and respond only to the extroverts in his audience. But, he also was responsive to what many introverts might have told him—that they feel more comfortable sharing in a small group setting, and that having the opportunity to verbalize their reactions to instructional material is a very important part of their learning process.

Some people will learn very little from a lecture, but, if given the promise that they will have a chance to react to a lecture through writing, sculpting, movement, or other artistic forms, they will pay attention to the material being presented.

Some programs are best internalized by the learner, if the presenter actually provides an opportunity for them to practice. For example, a workshop on good preaching ideally should include the modeling of excellent preaching by the leader, workshops on how to preach more effectively, and also small practicum groups where people can preach before their peers and receive feedback on what works. Providing three levels of pedagogical approach is more likely to lead to a satisfying, well-rounded educational experience for the participants, and will leave you, as a program planner, with more of a sense of success as your pedagogical objectives are satisfied. The evaluations should bear this out.

A Challenge

You can study the Holy Land, or you can take people there!

You can discuss getting congregations involved in direct service in the community, or you can take your workshop participants into the local community for a model mission project with critical reflection each evening, so that all can clarify what exactly they are learning from the hands-on involvement.

You can have a lecturer discuss world religions or you can convene representatives of several world religions and create a direct dialogue among them.

Why not? In each case, the second choice is certainly more work, but providing in-depth, direct exposure, an immersion learning experience, can be a most life transforming experience for the learner. The power of such programs may tell you that you need to let go of creating so many smaller one-day workshops and put your limited program planning energies into these more time consuming projects where the learning is likely to be more lasting and transformative.

How Can I Put This Program Together?

Ideally, you will not want to be the Lone Ranger, planning programs in isolation, based on your own intuition of what your constituency needs, and what will meet those needs. (One program planner friend said, "I get tired of hosting forty parties a year and hoping somebody shows up!") You may prefer to find your partners in planning each program and make the how-to question one for the entire planning team of stakeholders. Three or four heads often are better than one, especially if you select people with a high interest in or stake in the outcome of the proposed program. For instance, judicatory executives may desperately want a program that will assist small church pastors in doing local mission together. Convening them along with some small church pastors, as part of your planning team would make good sense.

If your institution does not expect you to create very many programs each year, this is the way to go. If, however, your institution requires that you create many programs annually and you don't have a lot of staff support, this may not always be feasible, but should be a possibility for some of your most treasured but risky programs.

If you are confident that a certain program will be popular and have high integrity with your mission goals and pedagogical objectives, it is easier and less time consuming for you. When you define an area of programming you wish to offer, you will need to find the right leader(s) to facilitate the program. Often, the more well-known presenters, generally published authors or theologians, will book their calendars one to two years in advance.

Pick up the telephone and call. Why not? Find out:

- if they ever do continuing education events, lectures, seminars or retreats;
- what they consider to be their cutting edge;
- what they may be working on right now about which they feel most passionate;
- when they are available;
- your institution's intended audience and program objectives;
- a possible schedule and flow of the program;
- compensation terms. (Do not forget this or they may, understandably, lose interest!)

If they are interested, follow up with a contract as soon as possible, so they will not be tempted to abandon your program for a more exciting offer elsewhere. It happens.

Next, give the leader(s) a deadline to produce an event title and description, which you can use in doing your publicity. I generally ask not only for a catchy title, but also for a description that includes something of the content to be covered, as well as the process to be used. If it will be three days of lectures and small group discussions, participants need to know that. If they will be asked to dance or do artwork in the process, or share their own writing, you must let them know well before they walk in the door or you will hear from them about being unpleasantly surprised. (Trust me.)

(Your institutional letterhead and logo)

CONTRACT FOR LEADERSHIP

At the invitation of (your center), _____

(Name of Presenter/s)

agrees to lead a workshop/retreat/seminar on the theme of _____

_____.

(Topic)

The program will take place on _____

(Dates)

(Your institution) and the Presenter/s further agree to the following Terms and Conditions as related to the program:

1. An honorarium of

$ _____

_____

will be paid to the Presenter upon the completion of the program at which time the contract will be terminated.

2. All transportation costs of the Presenter will be reimbursed upon presentation of travel receipts. Mileage is reimbursed at $.31 a mile or economy airfare, whichever is less.

3. All lodging and meals will be provided for the Presenter/s during the program.

4. (Your institution) will assume responsibility for promotion of the Program. Presenters are also encouraged to promote their program. (Your institution) will provide flyers upon request. The Presenter/s will provide a draft title, course description, and brief bio for promotional purposes. (Your institution) reserves the right to edit the Presenter's draft in consultation with the Presenter. Copy is due by:

_____.

5. (Your institution) will provide the Presenter/s with adequate physical space and necessary equipment for the implementation of the program. A questionnaire will be sent to the Presenter/s prior to the event to assess special needs/arrangements.

6. A leader/Presenter will be expected to:

    a. treat all event participants with equal respect and concern as loved children of God;

    b. honor the trust of event participants and observe appropriate boundaries.

7. In the event a minimum number of _____ participants do not pre-register by the two-week deadline prior to the event in question, (your institution) will have the option of canceling the event, in which case no amount shall be due to the Presenter. Nothing in this paragraph shall prevent the event from going forward if (your institution) and the Presenter are able to negotiate a mutually agreeable revised fee.

8. The terms of this Contract will be construed according to the laws of the state. Time is agreed to be of the essence in this Contract.

This contract is considered in full force and effect when the following signatures are affixed, dated below, and a copy received via fax or mail.

_____   _____

(Presenter/s)   Date

_____   _____

(Director of Your Institution)   Date

Presenter's Social Security Number: _____

Presenter's Address _____

Presenter's Phone Number:_____

Presenter's Fax Number: _____

Please sign both copies and return one to (your institution) at the address above as soon as possible.

If more than one Presenter is involved in this program, please supply the name/s, address/es, phone number/s, and social security number/s on reverse side of this page.

Do not be afraid to negotiate with the leader. You know your own institution's needs (and after a few years you will be able to intuit your constituency's needs) better than this leader. For instance, if the description is too academic or vague for your

(Your letterhead)

Dear Presenter,

We are excited that you will be leading an event here during the upcoming season. Though it may seem very early, we need to ask you to give some attention to the title, course, description, and brief bio about yourself that will be published in our catalogue. We will need your drafts by _____.

A few tips we've learned over the years about event descriptions in our brochure:

1. **Title:** The title is *the* most important piece. Think about how quickly you look through catalogues, and you'll realize how critical a catchy title can be. As we don't have a lot of photos in our brochure, and our product is not really something we can show by photo, we rely heavily on a snappy title to grab people's attention. Please give careful thought to your title, making sure it sounds appealing and yet also gives the person a sense of what to expect. *Please avoid long titles.* They prove cumbersome on display ads. If you need to say more, use a short title and a subtitle.

2. **Text:** The text describing your event should say a bit about the *content* you hope to explore and the methods or *processes* you intend to use. Remember to invite the reader in so that *they will know their needs will be met* by this workshop or retreat. The description does not need to be long. In fact, it is probably more likely to be read if it is not. The description can be as short as five punch, meaty sentences. A brief description also allows for graphics or photo options which help draw the reader's attention to the event.

3. **Bio:** We need just a few things about you: Your name as you wish to be known in the catalogue—e.g. Are you Suzie or Susan? Any degrees or expertise that relates to your workshop, any books you may have published on the subject of your program. We tend not to use more than four or five phrases about each leader so make yours count. If you are sharing leadership of your event with another person, be sure that we have accurate information about that person as well.

If you are repeating an event you've presented here in the past and like what we already have about you and your event, simply let us know to repeat what we've used in the past. But you may wish to use this checklist to take another look at that description and refine it.

If you are new to us, you may have to start from scratch or you may have an event title and description that worked well for you in another setting. Either way, we need to hear from you by _____. If we edit your description or have questions about your title, we'll call you to discuss our ideas before we publish.

With regard to **promotion**, we have found it to be extremely helpful to gather the suggestions of the program leaders themselves for publicity. Perhaps you know of journals, magazines, even newsletters, where notice of your event would reach the kind of people most likely to want to attend your event. Please send your suggestions to us along with your event title, description, and bio as some publications have early deadlines for ads or listings.

We also find that our best attended events are often those whose leaders do their own promotion in addition to ours. We will send you flyers which you can copy for distribution to your own mailing list or make available at other workshops you may offer prior to coming here.

Finally, enclosed is a **contract** restating my understanding of our expectations and compensation agreement. **Please review it and sign both copies and return one to me here by _____.** I'll keep it on file. If it does not reflect your understanding of our agreement, *please call me* as soon as possible so we can refine our understanding and I'll draw up a new one.

Thank you for taking some time to think through what you wish to say about yourself and your work to our constituency and how we can most effectively reach your audience. We very much look forward to working with you.

Peace,

_____, Director of Continuing Ed.

Again, we need from you **by** _____:
—one copy of your contract signed
—your event title, description, and brief bio
—any publicity ideas

intended audience, get back to them right away before they become too committed to their idea. And be sure to ask yourself as you read each event description if a specific need is being addressed by this program, and if the description communicates clearly how the program will meet that need.

Generally, this process results in a much better program and more effective publicity, recruiting the people who really want to be present because they have a good idea of what to expect and are assured their needs will be met by the program.

Within two months of the event, send the presenter a questionnaire regarding travel plans, specific audio-visual needs, a suggested schedule for their event (which they may want to modify), room setup, setup for worship, and any specific books they want you to sell during their program, so you have time to order them. The questionnaire serves the secondary purpose of reminding the presenter that they have made a commitment to your program, while it allows you to ask for their input. This is likely to ensure that your institution and the presenter are on the same page, and that expectations have been set with some room for flexibility, so that by the time the event begins, all is ready, and should flow smoothly.

Two weeks prior to the event, you should see that all registrants also receive a letter, making sure they know the schedule, directions, balances due, and other details as they also have made a commitment to your program, and you want to make sure they will show up!

Program Coordination and Intervention

Not every faculty person, writer, or theologian with whom you work will have excellent skills in all the areas that need to be covered in a given program you wish to offer. One leader may be a brilliant lecturer, but have limited people or process skills to help participants digest what they are hearing and make it relevant to their lives and ministries. Other leaders may be very good on group process, but make too many assumptions about participants' shared understandings of basic content. You, as program coordinator, will need to make sure that someone from your program is monitoring these concerns during the course of the

LEADERSHIP QUESTIONNAIRE

Please read this over carefully, disregarding any sections that are not applicable.

Leader: _____

Event: _____ Event Dates: _____

1. TRAVEL
   Please plan to arrive by 4:00 P.M. the first day of the event, if possible.
   Means of travel: ___ Car ___ Air ___ Bus
   If you are coming by air or bus, please give us the following information
   so that we can pick you up:

Place of arrival: _____

Flight #/Bus: _____ Time: _____

Will you need a ride back to the airport/bus station after the event?
___ Yes ___ No

If you need a ride, please give us the following information:

Place of departure: _____ Time: _____

Telephone number where you can be reached immediately before the event:
(___) _____

2. EVENT DESIGN
   Attached is a sample of an event design. Please indicate any changes that
   you would like to make in the design and return it to us with this questionnaire.

3. MATERIALS
   _____ makes the following materials available. Please indicate
   what you will need:
   ___ Easel   ___ 8½ x 11 paper   ___ Stereo/Tape Player
   ___ Overhead Projector   ___ Newsprint   ___ Crayons
   ___ Inclusive language songbooks   ___ TV/VCR   ___ Bibles
   ___ Slide Projector   ___ 16mm Projector   ___ Chalkboard

   Please let us know in advance if you need additional materials and list
   them below. We will let you know if we *cannot* provide them.

   If you have a modest amount of material that must be photocopied for
   program participants, please send us the originals at least two weeks in
   advance of the event. We will copy them and have them ready when you
   get here.

4. Write any additional comments on the back of this sheet. **Please** include
   the title, author, and publisher of any books or tapes you would like us to
   have in the Book Nest.

Please return this completed questionnaire as soon as possible.
Thank You!

seminar, workshop, or retreat, so that suggestions or feedback can be recommended to the leader between program sessions. Most leaders who want their programs to go well can handle gentle, constructive feedback, and will adapt their format, if you sense they are losing the group. Others may not be so flexible; in which case you may need to be more creative or diplomatic. And, sometimes you may just have to settle for a less than perfect program. My experience is that most leaders want their program to meet the needs of those who have come to their event and are open to changing gears for the sake of the educational process. My experience is that this sort of intervention is not needed, very often. But as the Boy Scouts say, "Be Prepared."

What Is Success?

If you feel your programs have been true to the mission of your continuing education program, have demonstrated pedagogical integrity, and have served the participants' needs well, then you have succeeded, whether or not they are blockbusters in terms of attendance. Remember that, as a program planner who is accountable to an institution, you may feel pressured to watch budgets and numbers of participants, but the smaller the group, the more attention each participant can receive from the leader or faculty person and their peer colleagues. More transformational learning may be going on in that smaller setting than in any given larger group. Bigger, while exciting, is not always better. Balancing that "mission vs. market" grid, like walking on a tightrope, will be your constant challenge.

Of course, the best way to know whether the programs you are offering are successes is to ask the participants! Be present around the edges of the event, during breaks, and at mealtimes so you can listen to participants. Take good notes. Each program should also have a well-crafted evaluation form. I find it easier to make these anonymous, so I can share them with the presenter if I hope to work with that presenter again in the future. Be sure to set aside time toward the end of your program, so that people have the opportunity thoughtfully to fill out an evaluation form. And let them know that you do take them seriously.

PROGRAM EVALUATION

Title of Event:

1. How do you feel about this event as a whole? Did it meet your expectations?

2. What was most valuable to you as a participant?

3. What was the least important?

4. How could we improve this event? Format? Schedule?

5. Please evaluate our food:

6. Please evaluate our facilities:
   Where were you housed?   Any problems?

7. Please evaluate our staff (including registrar, cooks, coordinator, others):

8. Other comments/suggestions:

9. How did you hear about this program? ___Catalogue; —— a friend;
   ___ a pastor; ___ Internet; ___ a flyer; ___ an ad in: _____

10. Did you come for the speaker? ___ or the topic? ___ or both? ___
    Was the speaker known to you? ___

11. Who would you like to see our institution invite as a program leader?

    What topics would you like us to offer?

Do not miss this opportunity to ask participants what programs they would like to see your institution offer. Beware: This is not the same, as asking them what they think your institution should offer. It seems like everyone loves the fact that my institution does peace and justice programming, and they all tell us we "should" continue to offer them. But, these same people do not tend to come for these sorts of events. It is as if they can relax, because someone else must be tending to these issues. What you really want to know from those who attend your programs, is what kind of program would meet their own needs. Ask for specific topics and specific leaders right on the evaluation form. You may not take all of their suggestions, but, over time after reading many, many evaluation forms, you will get a sense of the trends of what your constituents are seeking, and will gather a list of names of presenters who keep popping up as desirable. These suggestions will help keep your intuitive, imaginative process within realistic parameters as you plan for the future.

Is Sending Out a Survey a Good Idea?

Yes, and no. The results of a survey may provide you with information about what needs are out there in the constituency, but it does not guarantee that the respondents will actually attend events designed to respond to that feedback. The key is that the survey be carefully crafted. When I first arrived at the center where I work, I inherited the results of a survey that I found unhelpful. It was clear from the massive response to the survey, that people enjoyed having the opportunity to respond, so it may have been worthwhile from a relationship building perspective. However, the questions must have been posed in such a way that there was no way to quantify any trends.

I received five single-spaced pages of what looked like individual suggestions. It was overwhelming!

Now, members of my board and I are attempting to develop several survey instruments. One will go to people who have not come to any of our programs for several years, but used to be regulars. We want to ask them what sort of programs would meet their needs. We will suggest some specific categories and leave space for individual comment, so we can sense the trends while also being open to specific individual ideas. We are creating a different survey for people who always come to a specific type of program in an area in which the leadership is aging. We need to know who the next generation of leaders might be in that field. Another will be developed for clergy specifically.

We have abandoned the "one size fits all" type of survey approach so that the information we receive back will be easier to quantify and use. Codifying your computer database with information about which people attend which events and when makes these specific survey instruments a breeze to send out.

Again, the result of these surveys will not mandate what programs we will ultimately offer. If everyone says they'd just love you to invite a leader you know your institution will never be able to afford, well, at least you know the kind of topic they are seeking by the work of that leader. Or, maybe you can invite that leader for the "one shot deal" speech and use that opportunity to let participants know of the more in-depth program on that topic coming up soon which is led by a very creative and talented leader in that same field who may not be as well known. It just might work.

Is Program Development an Art or a Science?

As I enter my sixth year as a program planner, I find that, more and more often, my instincts are proving to be right. For example, someone visited me in person to explain the program he would like to offer. I liked the person and appreciated what he had to offer. In another case, a board member confidently suggested a program. But in the back of my mind, I suspected these offerings were risky, and I even knew why. But, I thought, I could be wrong. We offered these events and too few people registered to run them.

It turns out that, not only did I not do our institution a favor by offering programs which did not run, I also did the presenters a disservice as they dedicated precious preparation time for our programs and set aside time on their busy calendars in the expectation that they would receive income for that time.

I have learned to become more confident in my intuition about events. Indeed, program planners must develop this confidence, although we may still be wrong on occasion. But generally, after a couple of years of experience and keeping your nose to the ground, reading evaluations and sending our surveys, you will know more about program planning for continuing theological education than anyone else in your institution. It may feel intuitive when you would be more comfortable having objective predictors of success to follow. But, your storehouse of knowledge will be greater than you may believe. So, solicit suggestions and watch the trends, but, ultimately, trust your instincts.

Chapter 15

Assessing Needs and Interests: Individual, Church, and Society

Douglas E. Wingeier

This essay assumes that religious leaders are adults who want to learn and grow in order to become more effective in their ministry. As adults, according to Malcolm Knowles's theory of "andragogy" they have four characteristics: (1) They are moving from dependency to increasing self-direction; that is, they need less to be taught and more to be helped to learn. (2) They have gained a reservoir of personal experience, which can be a resource for both their own learning and that of others. (3) They are motivated to learn what they need to know in order to fulfill their roles and accomplish life's developmental tasks. (4) And, they have moved from a subject-centered to a problem-centered learning mode, that is, they no longer wish to study subjects assigned by others for delayed use, but rather seek to acquire knowledge and skills to solve immediate problems (Knowles, 1980, pp. 40-59; and Brown, 1977, p. 6).

Hence, assessment becomes a tool that religious leaders can intentionally utilize to ascertain their needs, set growth goals, and chart a course for continued learning and development of the skills, knowledge, and personal qualities needed to increase effectiveness and fulfillment.

Types of Assessment

Not all assessment procedures are based on these assumptions, however. Of the four basic types of assessment, only one is self-initiated (SACEM, 1978, pp. 4-6). The first, *market research*, is done by continuing education programmers gathering data on the kinds and formats of programs, which will attract participants.

Questions on evaluation forms ask both for critique of the present experience and for suggestions, improvements, and ideas for other events. Seminaries and study centers conduct focus groups to discover the needs of their constituencies, and to adapt their programs accordingly. Questionnaires are sent out to determine needs and interests in the process of program development. The common element in all these efforts is the quest for information for the benefit of those offering programs.

A second type of assessment is *performance appraisal*, which is conducted by congregational pastoral relations committees and denominational supervisors and certification boards, with a view to developing job descriptions, awarding credentials, measuring performance, and setting salaries. This procedure affords useful information on the person's strengths and weaknesses, and highlights areas for growth and improvement. However, it is essentially under the control of "employers" and supervisors, and can be used to reward and/or punish the pastor or leader through determining salary and promotion. The person being evaluated does not really "own" the process, and hence is tempted to be less than honest in acknowledging shortcomings and needs. The needs of the church for improved performance take precedence over the leader's need for growth and enhanced satisfaction and meaning.

The third approach is *group planning* in which colleague groups of religious leaders meet together to determine their needs and develop a study plan. This may or may not be based on individual self-assessment, and may or may not meet individual needs. The value of this approach is the mutual support and accountability it provides, but its drawback is that the needs of some individuals may be ignored in the "groupthink" process of reaching consensus on the goals and procedures to be followed, the areas to be explored, and the resources to be used.

The one self-initiated assessment process is that of developing *individualized plans* for professional development, in which leaders take responsibility for their own education, free from dependency on and control by other agencies. This approach fosters the leader's professional development through growth in knowledge and skills, in ways that are tailored to one's individual life and work situation, and in which one determines one's own direction, gathers one's own resources, and chooses one's own areas and goals for growth, gathers one's own resources, sets one's own timetable, and establishes one's own criteria and lines of accountability for measuring progress.

Purposes of Assessment

Each of these types serves a different purpose. The purpose of market research is to gather information, making possible the development of a continuing education program that will draw participants because it meets the needs of its constituency. The purpose of performance appraisal is to evaluate a leader's contribution to the overall goals and program of the church or institution, and thereby to motivate greater effort by the offering or withholding of rewards. The aim of group planning is to build consensus for common learning ventures that will enhance individual growth in effectiveness while at the same time building group solidarity and support. Finally, the aim of individualized planning is to facilitate intentional learning and growth toward greater personal and professional competence, effectiveness, and satisfaction in ministry.

Evaluation of the Approaches

Obviously, the advantage of the individualized planning approach is that the control of the assessment process is in the hands of the individual, which encourages openness, honesty, self-direction, and inner motivation. The disadvantage, from the standpoint of the institution, is that the leader can choose to disregard feedback and suggestions in favor of pursuing personal needs and goals. But a person performs better and maintains a higher satisfaction level when operating in a climate of trust and freedom than when under the threat of external judgment, and this positive sense of initiative and fulfillment is contagious.

The benefit of the market research type of assessment is primarily with the agency gathering the data, and only secondarily with participants in the programs offered, and the churches they serve.

Performance appraisal helps the congregation or judicatory assess the strengths and shortcomings of their ministerial staff, and to hold them accountable to common goals and standards for effectiveness in mission and ministry. And the group planning approach—often used in lectionary and colleague groups—while possibly overlooking some needs of individual members, and thereby reducing ownership and commitment, fosters a sense of acceptance, support, and accountability, which is much needed in what is too often a Lone Ranger profession.

Risks of Assessment and the Need for Accountability

The risks involved in most of these approaches to assessment are that persons will lack the incentive or support to follow through on the plans made; and thereby become discouraged or even depressed; will not be supported by families or congregations, who place demands on their time or insist on ministry priorities other than professional growth; will have energy and motivation sapped by interpersonal or role conflicts; or, will change or be changed to new ministry situations before having the opportunity to complete the professional development, planned by themselves, or expected by their supervisors or congregations.

These dangers point up the critical role of accountability in the assessment process—accountability to family, congregation, supervisors, colleagues, self, and God. For the entire assessment and planning process to be completed successfully, one must be willing to open oneself to feedback, on both goals and performance from all these sources. After examining the data, establishing goals, and making a development plan, the individual must submit the plan to family to ascertain whether the time and energy commitments involved are realistic and acceptable. The person's supervisor and the church's pastoral relations committee must be informed of one's goals and intentions, both for approval of the directions chosen, and for suggestions of means to pursue them.

One's ministry colleagues, whether on the same church staff, or in the same vicinity or judicatory, can be helpful in sharing their experience, filling in on ministry tasks when one is away doing continuing education, and holding one's feet to the fire when one is tempted to back off or divert from goals solemnly adopted. One can also keep a journal in the privacy of one's own reflection and devotional life, to measure progress and analyze obstacles in the achievement of growth goals. Moreover, one must turn to God in prayer for guidance and encouragement in persevering to accomplish aims for personal and professional development.

Sources of Assessment Data

When the individual is initiating and controlling the assessment process, one can seek data from a variety of sources to inform and resource one's development plan. Members of one's congregation who can be trusted to give straightforward, objective feedback can be asked to rate performance in preaching, teaching, administration, pastoral care, and other leadership roles and responsibilities. This can be done, either in candid conversation, open discussion in the pastoral relations committee, or through use of an instrument designed for this purpose. One can ask clergy colleagues or supervisors for evaluation of performance, in arenas affording opportunity for observation, and one may identify particular areas where feedback is desired—such as handling conflict, dealing with authority, or administrative follow-through on details. One's spouse and family can be helpful sources of information, because they are more inclined to be honest in a loving, supportive, relationship, although one must be cautious about expecting too much in this regard. Psychological tests and assessment instruments, provided by counseling and professional development centers, and the interpretation of these offered by trained personnel, give data which helps compare oneself with others on an objective basis in discovering strengths, shortcomings, and areas of needed growth and change. Professionals in other fields, sometimes members of one's own congregation, or in service professions in the community, who have experience in both giving and receiving assessment of all types in their own occupations, can share their perspectives, guidance, and advice on what to trust and what to avoid. And educational and training agencies and institutions, whether in the church or other fields, can offer their models, approaches, experience, and resources for the gathering, evaluating, and utilizing of information which can help in formulating one's professional development plan.

Criteria for Responsible Assessment

This leads to a final question: How does one evaluate the usefulness of all these data, approaches, and resources, as well as the relevance and value of the plan one comes up with through the use of them? Here are some questions to ask, in determining the extent to which one's assessment procedure and resulting plan are responsible, and likely to be both effective and faithful.

(1)   Are the needs of the larger society taken into account, along with those of oneself and one's church? One may tend to become too narrowly focused in the assessment process, thinking primarily the needs of oneself and one's congregation. But, "God so loved the world," and we are called to love and serve it, too. Ways of using our gifts and energies in addressing issues of poverty, injustice, oppression, and both physical and spiritual hunger, and a continuing education plan that expands our horizons and maintains a mission focus, are essential.

(2)   Is the individual being assessed the one primarily responsible for determining the goals, standards, and means of assessment, as well as who will do the evaluating, and what will be done with the results? Of course, pastoral relations committees and supervisors should have a part in the process, but they should not have a determining influence on the individual's life and ministry career.

(3)   Do the individual, committee, and supervisor agree in advance on what is to be included in the job analysis and evaluation procedure? Painful conflicts can arise if expectations and outcomes are not clarified and mutually affirmed ahead of time.

(4)   Does the individual know in advance the basis on which one will be evaluated, and have a voice in setting the criteria for evaluation? The best basis for determining assessment criteria is the mission statement, and the goals for ministry of the individual and the congregation he or she

serves. These must be defined and owned, before the assessment process begins.

(5)   Is the assessment taking place within a supportive relationship in such a way as to strengthen that relationship? Only if those doing the evaluating genuinely care about both the person and the program, and, if a climate of trust prevails, will honest feedback aimed at contributing to personal and professional growth be given, constructive achievement of mutual ministry goals achieved, and the relationship itself nurtured.

(6)   Is the primary purpose growth? If the assessment is perceived as a threat, it will be counterproductive. Growth in the direction of self-understanding, inner-direction, and intentionality is desirable for ministry, inasmuch as these qualities are essential to effective functioning in an other-directed, authoritarian society.

(7)   Are spouse and family intentionally and fully involved in all stages of the assessment, planning, and implementation? Ministry begins at home. When family members are left out of an individual's growth process, they may feel rejected or ignored, begin to move in other directions, and develop resentments that may interfere with wholesome relationships and effective functioning.

(8)   Does the process allow for periodic revisions, so that objectives are challenging, reachable, and continually updated? Neither the individual nor the congregation or judicatory should be so rigid as to be unwilling to take account of changes in circumstances, interests, needs, or motivation which suggest a shift in goals or directions.

(9)   Does the assessment, rather than focusing on weaknesses, emphasize problem analysis, diagnosis, and future-oriented action planning? It is said that, because of the way most people in the American culture are conditioned to a negative self-image, it takes seven words of affirmation to overcome the effects of one criticism. Hence, assessment that helps persons believe in themselves, identifies gifts and potential, and fosters growth toward goals which are

both stretching and realizable, will contribute to personal as well as professional development.

(10) Does the assessment include ways of spotting growth needs of both leader and congregation? Evaluation of only the individual leader lets the congregation off the hook, in terms of dealing with their needs for correction or improvement, and allows them to make the professional leader the "identified patient" to be blamed for their systemic problems (Friedman, 1986, pp. 19-23).

(11) Does the process give the leader support to deal with what it discovers? Persons need a framework that is firm, encouraging, supportive, and yet unrelenting in holding them to the goal and task, if the assessment is to produce the desired results. No one can grow alone.

(12) Is training provided to enable both leader and congregation to develop the skills necessary to determine goals, develop criteria, make and carry out plans, and measure progress? Assessment and planning do not come naturally. Those requiring or facilitating assessment must be prepared to train the persons undergoing it to accomplish it successfully.

(13) Does the assessment focus on the future rather than the past? To affirm the minister's potential, rather than just problems, is much more productive.

(14) Is the assessment and planning seen as means for more effective expression of one's values and commitments? A career is a life statement, not a planned sequence of upward mobility. The pursuit and fulfillment of one's call, not one's ambitions, must be kept central to the whole process.

(15) Is the focus on ministry as a service vocation? Career assessment and planning, done primarily for purposes of self-fulfillment or advancement, do not do justice to those engaged in the ministry of Jesus Christ. The aim must be to enable the leader to become better equipped, personally and professionally, to give oneself on behalf of others and the Reign of God.

Serious attention to these criteria for responsible assessment, using the individualized planning approach, will provide reliable guidance to both those seeking assessment and those offering it, in order to ensure productive, reliable, and positive outcomes.

Ministry Assessment Lab: A Model for Individualized Planning

An approach to assessment that seeks to meet these criteria is the Ministry Assessment Lab, developed and conducted by the writer over many years at Garrett-Evangelical Theological Seminary.* It was based originally on the Career Development Labs, pioneered by Thomas E. Brown at Lancaster Theological Seminary, but has been modified considerably by the incorporation of fantasy exercises, to balance the rational with the intuitive, use of assessment data from peers and parishioners, theoretical input on adult learning and development, and biblical and theological reflection.

The objectives of the Lab are to help participants: clarify their professional role priorities; identify strengths and weaknesses in knowledge, ability, and personal characteristics; identify goals for ministry; analyze and prioritize feedback from those who serve as peer evaluators; translate growth areas into learning goals and a continuing education plan; and find resources for pursuing these goals. These are accomplished through a process combining other-assessment, self-assessment, test-assessment, consultation, private reflection, planning, and contracting. The Lab helps participants plan for personal and professional development *in ministry*, not to decide on a possible career change.

The Lab begins with a meditation, "Planning as an Act of Faith," based on the story of Jeremiah's purchase of a deed to a plot of land in occupied territory, where there is no apparent hope of ever taking possession. This act is symbolic of his faith that the God who led the Israelites out of Egypt would again be faithful to restore them from exile to their homeland. So, Jeremiah stakes his claim on the future, based on God's promises.

---

*Note: The author is happy to provide copies of the "Professional Assessment Process" rating instrument and other information about the Lab. Please write to 36 Bust-O-Dawn Drive, Waynesville, NC 28786.

Likewise, planning in this Lab is for an unknown future, but is done in faith that the God, who calls and provides gifts and opportunities for ministry, wants us to develop and use them. So, we take stock of our gifts and needs in order to equip ourselves for the next phase of our ministry. We make a plan (buy a deed), although we cannot see where our next steps will take us. We trust God to make a way for us to fulfill the plan—just as God brought back the people from exile, so they could plant and harvest again in the land.

While these are the opening words spoken in the Lab, participants have been preparing for about two months. They complete a planning workbook, *The Parish Minister's Guide to Planning for Continuing Education*, available from the Office for Church Life and Leadership of the United Church of Christ, with supplemental exercises taken from Thomas E. Brown's *Survey of Resources for Development in Ministry Plan Book*, published by the Center for Professional Development in Ministry, Lancaster, Pennsylvania. They also take psychological tests, including the Minnesota Multiphasic Personality Inventory (MMPI), the Shipley intelligence test, and the Learning Styles Inventory (or sometimes just the latter plus the Myers-Briggs Type Inventory). Finally, using my own "Professional Assessment Process," they tabulate ratings of all aspects of their ministry by laity and clergy peers who know them well.

Self-introductions at the start of the Lab begin a three-day process of becoming vulnerable, developing trust, deepening relationships, and engaging in mutual consultation and support. An exercise called "chapters" helps participants get in touch with significant turning points in their own and each other's journeys. In a meditative mood, they jot down significant events, memories, and highlights, then pick one to journal about. They describe, analyze, and theologize about it, and indicate the kind of person they are as reflected in the experience. These "chapters" are then shared, in groups of three, after which the total group hears highlights of these conversations.

Participants next turn to the list of ministry roles in the workbook, and write all their present roles on a grid, indicating whether or not they are meaningful and required, choosing three for special, developmental attention, and estimating the percentage of time devoted to the roles in each category. These charts are put on newsprint and presented to the group, who respond with feedback and suggestions. This begins the process of group consultation.

The next step is developing a sense of strength in abilities. In the workbook, participants have named five significant achievements, identified the abilities used in each, and then drawn from these their most effective abilities. Each now describes in detail one of their achievements, after which the group identifies the abilities used. This becomes a very affirming experience, as participants receive recognition for things they have done, and discover abilities they did not know they had.

A similar process is followed in relation to areas of significant knowledge. In the workbook, participants have identified their knowledge strengths—in which they are relatively current, can hold their own with peers, and maintain a regular interest. They now review these in terms of further criteria—current in theory, as well as practice; able to resource laypeople; awareness of what they do not know; knowledge *of* not just knowledge *about;* what they have read in the area since seminary; and feeling no need to develop it further during the next two years. They are advised to avoid the twin dangers of over-confident belief that they have mastery when they really do not, and the too cautious feeling that they lack competence when they really are proficient. These lists are presented to the group on newsprint in what is sometimes the most difficult part of the Lab, particularly for those who have not done much studying since seminary. Some try to claim more knowledge than they have, while others have to be pushed to acknowledge their expertise. The leader and group help them test their knowledge and revise their lists by either adding or removing items.

The group is then pointed to the workbook pages, where the knowledge and abilities normally required for each of the ministry roles are listed, and asked to compare the lists under their three roles chosen for developmental attention, and compare these with the strengths they have identified. Then, on a summary page, they note the areas of knowledge and ability required by their roles, which are either: (a) strengths they want to develop or (b) areas of weakness needing attention. This begins to identify areas that they will work on in their continuing education plan.

Next, attention is turned to the feedback from lay and clergy raters. Group members select from their tabulations a short list of competencies that are either strengths to be developed, or weaknesses needing attention. The outcome sought is a short list of five or six strength areas, and the same number of weaknesses, which are first put on newsprint and shared with the group for feedback and consultation, and then added to their summary sheet.

The Lab thus far has been heavily analytical and "left-brained," so for a shift in approach, participants are asked to imagine themselves at a banquet in their honor on the occasion of leaving their present ministry situation. They are to think of the person there they most admire, and then write his or her laudatory speech, pulling out all the stops, to record all the praise they would like to hear about their ministry. Then they re-engage their left brains, and identify the goals for ministry implicit in the speeches and the strengths and shortcomings to be developed in order to achieve them. Again in groups of three, the speeches, goals, and areas for development are shared and analyzed for further goals and needs. Participants find this a welcome change of pace from the rest of the Lab, and discover things about themselves that the more rational process had overlooked.

The stage is now set for the most intense and potentially threatening part of the Lab—the session dealing with personal characteristics. This session is best conducted by a colleague with experience in psychological testing, who has scored the tests and drawn up participant profiles. In this session participants compare self-ratings on the eighteen items in the "Survey of Characteristics" with those by leader, group, and tests, discuss discrepancies and concerns in the group, and then meet with the leader for individual consultation. At its close, they identify personal characteristics that they consider to be either strengths or weaknesses, and enter these on their summary sheet.

Participants are next given personal reflection time to complete their summary sheet, as well as a planning chart on which they identify three priorities for professional development. This chart has space to fill in five types of processes that they may utilize—independent readings, on the job activities, contracts with colleagues, personal and family activities, short-term seminars, and formal courses and degree programs.

At the final session, participants share these summaries, explain their needs and priorities, and receive suggestions on ways to address them in their continuing education plan. All are given a Ministry Development Resource List of books, journals, and training and resource centers. As suggestions come from the group, participants write them down on their planning charts. They are then urged to establish covenants of accountability for implementing their plans, both with each other and with ministry committees, family members, supervisors, and/or staff colleagues back home.

Several devotional and theoretical resources are used along the way. The words of Isaiah 43:18-19 ("Remember not the former things, nor consider the things of old. Behold I am doing a new thing; now it springs forth, do you not perceive it?" (RSV)) are used with the speech fantasy to encourage creative visioning. The image of the pilgrim people, based on Hebrews 11:8 ("By faith Abraham . . . went out, not knowing where he was to go") RSV is used in conjunction with a diagram of the transitions and life structures of the human pilgrimage, drawn from Daniel Levinson's *The Seasons of a Man's Life* and Daniel and Julia Levinson's *The Seasons of a Woman's Life*. The story of Nicodemus and the Spirit blowing like the winds of change (John 3:1-8) is told to open participants to awareness of God's presence in painful crises and role conflicts, which are presented in a diagram called "Crossfire: Clergy Role Conflict," and a list of clergy crises. And, finally, the Lab is closed and persons are sent forth by reference to 1 King 19:9-15a (KJV), in which, after defeating the prophets of Baal and hearing the still small voice, Elijah is told by God to "return . . . to the wilderness of Damascus" to take up God's appointed work once again.

Persons come to these Labs for a variety of reasons—conflict in the congregation; recommendation of a supervisor; doubts about ability or suitability for parish ministry; search for new directions; transition in life situation; or, as one put it, "My church needs a new pastor, and I want to be that pastor," that is, the desire to grow to meet new challenges in one's present situation. Most leave with a sense of recharged confidence; a new vision of the ministry needed in their situation and how they can rise to the challenge; and concrete ideas about books, courses, projects, and resources they can draw on, to enhance their ministry. They also have the workbook and experience with the process, so they can repeat it later on their own.

Overall, this model for clergy assessment and planning has several significant features: (1) It is grounded in theological reflection, so that participants base their planning in a faith perspective. (2) A sense of community is developed which fosters honest feedback, personal affirmation, serious self-examination, and covenanting for accountability. (3) The congregation is involved—in both rating performance and competence before the Lab and supporting growth afterwards. (4) The rhythm of the process, flowing from rational assessment to imaginative fantasy to group sharing to moments of worship, is holistic and balanced. (5) Attention is given, not only to plans for skill development, but also to needs for personal and spiritual growth. (6) The process is not leader-dependent, but the resources of the group are drawn out and utilized. (7) Participants feel affirmed, grow in self-confidence, and gain support for making significant decisions and adopting sometimes life-changing directions.

In sum, my many years of experience with this approach have demonstrated that it effectively achieves the aim of the *individualized planning* approach to clergy assessment, which is "to facilitate intentional learning and growth toward greater personal and professional competence, effectiveness, and satisfaction in ministry."

References

Brown, George C. *Planning for Adult Learnings: An Introduction to Andragogy.* Boston: Ecumenical Leadership Education Program, 1977.

Friedman, Edwin H. *Generation to Generation: Family Process in Church and Synagogue.* New York: The Guilford Press, 1986.

Knowles, Malcolm S. "Chapter 4: What Is Andragogy," in *The Modern Practice of Adult Education: From Pedagogy to Andragogy*, revised and updated. Chicago: Follett Publishing Company, 1980.

Levinson, Daniel. *The Seasons of a Man's Life*. New York: Ballantine Books, 1979.

Levinson, Daniel and Julia Levinson. *The Seasons of a Woman's Life*. New York: Alfred A. Knopf, 1996.

Society for the Advancement of Continuing Education for Ministry. *Planned Continuing Education: A Study of Needs Assessment Processes*. Collegeville, Penn.: SACEM, 1978.

Chapter 16

Effective Marketing

Doris J. Rudy

"If you build it, they will come" may be applicable to remote baseball diamonds and sports heroes from the past, as in the popular movie *Field of Dreams*, but seldom, if ever, is it applicable to continuing theological education. As you probably have learned already, "getting them to come" requires almost as much of the provider's attention as any other aspect of the job—more, in fact. For once the program is in place, marketing (more often called publicizing and promoting) the program is a full-time job. It is likely that this "full-time" job is included in your already full job description, with the expectation that you will do whatever is necessary to attract program participants.

Shortly after graduating from college with a degree in corporate communications, my daughter went to work for Youth Organizations Umbrella, a not-for-profit youth drop-in center. Her responsibilities included editing and mailing the center's quarterly newspaper. With the current issue spread all over our family room floor one evening, she was complaining about all the work it took to publish one issue. In response to my question as to why they did a newspaper, she unknowingly stated the purpose of marketing: "It tells what's going on at the center. It gets people interested in what we're doing so they'll support us and get involved in the center's work." Floyd Craig of Craig Communication, Inc., Nashville, offers a tongue-in-cheek definition of marketing as "getting the organization to have what it can get rid of." *Webster's New World Dictionary* defines marketing as "all business activity involved in the moving of goods from the producer to the consumer, including selling, advertising, packaging, etc." (Second Edition, 1984, p. 868). Both of these definitions are correct, for they emphasize the need to consider the all-encompassing nature of marketing, for, as you will see later, everything you do before, during, and after a continuing education event affects the appeal of your program to potential participants.

Getting Started: The Marketing Plan

Writing your marketing plan is your first step to effective marketing. Various writers and marketing specialists include different components in their marketing plans. You may want to visit the marketing section of your local library or bookstore, which has dozens of resources on the subject. In the interest of space, I've included only a skeletal outline for you to follow in developing your marketing plan.

Every plan needs to begin with a *mission statement*, so if program doesn't have one, start working on it now. If your institution has a mission statement, is it applicable to your program or do you need a separate one? If you have a mission statement, but haven't reviewed it for a number of years, do it now. Does it still describe your mission? Is it complete? Is it concise enough to use in your written materials? Does it need some reworking or rewording? Once your mission is clearly defined, you are ready to continue working on your plan.

The next step is to *analyze your market situation*. Are you the only program or one of several programs in your geographic region or denomination? What is your position in the market? What would you like your position to be? Is your program new or well established? What are your program's current strengths and weaknesses? How does your target audience feel about your program? What does your target audience need and want? If you don't have accurate answers to these questions, do whatever research is necessary to get them. For instance, if you do not know how your target audience feels about your program or what they want or need, ask them. Send questionnaires, form focus groups, telephone key persons, or revisit evaluations of earlier programs. Gathering this information now will provide grist for your planning mill for a long time to come.

Determine *the goals and objectives* of your marketing program. While goals are statements of intended long-term outcomes, objectives are statements of shorter-term outcomes that support the goals. An objective is measurable and usually has a deadline. You may want to write goals and objectives at the start of each year or two or you may want to up-date your goals and objectives every two or three years as staff, finances, participant needs, and other circumstances change.

Finally, your marketing plan must include *a plan of action or strategies* you will employ to achieve your objectives. Be sure to establish the deadlines by which each action will be completed and the budget for each action step. If you have a staff of any size, name the person responsible for each action step. Post this plan in a prominent place in your office, and check in with your staff frequently to make sure you are on schedule. No one needs to tell you that the plan of action has the most direct effect on whether persons enroll in your programs. Be realistic in defining your plan of action. If you have staff and budget to complete only three large mailings a year, limit your mailings to three. Three mailings done well and on time will probably be more effective than five mailings that look as if they have been hurried, and are delivered too late to have any impact. If your budget allows for only one targeted mailing, combine that mailing with other less labor-intensive and expensive forms of contact.

Multiple Strategies

When I joined the continuing education staff at Garrett-Evangelical Theological Seminary in 1979, the first workshop I attended was on publicizing and promoting programs. One important learning from that workshop was the "three-contact" rule, which referred to the number of contacts we need to make with our target audience if we are to motivate them to respond to an invitation to a continuing education seminar.

Along with the "information age," which exploded onto the scene less than a decade ago, came the fax, the email, community television, cell phones, web pages, and beepers. They have flooded our internal and external communication systems with so much information that some marketing experts say that the three-contact rule has now given way to the seven-contact rule. Is it reasonable to think that any of us have the time and financial resources to contact our constituents seven times about our programs? Probably not, though I believe that an effective plan of action does usually include multiple contacts of different forms.

Competition for people's time and financial resources has increased immeasurably. The number of continuing education opportunities has increased, especially in the commercial sector, where faith-related continuing education competes not only for people's time, energy, and interest, but competes also with the large amounts of money corporations spend to attract persons of international note. Everyone's doing it. If you don't believe me, watch your mail more carefully. Every day it brings a brochure, letter, or flyer announcing such an event.

So, what will be included in your effective plan of action as you enter the twenty-first century? You will have to find more than the usual one or two effective ways of communicating the same piece of information to your target audiences if you want to get their attention and expect them to enroll in your programs.

Several marketing strategies are available to all of us and the ones you employ will differ according to your situation in the market, your financial and human resources, and the type of program you offer. Here are some possibilities for you to consider:
- direct mail
- brochures/flyers
- news articles/newsletters—church-related/public
- community cable and commercial radio and television
- electronic media
- reminder cards/letter inserts
- hospitality

A more detailed look at each of these may be useful to you.

Direct Mail

The computerized database and mail merge have revolutionized the direct mail process. You may remember what it was like to update the "master list" manually and run off labels on the copy machine. Keeping more than one such list was next to impossible. It is easier now, though "entering" data is still subject to input error and frequent revisions and corrections are essential—and expected.

Your database probably will include at least six or eight or more different target audiences, which makes it possible for you to segment your mailings. When a target group has been identified and all addresses gathered and entered into your database, a letter by first class mail is an effective way of getting people's attention. Address each letter individually with the use of mail merge, and be sure to sign each one individually, too. Add a handwritten note to those persons you know; people appreciate a personal touch like this. The letter has to be a "grabber," to which is added a P.S., which most people are likely to read first. Enclose a flyer or brochure, which is easily tacked to the recipient's bulletin board.

Bulk mail letters are not as likely to be read as first class letters, and may end up in the recycle barrel before they are even opened. So, if your budget allows, first class postage is always preferable to bulk mail for direct contacts. If you use the latter, make certain you know the bulk mail regulations well. They change frequently, as I discovered one time when I sorted and bagged a mailing of more than 8,000 pieces incorrectly and spent four hours at the post office re-sorting and re-bagging every last piece!

Even better than doing the bulk mail yourself is to use a professional mailing company. They know the latest mailing regulations, have the staff and equipment to prepare the mailing quickly, and will deliver it to the post office in a timely fashion. They will add the up-to-date bar code, which allows them to sort more specifically than you can, thereby cutting postage costs. You will find that having the professional prepare the mailing will cut your overall costs, especially when you include all the person-hours a large mailing requires. All you have to remember is to make sure you have enough postage on your permit account to cover the mailing. A word of caution: professional graphic designers don't always know the mailing regulations that relate to such things as placement of the fold and blank space on the mailer. You may want to suggest that your graphic designer consult with your mailing company about such matters.

Brochures/Flyers

One of the most popular marketing strategies is the distribution of a brochure or flyer, which is relatively easy to do if your staff is familiar with desktop publishing. You may prefer to work with a graphic designer who, using copy you have provided on a disk, creates the brochure or flyer and follows it through the printing and mailing processes for you. If you are creating the piece yourself, I suggest that you purchase one or two good resources on brochure design and production for your library. You will soon learn what works and what does not work with your audience. I discovered over the years that a neat, attractive, and simple brochure format, which contains accurate, complete, and well-written copy, and is delivered at least six to eight months ahead of the event, drew as many participants as a slick, costly piece did. Maybe it's because church leaders, both ordained and lay, are conscious of good stewardship practices and appreciate your efforts to use your resources wisely.

Regardless of who designs or produces your brochure, you are responsible for copy. Here are several more important things to remember when writing copy.

Count to seven, slowly. Marketing consultants will tell you that this is how long you have to get your reader's attention. An *attention-getting opening statement or graphic*, which focuses on the needs of the reader, is essential; Floyd Craig (Craig Communications, Inc.) says that four out of five people never get beyond it. Colored paper and neutral paper with two-colored printing are attention-grabbers as well. One brochure I will always remember was printed on neon green. The graphic on the outside showed the top of a person's head, two eyes, and fingers curled over the edge of the fold, and the words "It's time." Of course, I opened the brochure, to be greeted with the words "to come out of hibernation." In the middle of February, in Evanston, Illinois, I was going to read whatever followed. The sender had already met one of my needs.

Benefit-oriented copy is essential. Tell recipients how this particular program relates to their personal or organizational needs. (If you've asked them what they need, you'll have no trouble with this.) Use brief, descriptive statements, which contain several references to "you." Include words that have the best appeals—gift, saving, adventure, ease, enjoyment, dependability, efficiency, newness, authority, creativeness, self-expression, self-improvement, advantage, leadership, privilege, influence—and the list goes on. Use audience, not institution, language.

Proofread, proofread, and proofread! Need I say more? Though my publisher friend, Greg Pierce, has helped me understand his theology of imperfection, a typo in anything that is distributed to eleven thousand (or one thousand and one hundred) clergy and laity is still an embarrassment—not to mention the fact that it does not reflect positively on your program *or* your institution. Make sure someone who is not as familiar with the copy as you may be proofs it as well. Two sets of eyes are always preferred when it comes to proofing copy.

Always *ask for a response*. If you don't already have an 800 number, get one immediately—one that is simple to remember, perhaps one that says something about your program or institution. You want to make it as easy as possible for people to contact you, so be sure to include a fax number, an email address, the option to pay by credit card or check, and the name of a contact person—whatever will facilitate a quick response. If you list a "register by" date, always let recipients know that it is possible to register after the deadline.

Let your audience know that you believe it is important to *acknowledge a registration* and that their registration will be acknowledged 24 hours after it is received. The easiest way to do this is by E-mail, of course, if an email address is available (be sure to ask for it on the registration form). The next best way is by a simple, generic postcard, which states "Your registration for (fill in the seminar name) has arrived. Travel directions, a list of participants, and (whatever else you mail in advance) will follow." This acknowledgment will prevent unnecessary phone calls from registrants who keep track of such things.

News Articles/Newsletters—Church-related/Public Press

Whether you rely on direct mail of letters or brochures, you will want to prepare news articles about your program or event. Nearly every synod, district, diocese, conference, presbytery, or area has either a newspaper or newsletter or both. The advantages of using an already-existing newsletter to publicize your event are obvious.

It communicates to a more specific audience. It communicates the judicatory's support of the program. It is low in cost for you.

The editor of any newsletter reserves the right to decide whether to include your article, of course, because most editors are willing to include two or three a year from any one source. It is better to submit one and not have it published than to overlook this important possibility. Try to get to know the editors in your judicatory. Talk with them about their deadlines, the desired length of news articles, and to what extent they are willing and able to include your submissions. Be sure to get each editor's fax number and email address, which, when used to communicate the facts about your event, do get the attention of most editors.

News articles serve as excellent reminders about your program, especially if you have just mailed a letter or brochure to persons in a particular geographic area. If your audience has just received a first class letter with a brochure enclosed, and a week later reads about the event in the district newsletter, the impact will be more than double.

The news article must be short and contain only the most important facts about the event or program. Always include the name of a contact person and a fax number, email address, or toll free number where the contact can be reached. Enclose a black and white, glossy photo of the primary presenter, if you like, though it may not be published and you are not likely to have it returned. Acquaint yourself with the style used in any given newsletter and pattern your news article after that style.

While these general principles apply to news articles submitted to the public press in your area as well, it is much more difficult to get an article published in this medium. Get to know the religion editor, if at all possible, since he/she may be your best entrée to the local newspaper. A nationally known presenter or a topic of local public interest may be the only way you'll be able to break into this scene. Don't be surprised if your brilliantly written article submitted by email finally emerges as three sentence filler buried in the fashion page.

Community Cable, Public Radio, and TV

Church professionals often overlook this medium, which is more widely viewed than newspapers are read. We usually think it is too expensive and too technical a medium for us to use. We often do not realize that 100 percent of the programming on community television stations is committed to just that—the community. In Evanston, Illinois, a city of 73,000 people and 80 churches, synagogues, and church-related educational institutions, not more than five or six local congregations use our community channels to publicize their programs on a regular basis and it is there for the asking!

In most cases, all you need to do to initiate the process is call your community's cable station, make an appointment with the director, and talk with him/her about your program. Find out what you need to know and do in order to have an announcement in the form of either a graphic or a recorded message run on the station. Most community stations have trained volunteers who are willing to help you prepare your ad. If you want the graphic to include a still shot of your participants, leaders, or facilities, ask a volunteer with a video camera to visit your shop, or submit your own photograph to be used as background for the printed message.

Commercial radio and television stations are required by the Federal Communications Commission to offer a percentage of their programming every 24 hours for public service announcements (PSAs). These announcements are usually in the form of pre-recorded messages that are run at times decided by each station. So, your announcement is run at 3:00 A.M. You would be surprised at the size of listening and viewing audiences at that hour! Call your local stations and get to know the personnel there. In addition to running a PSA now and then, you may want to consider buying time on one or more of your local stations to promote your program. Two hundred thousand persons, commuting to work at 8:00 A.M. on Monday morning, listening to their car radios, represent a sizable captive audience!

Electronic Media

If your institution doesn't already have a Web page, contact a Web master immediately! Look first for someone who will do it for you *pro bono*. If that doesn't work, ask friends and professional colleagues for persons they might recommend. Design the most attractive, eye-catching page you can afford. Just as important as the quality of the page itself is whether your institution has the capability of keeping it up to date. A Web page with last fall's events listed is worse than no Web page, believe me. Include a number of contact persons and their E-mail addresses. (Cyberspace users don't want to waste time trying to reach someone by phone.) You may want to provide an option to register for a seminar via the web page.

If I were starting my continuing education days anew, I would do whatever it took to establish an address book with the names and email addresses of everyone who had passed through our doors during the last two or three years. (E-mail addresses don't change as often as street addresses.) Every marketing expert will tell you that the satisfied customer is the one most likely to return. As soon as a program is confirmed, send a notice to everyone in your address book under "recent attendees." Give them the details of the seminar, offer them an opportunity to register early (at a reduced fee, if you can afford it) and ask them to forward the message to ten others who might be interested. The immediacy of the email is critical in spreading the word about your programs.

Reminder Postcards and Mail Inserts

In the best of all marketing worlds, each of us would have the staff and budget to mail reminder postcards (first class) to a segmented market a month before a given seminar. Those who have been waiting to see what else comes along (and we all know church folks do that) may be motivated to register upon the receipt of this final reminder, if they've been thinking about it at all. Remember that the postal service has regulations about the minimum and maximum size of a postcard, especially if you are using bulk mail. Printing on neon-colored cardstock, while a bit more expensive, catches the recipient's eye quickly.

If your budget doesn't allow for mailing reminder postcards, prepare reminder cards the size of #10 business envelopes and make sure one is inserted in every piece of mail that leaves your institution every day. This is not the same as segmenting your market with a particular mailing, but you never know when a vendor, for instance, will pass the reminder card to a friend. Provide cards for all the departments in your institution and enlist their help in spreading the word about your program.

Journal/Magazine Ads

If you have a substantial marketing budget, you may be able to afford journal and magazine ads. They are initially expensive, though the circulation numbers usually warrant the expenditure. If you invest $800 on an ad and the publication goes to 30,000 pastors or laypersons in your denomination, the ad costs about three cents per person. That's a fairly inexpensive contact, even though you know that not all journal readers scan the ads. A classified ad is even less expensive and more likely to be read. If you do use this form of contact, select your journals carefully and make certain your ad is attractive, accurate, eye-catching, and of high print quality, a result that may only be achieved by employing a professional designer. Make sure he/she has a copy of the ad specifications provided by the publication, for they must be followed exactly. Deadlines for such ads are often three to five months prior to the publication date, so plan accordingly.

Hospitality

Elsewhere in this resource, you will find a chapter on the welcoming environment, so here I will only remind you of the importance of hospitality to your marketing strategies. It is a year-round endeavor, has a daily deadline, and must be on the minds of every single person involved in your institution. It doesn't just happen. It requires careful, intentional planning and action. Hospitality is embodied in the advance information you send; the quickly returned telephone call or email message; the condition of the sidewalks on a snowy day; the correctly-spelled nametag; the room temperature; the quality of dining room food; the clean hallways; the receptionist's attitude; the working smoke detector; the classroom setup; the delivered emergency message; and the ability to greet participants by name when they arrive. Hospitality is communicated in all we do and say to create an educational environment to which persons feel welcomed and wanted. Do not take it for granted! Be intentional about training the entire program and maintenance staff in the characteristics of hospitality and the role each person has in providing it. The return is unlimited.

Measure Effectiveness

If you are using multiple marketing strategies, be sure you have a way of measuring the effectiveness of each. You may want to add a "How did you hear about this seminar?" question at the end of the evaluation/feedback form completed by each participant at the close of the seminar. When one strategy works well, double your efforts in that area. If a strategy doesn't work at all, eliminate it.

Summary

Peter Brinckerhoff, in *Mission-Based Marketing*, points out that "the customer is not always right, but the customer is always the customer" (p. 166). This may be the most important thing to remember if your marketing efforts are to be effective. The layperson, the pastor, the Christian educator, and the church musician are your "customers." They have unmet educational needs. Find out what those needs are, design programs that will meet those needs, tell your story, focus all you do on serving your "customers" well, and your marketing efforts will be effective.

References

Brinckerhoff, Peter C. *Mission-Based Marketing: How Your Not-for-Profit Can Succeed in a More Competitive World*. New York: John Wiley & Sons, 1997.

CareerTrack, Fred Pryor Seminars, and LERN all offer workshops and print, audio, and video resources on marketing programs, brochure-designing, and effective communication. Call 1-800-488-0928 to get on the CareerTrack (www.careertrack.com) and Fred Pryor mailing list. Contact LERN at 1-800-678-LERN or angela@lern.org

Craig Communications, Inc., 4235 Hillsboro Road, Suite 101, Nashville, TN 37215, is an excellent marketing consulting firm.

Chapter 17

Welcoming the Whole Person

Carolyn Henninger Oehler

From first contact through final evaluation, a welcoming environment can be intentionally created to appeal to adults serious about their continuing theological education. Marketing, registration procedures, facilities, and learning ambiance may be designed intentionally to attract and satisfy adult learners. When body, mind, and spirit are considered as integrated parts of the whole person, adults are more likely to learn at their maximum capabilities. Often, the intangibles and peripherals make the difference between an okay experience and an empowered learner who will want to return for more.

Both the Hebrew and Christian scriptures contain stories that dramatize the central place of hospitality in communities whose faith journeys are told there. Abraham welcomed the Lord, in the guise of three men, by the oaks of Mamre. He saw to their comfort and refreshment himself, offering them the best he had (Genesis 18:1-8). On the other hand, to violate the norms of hospitality could result in the death of individuals or even whole cities. Sodom and Gomorrah were destroyed for the sinfulness of their inhabitants, the lack of hospitality primary among them (Genesis 18:16–19:29). In order to share her most profound understanding, Wisdom prepares a feast, and offers a banquet to all who would sit with her to become wise (Proverbs 9:1-6).

Jesus and his disciples received the hospitality of many in their journeys. They probably could not have continued their ministries without regular offerings of food and places to sleep. Jesus performed his own act of hospitality when he fed thousands of people. He showed "compassion for the crowd, because they have been with me now for three days and have nothing to eat; and I do not want to send them away hungry, for they might faint on the way" (Matthew 15:32). He understood that teaching included caring about whole persons.

Today, the eucharistic meal is still characterized as a feast, God's gracious act of hospitality and welcome in the name of Jesus Christ. Those of us who plan and offer continuing theological education can do no less than reflect that hospitality in our offerings to those who come hungry for knowledge, for nurture, and for self-respect.

One continuing education program presents itself in this holistic manner. Their brochure characterizes their program as one that "provides a creative, nurturing, welcoming, and empowering environment for the people of God along their journey.... A sacred place where refreshment of the spirit, care of the soul, renewal of the mind, and rest for the body may be experienced through retreats, worship, prayer, the arts, and hospitality." With this as a goal, this program will indeed welcome the whole person.

The process of learning is emotional as well as intellectual. The power of place can be an ally in creating a positive learning environment or physical surroundings can be a distraction in the learning process. Attention to them can make a critical difference in the participants' feelings of satisfaction regarding the program.

The single most important ingredient in the learning environment are the people with whom the potential learner interacts, from the first contact, through registration, meals, class, housing, and other contacts. The place and the people will work together to create a positive learning environment.

Staff who are trained in hospitality and customer service are an essential ingredient in a welcoming program. The first contact is a key person in the process, and should be gracious and welcoming, as well as knowledgeable. Housekeeping, maintenance, and food service personnel may have more contact with guests than so-called executive staff. All need training in hospitality and service.

Becoming User-Friendly

Who is seeking continuing theological education in these days? What will attract them to your program, again, and again? What does the whole person expect from the experience? Answering these questions from the standpoint of your specific context can set you on the path to becoming a growing program with repeat learners.

Often, it's the little things, done well, that add up to a worthwhile experience, even before the leaders have opened their mouths for the first time. Taking care of details such as the registration process, parking, signage, and accessibility can signal respect and welcome, preparing participants for a positive experience. When some details are omitted or done poorly, event leaders must work harder to overcome a negative first impression.

Easy advance registration, whether on the Internet, over the telephone, or by mail, will set the tone for the experience. Before they spend their precious continuing education dollars and time, learners often have many questions. Potential registrants may call several times, trying to decide if the program is right for them. Questions need to be answered promptly, patiently, and accurately, so that potential learners feel that they will be nurtured and respected in the program.

The younger the target learners, the more likely they are to respond to, and even demand, a technology-assisted registration process. Registration via the Internet, or at least a registration form available on the Web, will attract these persons and allow them to register while they have the motivation to do so. By the time they wait for that brochure they requested to arrive in the mail, they may have cooled off, or found another program whose registration process is easier.

Telephone registration, including 800 numbers, also attracts those who want to take action immediately. Capturing that first phone call and routing it to someone who is knowledgeable and welcoming is essential; the potential registrant may not make a second call. Offering the option of paying by credit card benefits the program by receiving immediate payment, and offers the registrant the convenience of completing the registration by telephone. Careful, confidential handling of checks and scholarship requests are additional aspects of sending a welcoming, respectful message before the learner ever arrives on site.

Parking availability can affect a program's attractiveness to potential learners. In urban and university settings, occasional visitors may find themselves uncertain where to go or unable to park in lots or facilities reserved for daily parkers. Clear instructions about the possibilities and problems of parking may forestall exasperation and frustration that gets directed toward the entire program. Be honest about what your guests will face; suggest public transportation or alternatives, if that is feasible. Getting a ticket or having one's car towed can ruin the entire experience!

Reading the "signs of the times" may be easier than finding the way to a meeting room or a registration table. When we become familiar with a process or a place, we may tend to assume that everyone knows what we know. It may seem so obvious that it needs no explanation. Ask someone for directions to a place familiar to them, and you may get the response that they know how to get there, but don't remember the names of the streets to turn on or how many blocks to travel. Familiarity can breed lack of awareness, as well as contempt. Try to look at the meeting site with fresh eyes, and ask where signs need to be posted—temporarily or permanently—to guide the occasional guest to places that the regular finds without thought.

Don't assume that everyone who will attend the event has been to your facility before. Even if alumni are your main attendees, others may be interested in something you offer. If they are made to feel like outsiders and like the only ones who don't know where to go and what to do, they will not return. In addition, signs can alert staff and faculty that something important is going on. Even persons not directly involved in the continuing education program may be called upon to provide directions or other information. Make sure they're informed as well.

Do not forget to visit the sleeping rooms occasionally and ask if you would want to sleep there. Are they clean, well lit, and supplied with necessities? Are bathrooms clean and towels of decent size? If you use empty dorm rooms, think about how they can be made more inviting to adults. A treat for the pillow, a mug for water and other beverages, and personal products in case of emergency can communicate welcome. If you are recommending hotels, check on their accommodations periodically. Do not recommend anywhere that doesn't meet the basic test: Would I like to sleep here?

More and more often now, participants in continuing education want to use computers as part of their learning process. Taking notes during a day meeting or writing reports or papers for a longer course may call for a computer. Easy access to power for notebooks and a printer for documents sends a message that you are up-to-date, not only in technology, but in other aspects of the program as well. Being able to send and receive email, and even surf the Internet, either through their own phone lines or at computers made available for guests, is rapidly becoming an expectation for a quality educational experience.

Make the safety and security of your participants a top priority. Be clear about what precautions need to be taken for personal safety and for security of belongings. If you have concerns about general security at your site, work with your administration to address these concerns. Feelings of safety and security, which may be subliminal, will affect the program in positive and negative ways and affect the return rate.

Creating and Sustaining an Optimum Learning Environment

The process of learning may be described as an experience which occurs inside the learner and for which the learner has responsibility. The adult learner is one of the richest resources for learning, as she or he cooperates and collaborates with the leader in the learning process. This learning process is the precious gem at the heart of any educational enterprise. The setting in which this gem is placed can make a great difference in whether the experience is productive, or whether it is less successful and forgettable.

The conditions that create a positive learning environment and facilitate learning, when working together, create an atmosphere in which learners thrive and in which the continuing education program has maximum impact on learners, leaders, and the program developers. Some of those conditions are respect, acceptance, openness, and valuing difference of opinions and learning styles.

Creating a Respectful Atmosphere

Respect is that overarching ingredient that makes possible all the rest. Respect is present when the potential participants' needs and interests are taken into account in the development of the courses and the program. Even in situations where clergy and lay professionals are required to earn a certain number of continuing education credits to remain in good standing, they have many choices. Including potential participants in planning communicates respect for what they know and what they believe they need.

One way to help assure this is through involvement of potential learners in planning or in focus groups. In a planning group, the potential learners will have the opportunity to shape a particular offering, knowing what will appeal to persons in their situations. Once involved, they are also likely to become participants in the offering and to recruit others for it. In a focus group, planners can gain more general knowledge abut what kind of program and program offerings will appeal to the persons they are targeting. Listening to the customer and then acting on that information is a key way to communicate your respect for the learners, as well as to develop viable programs.

Respect for the learner who decides to take the class includes offering a setting that communicates that this class and these learners are important to the institution and to the program. Adequate space, heat or air-conditioning supplied as appropriate, comfortable and adequate furniture, resources ready and available to all, faculty chosen with care and fully briefed on the nature of the class and the needs of the participants—all convey respect for the learner and for the program itself. Their absence conveys a lack of respect for both the learner and the program.

The Role of Faculty and Other Leadership in Setting a Climate of Respect

Respect for the learner must also be a high priority for the leaders and faculty in the program. Those who engage in continuing education for ministry, even in systems that include requirements, are almost always motivated to choose specific courses and classes by their own curiosity and interest. They are readied to learn by their situations and the problems or tasks they are confronting. They are usually self-directed and responsible for their own learning path. Faculty who assume pedagogical approaches that tend to be subject-centered and authoritarian can damage the climate of respect the program is attempting to achieve. Trusting the learner, and what the learner brings to the table, is an essential posture for the faculty/leader to take in setting a climate of respect.

In order to sustain and extend the atmosphere of respect essential for effective learning, faculty who know their subjects must also know their learners and something about how adults learn. Qualities desirable in faculty include openness to opinions and ideas different from and even in conflict with their own. Faculty should be able to come out from behind a lecture format and model vulnerability and a learning posture. Lectures are usually the easiest way to deliver material, and the least effective method for retaining what is delivered. Respect includes willingness to expose ideas and conclusions to debate and discussion, and even to conflict. Faculty who are well prepared and who believe in continuing education and lifelong learning are more likely to communicate respect and enthusiasm for this learning situation.

Learners who received their degree educations at certain periods and/or in certain institutions may need to be empowered by the leader to take responsibility for their own learning. Offering them respect is a key way to generate self-respect in the learner. If learners leave with greater respect for their own experience as a resource for learning, and for themselves as learners, they will have learned an invaluable lesson.

Creating an Accepting Environment

By the time we reach the status of adult learner, we have usually acquired certain attitudes about our ability to learn, particularly in structured situations. Even a successful academic career can leave us with feelings of inferiority and anxiety about what kind of learners we are. If we didn't like our formal educational experience or struggled with certain courses or ideas, we may need reassurance before we can give ourselves permission to learn up to our capacity.

Acceptance by faculty can make a difference in the amount of learning that occurs and the chances that the learner will want to return another time. Aspects of an accepting attitude include a nonjudgmental approach to ideas and questions from learners and a realization that persons learn in different ways and at different paces. Creating an accepting environment includes providing a learning experience that appeals to various learning strengths.

Some are most comfortable and effective learners through personal involvement with people in everyday situations. This learning from feeling rather than through a systematic approach places an emphasis on learning from specific experience, relation to people rather than to ideas, and being sensitive to feelings and people. Others may prefer to learn by watching and listening. They observe carefully before making judgments, like to view issues from different perspectives, and look for the meaning of things.

Still others prefer to learn by thinking, by logically analyzing ideas, and doing systematic planning. Then they are ready to act on an intellectual understanding of the subject or situation. And yet another group learn best by doing. These are the hands-on learners. They have a great ability to get things done, are risk-takers, and try to influence people and events through action.

Most people are able to learn in any of these four modes, they just prefer and probably learn best in one over others. Ideally, a learning experience will provide something for each of these learning styles. This may not be practical in a short or confined offering, but it is an important goal to place before faculty and program planners. At another level, continuing education experiences are excellent venues for strengthening less preferred learning styles and learners can be encouraged to widen their comfort zone by participating in and learning in other modes. Learning to learn is an important, yet usually invisible part of continuing education. Faculty, then, must be skilled in how to teach as well as what to teach.

Planning for Spiritual Needs

Welcoming the whole person includes attending to spiritual needs. To do this well, worship must be a forethought, not an afterthought. To make the experience truly continuing education *for ministry*, the experience should include the opportunity for worship, for meditation, and for prayer. It would be unwise to generalize too strictly on what brings persons to continuing education experiences, yet many will come from busy, stressful situations. If they have been sent by a supervisor or a congregational committee urging them to address some deficit of skills in ministry, there may be pain and anxiety present, as well. Worship experiences designed to offer healing, hope, and a time apart will minister to the whole person. Without them, there is less chance that persons will be ready to turn their attention to learning. More important, without worship done thoughtfully and well, the program misses the opportunity to provide nurture and care for the souls of those who come. Choose worship designers with as much care as faculty are chosen. What they offer is as important.

For an extended program, consider making a spiritual director available for conversation and guidance to those who wish to pursue this avenue. We need to ask the old question of each other: How is it with your soul? Not only will this free up participants to learn at their highest capacity, it will communicate in yet another way that you care for the whole person. This added value to a program expresses the value placed on each person and communicates respect for each one's unique spiritual journey and needs.

Worship experiences and attention to the spiritual needs of the learner are part of a larger emphasis on community. The opportunity to be with peers is a key reason why learners choose a program. Talking with someone who is having similar experiences and struggles, laughing about the aggravations and stumbles of ministry, sharing concerns about family and future are invaluable parts of the continuing education experience. To facilitate community, time and space need to be provided. People will probably seek each other out, no matter what the situation. A well-run program gives opportunity and comfortable space to enhance the experience. In a classroom, introductions, personal storytelling, even name tags, can be part of intentional community-building. Meals arranged so that conversation is encouraged also enable community. For those experiencing loneliness in ministry and/or in high stress ministries, this aspect of the program may be more vital than the content of the course.

Remembering the Body

In addition to the comforts mentioned above, a program that welcomes the whole person will make provision for physical activity and attention to the body as well as to the mind and spirit. If there is a place for recreation on site, allow time for exercising, swimming, and running. Develop a schedule that acknowledges the need for physical activity and realize that such activity aids the learning process. If nothing else is possible, consider board games, jigsaw puzzles, team competitions. Make play a part of the learning experience.

If the program and situation allow, consider teaching basic Tai chi or other exercises. Perhaps the opportunity for massage would give stressed-out participants a new lease on learning. Even a foot massage or a back rub can change perspective and get tired bodies ready to learn.

A break for the group to attend a play or a concert, a dinner out together, a visit to a place of historic or natural interest—each can serve multiple purposes of learning, community building, and getting bodies off chairs and moving around.

Conclusion

Remembering that the whole person is involved in any continuing education for ministry will keep before the planners needs to be met in a wide variety of areas. Processes that need to function well each time there is a program offering can be systematized to assure quality. Registration, parking, signage, sleeping quarters, and quality of space can be designed to communicate a welcome to those who participate. Creating and sustaining an optimum learning environment includes choosing faculty who will use empowering teaching methods. Faculty and leaders who are comfortable with diverse opinions and respectful of the uniqueness of each learner are key parts of creating an accepting learning environment.

Attending to spiritual needs through well-planned and executed worship, time and space for prayer and meditation, and, perhaps, even providing opportunities to work with a spiritual director will nurture and support learners and communicate care for the whole person. Space and time for community-building and physical activity—even fun!—will produce a well-rounded program and well-rounded learners. Welcoming the whole person makes continuing education for ministry a true ministry of hospitality.

Chapter 18

It's Worth the Risk Management

Doris J. Rudy

Better safe than sorry.
A stitch in time saves nine.
A penny saved is a penny earned.
An ounce of prevention is worth a pound of cure.

We are all acquainted with sayings like these. We remember them and they crop up in our conversation today, because they were, for our parents and grandparents, ways of telling us that we should take steps to prevent serious consequences. These reminders were surely the precursors of what today is referred to as risk management.

Risk management is defined as the identification, measurement, and treatment of exposures to potential accidental losses (Williams and Heins, p. 4). The purpose of risk management is to take steps prior to an accidental loss to minimize the hurt at minimum cost to the institution or organization.

Exposure is any situation, which has the potential for injury, damage, or loss. There is a certain amount of inevitability that, given a certain set of circumstances, loss will occur. We sometimes refer to these circumstances, or exposures, as "accidents waiting to happen." A car without lights, being driven the wrong way down a one-way street at night is such an "accident." Likewise, there are situations or sets of circumstances around our institutions that are also "accidents waiting to happen." It behooves us all to try to identify such "accidents" and do whatever is needed to prevent the occurrences.

Managing risk, then, is identifying existing exposures and taking whatever steps are necessary to reduce the exposure.

Why Bother?

Current resources on risk management approach the topic primarily from a business perspective and show how losses will affect insurance premiums, the margin of profit, employee work hours, and related concerns. But risk management is just as applicable, if not more so, to the not-for-profit institution. In fact, having fewer financial resources at our disposal makes risk management even more important to us, since losses of any kind almost always have serious financial implications.

All institutions, including the not-for-profit, face the threat of losses that a program director or facility manager hopes will never occur. A visiting student falls on a wet floor, where no caution marker has been placed, and breaks an ankle. A compact disc player is stolen from a participant's locked room. A visitor breaks a tooth on a piece of extra crisp bacon prepared in the dining facility. That more accidents don't occur around our institutions probably means that one or more persons have taken the steps necessary to manage the risks to the benefit of the entire organization.

Risk management frees a company or institution to pursue more aggressively and intelligently its regular activities. It enables any business where economic survival is of utmost importance to handle its exposures to accidental losses in the most economic, effective way. In the not-for-profit world, we are, or should be, concerned not only for the economic survival of the institution, but also for the personal, bodily survival of the institution and all the persons involved therein.

Risk management is also important because you are likely, at one time or another, during your tenure as continuing education director, facility manager, or program coordinator, to be involved as the risk manager, officially or otherwise. The very nature of continuing education for ministry requires it of us. You will benefit both personally and professionally from some knowledge of risk management. While some loss is inevitable, managing to reduce the losses is highly desirable.

Risk management contributes to a business, organization, or institution in a number of ways:

(1) It makes a difference between survival and failure. Liability suits may be so damaging as to force the closing of an institution's doors. Insurance costs can be kept lower, freeing up much-needed funds for programming.

(2) It can contribute to operating efficiency. Employees injured on the job cause a disruption in services that cannot be recovered. Time is money. When a maintenance person is absent, it usually means hiring a substitute or delaying projects, which would otherwise be completed in an efficient way.

(3) It can reduce fluctuations in cash flow. Paying a temporary office worker requires unexpected payment of costs. If a visiting seminar leader does not show up in time for the seminar, registration fees will be lost.

(4) Employees prefer to work in an organization that strives to protect them against risk. An organization's record and reputation for caring for their employees is often well known beyond the walls of the institution. The applicant pool for any opening tends to decrease as safety infractions occur.

(5) Knowing that you have done all you can to manage risk on your campus, center, or church offers the peace of mind that improves the physical and mental health of the management and owners.

(6) Risk management helps satisfy the institution's sense of social responsibility or desire for a good public image.

(7) Finally, risk management helps satisfy externally imposed obligations such as safety regulations set by the Occupational Safety and Health Act (OSHA).

Steps in Risk Management

Risk management requires five very important steps: (1) identifying the exposure; (2) measuring the potential loss; (3) considering which tool or combination of tools to use in attacking the exposure; (4) implementing the decisions; and (5) monitoring the decisions.

Identifying the exposure means naming the areas in which your program could suffer loss. It is the process by which a business systemically and continuously identifies property, liability, or personnel exposures, as soon as or before they emerge. Are halogen lights or candles allowed in housing spaces? Do stairways have adequate lighting? Is it important for your visiting faculty to know your policy about sexual harassment? Can you keep all the promises you make in your written material? Are there areas on or around your campus that are unsafe at night? Are all steps and handrails in good repair? Do you offer off-campus or international seminars? Is the stairway carpet loose? Have you experienced theft on your campus? All these situations have the possibility for loss. Keep an ongoing list of the exposures you and others on your staff identify. Update the list on a regular basis. Consult regularly with full-time staff members, seminar leaders, program participants, and program colleagues about loss exposures they have observed.

Measuring the losses associated with these exposures is the next step in risk management. It means trying to determine the probability or chance that the loss will occur and the impact the losses would have upon the financial or personal affairs of the organization, should they occur. This step, while more difficult than any of the others, is important because it helps you set priorities as you establish policies and procedures to avoid the loss. For details about determining probability, we suggest that you consult a risk management or insurance resource.

Next, consider the various tools or combination of tools of risk management that should be considered in attacking the problem. You have several choices.

- Separate the exposure
- Transfer the exposure
- Reduce severity of the loss
- Avoid the exposure
- Prevent loss

Each of these tools is explained in detail in the next section of this chapter.

The next step calls for *implementing the decisions* made. This step calls for a great deal of consultation and collaboration, in order that your entire institution is involved in controlling the potential losses that affect all of you. Administrators will need to be consulted if policy changes are called for. Be sure to involve the facility manager and housekeeping department, if physical repairs or changes need to be made. When our insurance company conducted a risk management seminar for us, they made individual appointments with every department chairperson and program director on our campus. Following that consultation, they prepared and mailed to each of us their recommendations for risk management in the respective departments and programs. It was a very helpful process for raising everyone's consciousness to the need for all of us to be involved in risk management all the time.

If, for instance, insurance is to be purchased to cover an unavoidable loss, such as that caused by fire, it will be important to establish proper coverage, obtain reasonable rates, and select an insurer.

Finally, you will need to *monitor your decisions* in order to evaluate the wisdom of those decisions and determine whether changing conditions call for different solutions. If you decide that purchasing additional liability insurance is required when you are offering international seminars, and then you decide not to offer such seminars in the future, the potential for exposure to loss changes. You would, no doubt, decide to reduce your liability insurance costs by canceling that particular insurance.

Risk Management Tools

As we mentioned in the preceding section, you have at least five tools available to you in your risk management efforts. Let us look at each one of them in more detail.

• *Separate the exposures*—When you place important documents such as your birth certificate, passport, deed, marriage license, or pictures of personal property in a safety deposit box at a bank, you are separating your exposure. In the event that fire destroys your home, these documents will be safe. You will want to do the same with important documents related to your program or facility. Be sure to make duplicate copies of computer files that contain documents that are impossible to reproduce and store them at another site. Store the originals of historical documents in a safe place off-site. Another way to separate the exposures is to insert a material barrier between the hazard and the person or item which is to be protected. For example, if a maintenance person is allergic to cleaning fluids, separate the loss by requiring that the maintenance person wear latex gloves when using the cleaning fluids. What additional items do you think of that need to be separated from a potential loss hazard?

• *Transfer the exposure*—When you hire piano movers to move the piano into the seminar room, you have transferred the exposure. You have transferred the exposure to possible personal injury and the possible destruction of property to someone who already carries liability and property damage insurance. When you ask your program participants to sign a waiver of responsibility before the start of the off-campus seminar, you have transferred the exposure from your program or institution to the individuals who are participating in the program. While you probably would not ask on-campus participants to sign waivers, it is perfectly understandable that you do it when you have little or no knowledge of what exposures might exist in the off-campus site. You may be able to transfer the exposure by simply posting a sign notifying program participants that your institution is not responsible for items removed or stolen from a particular place.

• *Reduce the severity of the loss*—Smoke detectors are designed to reduce the severity of loss. Closing fire doors does the same thing. A few years back, our program began the policy of placing occupant names on the doors of all the dormitory rooms. In case of an emergency evacuation, we had a record of who needed to be accounted for. Take two vans or two cars rather than trying to crowd everyone into a single vehicle. Two leaders of the same seminar should be encouraged to fly on separate planes. In the event one flight is delayed or canceled, at least one leader would be available to proceed with the seminar. My brother and sister-in-law always flew in separate planes when their children were young. It seemed silly at that time, but now I understand the wisdom of such a decision.

• *Avoid the loss*—There is no guarantee that loss will be avoided, no matter how careful you are or regardless of how many precautions you take. We do know, however, that the chance of loss decreases when all employees are required to wear seat belts; when doors to private rooms are kept locked; when valuables are removed from coats kept on public coat racks; and when safety standards are strictly enforced. And, if your organization does not want to assume the potential loss present in off-campus programs, it is wise for you to avoid offering off-campus programs. Have your employees been trained in proper lifting techniques? Do you caution your program participants in writing about leaving valuables lying around? Have you posted evacuation procedures in every room in your buildings? Have you taken necessary steps to seal windows near library resources? Do you have clearly communicated procedures for reporting an emergency? Are snow and ice removed from sidewalks immediately? These are all ways to avoid loss.

• *Prevent losses*—Everyone knows that when halogen lights and candles are prohibited in living quarters, there is no likelihood that fires will be ignited by them; that's the way you prevent loss from this particular cause. Likewise, visiting faculty need to know your expectations about appropriate behavior around students. Since visiting faculty are expected to abide by all your institutional policies, let them know that acts of racism and sexual harassment will not be tolerated. Do you have failsafe security for library resources? Have you checked the secretary's offices to make sure chairs and computers are placed properly to prevent eyestrain? Have staff members been trained to take frequent breaks from computer input? Do they know how to prevent carpal tunnel syndrome caused by repetitive wrist movements? Are all drivers to seminar-related field trips licensed and registered with the institution?

You will find that the use of one or more of these tools will reduce your losses considerably. You leave nothing to chance when carelessness or oversight may result in serious loss of personnel, time, or money—or all three.

Contracts

Contracting with leaders is a major risk management area. Therefore, it is important to spend the time necessary to write contracts carefully. Since the leader is key to the effectiveness of any seminar, you do need to have a written contract with each seminar leader. Be sure to keep a copy of the exact contract mailed to the leader. If you are currently using a contract form, it is a very good idea to look it over and try to identify any risk exposures it contains. Be sure to include the following items: expected arrival time, exact seminar schedule, the minimum number of registrants required, your cancellation policy and cancellation date, the leader's responsibility for securing permission to photocopy handouts, exact honorarium, provision of meals and housing or reimbursement for same, reimbursement for incidentals, and mileage rate or travel expense limits (coach or first class fare). Attach a copy of your sexual harassment policy, racism policy, faculty policy regarding appropriate behavior on campus, classroom and worship inclusive language guidelines, and any other document that is usually made available to your full-time staff or faculty. Indicate on the contract the date on which the honorarium is to be paid, either immediately following the seminar, or on a specified date. If you require a Saturday night stay-over to reduce travel costs, let the leader know about it in advance. You may wish to include a signature form to be returned to you, indicating that the seminar leader has received and read these policies and is responsible for following them.

Always require that the leader sign the contract, keep a copy, and return a signed copy for your files. Additional follow-up will relieve your mind as the seminar date nears. Call the seminar leader a week in advance to confirm arrival time, check to see what, if any audio-visual equipment is needed, and to let the leader know how many registrations you have received.

You may already know that even a perfectly shaped contract will not ensure excellent seminar leadership. Before you contract with any leader, check with other continuing educators to see if anyone has had first-hand experience with that leader. It is a known fact in our business that the best authors are sometimes the lousiest seminar leaders, so just because someone has written a popular book on the Dead Sea Scrolls, that author may be deadly boring in a seminar setting. You may be able to avoid leadership catastrophes (and thereby seminar catastrophes) if you work the continuing education network for references in advance of contacting a prospective leader.

Your Role as Risk Manager

While you may not be the designated risk manager in your organization, nearly everyone in any form of program direction, program coordination, or facility managing functions at least part of the time as a risk manager. It is to your advantage to take this role seriously. Generally, it means eliminating or reducing as far as practical the conditions and practices which cause insurable losses and then insuring what cannot be avoided. To do this requires, first of all, an awareness of the potential for loss in every aspect of our job—property, finances, personnel, time management, and print information, leadership contracts, and marketing.

Spend some time with your staff focusing on what exposures exist in each of these categories. Better yet, invite your institution's liability insurance company to send a risk management consultant to spend a day with you and others on your staff. The professional consultant will raise concerns you might overlook and give you helpful recommendations following the consultation. This is an inexpensive way of identifying your risks and finding solutions for reducing them. Here are examples of the kind of recommendation an insurance company may have for you:

(a) Consider developing a policy and procedures to prevent and deal with highly contagious diseases.

(b) Consider reviewing the personal safety risks present with employees who work evenings and leave the building after dark.

(c) Consider developing written emergency procedures for groups who use your facilities when few seminary employees are present.

(d) Consider requiring residence hall occupants to state if there is a need for medical sharps (such as needles) disposal containers.

(e) Consider requiring all approved drivers (for off-campus events and field trips) to participate in ongoing drivers' training.

(f) Consider developing an emergency plan for the loss of a utility or a major building on campus.

In addition, it is very important for the continuing education director to orient seminar participants who are not familiar with the campus about emergency evacuation procedures: where to go when the fire alarm sounds, which exit to take to reach the outside quickly and safely, and what to do when they get outside. A consultant to my facility also emphasized how important it is to report accidents and incidents immediately, since workman's compensation is affected when a lapse in reporting occurs. The day you spend with the insurance risk management consultant will be an extremely helpful and productive time.

Summary

The risk management function in church and society continues to grow in importance and complexity. Top management in business and not-for-profit sectors is becoming more cost conscious and more aware of how sound risk management helps to minimize expenses. Society in general is more litigious now than ever before. A whole new genre of exposures has emerged upon the scene with increased use of technology. All employees must accept their share of responsibility for identifying exposures and taking steps immediately to report and reduce the risks that most likely will result.

References

Dorfman, Mark S. *Introduction to Risk Management and Insurance.* Englewood Cliffs, New Jersey: Prentice-Hall, 1994.

Dunklee, Dennis R. and Robert J. Shoop. *Primer for School Risk Management: Creating and Managing District and Site-Based Liability Prevention Program.* Boston: Allyn and Bacon, 1993.

Williams, C. Arthur, Jr., and Richard M. Heins, *Risk Management and Insurance,* 5th ed. New York: McGraw-Hill, 1985.

Williams, C. Arthur, Jr., Michael L. Smith, and Peter Young. *Risk Management and Insurance,* 7th ed., New York: McGraw-Hill, 1995.

Youngbery, Barbara J. (ed.) *The Risk Manager's Desk Reference.* Gaithersburg, Md.: Aspen Publishing, 1994.

Directions and Resources for the Future

Chapter 19

Collaboration in Continuing Theological Education: Creating Communities of Moral Deliberation

Ward Cornett III

Continuing theological education for clergy and church leaders in North America consists of a diverse and wide-ranging market of possibilities and opportunities. Traditionally, the focus of continuing theological education has been upon programs that served the needs and interests of pastors involved in the daily work of parish ministry. Today we understand the arena in which continuing theological education functions in a much larger sense—as a contribution to the church's work in dialogue with the society in which it is located. An important aspect of this work is to structure continuing theological education programs as collaborative enterprises with various other sectors of society. Such collaboration will, in fact, result in the creation of temporary communities of moral deliberation.

Throughout its history, the church has struggled to define its relationship to society. An isolationist or sectarian position is, for most Christians, unworkable as they and their church communities are too fully integrated into the surrounding culture. Conversely, a posture of uncritical accommodation of all that happens in society is also unacceptable. The challenge for the church is to assume an active, but critical, engagement in the world around it. The collaborative enterprise of continuing theological education is one way in which the church can actively engage the world.

Collaboration in continuing theological education challenges the church to rethink its traditional boundaries and its natural tendency to turn inward in order to engage the larger culture in which the church is located. The world is multicultural, multiracial, and religiously pluralistic. Our society is served by governmental agencies, nonprofit organizations, varieties of religious organizations, social service and healthcare organizations, professional associations, businesses, industry, and community service organizations. Our culture is also politically diverse, ranging from ideological extremes of the far left to the far right with a broad middle ground. A wide range of organizations, reflecting that political diversity, routinely engage in major research projects and political advocacy on behalf of their constituencies.

Collaborative efforts in continuing theological education invite the Christian community to build bridges into the community and undertake learning partnerships with organizations, agencies, institutions, and individuals beyond the boundaries of the religious community. Collaboration suggests that continuing theological education can be planned and facilitated in conjunction with other groups in society that may contribute to the ongoing conversation within the religious community. Likewise, those groups will benefit from their participation in educational projects conducted in collaboration with the religious community.

The rationale for creating a broader arena for discussion through collaboration is affirmed by the psalmists who suggest that anything and everything is subject to theological analysis. To quote Psalm 24, "The earth is the LORD's and all that is in it" (24:1a). Psalm 8 reminds us that God has created humanity a little lower than the angels and given us dominion over the works of God's hands. The psalmists provide a clear mandate to be about the business of the world. From a theological perspective, nothing in all of creation is out of bounds for discussion. God has endowed humanity with responsibility for everything that exists. The church's service in the world can be greatly enhanced, as the faithful become more familiar with the rich diversity of God's creation.

Theology is always contextual. Therefore, it must naturally be in conversation with its respective cultural setting. Canadian theologian Douglas John Hall commends the North American church to a "genuine give-and-take, in which the world is permitted to speak for itself" (Hall, p. 79). Only in this way can the disciple community learn something of the spirit of the times, or *Zeitgeist*. By listening to the "host culture," the community can come to a better understanding of the forces at work upon the human spirit. "The disciple community sees its socio-historical habitat, not only as a field to be investigated, but as a partner in the investigation—and therefore as a contributor to the theological task itself" (Hall, p. 79). Through such a contextualizing exercise, the church is able to find common cause with the culture.

Contextual theology can take a variety of forms beginning with the basic task of listening to and observing the surrounding culture in order to inform the church's teaching, preaching, and witness. Another form of contextual theology is the exercise of collaboration in continuing theological education. Representatives of various community organizations or institutions and leaders in continuing theological education sitting down together to plan and produce an educational event is collaboration that puts theology to the test of listening to the culture. This is fundamental to theological education and the life of discipleship. Hall states with force and clarity the need for such an undertaking: "The church can become a theologically alive and obedient disciple community only as it permits its thinking to be receptive to and re-formed by the realities of the world" (Hall, p. 85).

The collaborative effort can be mutually beneficial to everyone involved in a given project. For the church's purposes, it is immediately beneficial to the enterprise of continuing theological education. As Hall notes, contextual theology enlivens the church. The church can only be enriched in its understanding as a result of such an enterprise.

The collaborative model represents what the church has always done: conduct a public witness. Historically the church has carried out a public witness through its social ministry and on-going work for justice for the poor, the oppressed and exploited peoples. However, at the end of the millennium, issues of justice have become much more complex, sometimes polarized, and not as easily addressed by the church without extensive specialized knowledge, expertise, and increased understanding of the issues at stake. The most legitimate prophetic witness in the late-twentieth-century North American church was that which is best informed by the broadest possible knowledge of cultural trends and ideas. Further, it is expressed within the framework of civil society that exercises mutual respect and appreciation for diverse points of view. Certainly civil action has been part of the church's repertoire for effecting social change. It has played a role in the past in the civil rights movement and opposition to the Vietnam War. However, those events were high points of civil crisis that called for the use of extreme measures. In the more mundane day-to-day business of addressing the social problems of our time, it is the carefully considered and measured civil exchange that will have the most impact. The enterprise of collaborative continuing theological education is one arena where this exchange can take place.

The church has a unique relationship to its surrounding culture. It has no legal authority, but significant moral authority. Its authority is exercised not as coercion but as persuasion. However, this authority is eroding as Christianity, specifically, and religious faith more broadly, are marginalized and diminished in an increasingly secular, ethnically and religiously pluralistic culture. The church is also unique in that it is the one institution charged, by public consensus, history and tradition, with the responsibility of promoting humane values. The church has been the repository of concern for human dignity, love and justice, hospitality to the stranger, care for the neighbor and issues of community cohesion. Clearly, these are not simply private values, but matters of great public import. Ronald Thiemann contends that public theology is actually not a specialized discipline or a technical subspecies of theology. Rather, he says, it is guided by the Anselmian credo, "I believe in order that I may understand." Public theology, according to Thiemann, is faith seeking to understand the relationship between Christian convictions and the broader social and cultural setting in which the Christian community lives. In order to understand that relationship, the theological challenge is to offer a careful and detailed description of the entities in question. The goal is not to provide an overarching theory about church and world, but to identify those places where Christian convictions intersect with practices that characterize contemporary public life. Thiemann has stated concisely the rationale for the collaborative model of continuing theological education (Thiemann, pp. 21-22).

Collaboration involves bringing the religious perspective into the public arena. It is especially troubling for church people today that the religious community, its message and its activities are becoming increasingly less significant in contemporary society. Numerous writers and scholars have documented recently the concern for both the fragmentation of the religious voice in the public arena, and the complete dismissal of religion as a legitimate participant in the cultural and civic enterprise. Religion, as a significant voice in the public arena, suffers from a number of hindrances. First, the faith perspective is typically compartmentalized by religious people. The tendency is for the religious person to segregate the practice and understanding of religion from the rest of her or his life, that is, to confine religion within the walls of the church. Especially for Christians, this tendency reflects a shortcoming of religious education. Parishioners, typically, are not instructed or urged to think about their vocation or their place of work as the arena for living out their faith. Only in recent years have we observed a movement toward a religious understanding of vocation or ministry in daily life. Otherwise, the normal practice is to leave our religious beliefs at home and at the church. Religious self-understanding and expressions of faith are not particularly welcome within the work place and public arena, nor are expressions of one's faith perspective readily shared openly by many Christians.

Stephen Carter has documented this tendency to privatize and compartmentalize religious faith in *The Culture of Disbelief: How American Law and Politics Trivialize Religious Devotion*. Carter deals extensively with a number of different aspects of religion and culture, including the church-state debate, religious expression in the public schools, and the resurgence of Christian evangelical demands for recognition and rights. Although he is sympathetic to some of the difficulties Christian Evangelicals have experienced with attempts to limit their public expression of religious faith, Carter does not limit himself to the problems of only one particular religious movement. He is more broadly concerned about American culture and its inability to recognize the place and the importance of religion in the overall cultural scheme. Not only do law and politics trivialize religion, the culture itself treats religion as if it has nothing substantive to contribute. Carter sites numerous examples of open hostility to religion and religious expression in American culture, including academic treatises that engage in the disparagement of religious belief. There is little tolerance for religious belief and expression in various sectors of society. The wholesale indifference toward religion that is evident in other corners of American culture is just as harmful and insidious. Noting this tendency, Carter repeatedly makes reference to the idea of religion as a hobby. In other words, religion is understood as being primarily a private and personal matter that has little public or political consequence (Carter, pp. 51-84).

There is also evidence of the public's attitude of indifference toward specific institutions of the church. Theological education is uniquely the province of the church, its judicatories, and its educational institutions, including church-related graduate schools of religion and theology, and theological seminaries. These same institutions serve as venues for continuing education. A recent study conducted by Auburn Theological Seminary determined that many community leaders were simply unaware of the presence of seminaries in their communities. According to Barbara G. Wheeler, president of Auburn and Director of the Auburn Center for the Study of Theological Education, "seminaries are virtually invisible to leaders of secular organizations and institutions, even those in the seminary's own city and region." Wheeler reports of one community activist, who lives in a city with several seminaries, "The seminaries don't appear often on people's radar screens." A businessman in the same city said, "I don't know that anyone in this town knows that (the seminaries) are there." The study documents thoroughly the invisibility of theological seminaries and the more general tendency of religious leaders, including parish pastors and church-related institutions, to be increasingly disengaged from issues in the public realm (Lynn and Wheeler, p. 4).

Part of the challenge in collaborative continuing theological education is convincing the secular community that the church has something important to contribute. Similarly, it is a challenge to convince the church that it has anything to gain by participating in the public arena through a collaborative approach to theological education. In order to "make the case" for collaborative theological education, the church must be clear in its rationale for such an undertaking. Otherwise, it will not be convincing to the world or to its own constituency.

Of course, there is more at stake than the church's public witness and presence. To name a few, the church needs to support efforts to renew civic life, cultivate common ground for mutual conversation, and encourage the exchange of diverse viewpoints on a series of topics, including some that are highly controversial. Social isolation and public fragmentation has been addressed by historian Arthur M. Schlesinger, Jr. in his reflections on multicultural society, *The Disuniting of America* (1991). He notes that the United States has been incredibly successful, up to now, at nurturing and maintaining an amalgamated society consisting of a rich diversity of ethnic origins, European, African, and now, South American. That unity has been served by the emphasis upon individual identity with the larger culture of the country, rather than with ethnic origin. Individuals desired to shed their ethnic identity and assimilate, unnoticed, into the American milieu, "to forge a new American culture" (Schlesinger, pp. 12, 13). This has been accomplished despite the "curse of racism" that has prevailed over centuries of American development. Schlesinger laments the fact that this assimilating capacity has diminished significantly as more people are finding their identity primarily within ethnic and linguistic subcultures. This occurs often at the expense of broader cultural and nationalistic sources of identity. The consequence of this trend is that tribalism will continue to grow and different groups in society will focus exclusively on their own interests and concerns.

In *Habits of the Heart*, sociologist Robert Bellah and his associates conducted a series of in-depth interviews with a wide range of people. The interviews were designed to measure the degree of independence and individualism versus commitment to communitarian values. Following the interviews, the sociologists engaged in extensive analysis of the results. Part of basis for their analyses was the nineteenth-century study of American culture and character, *Democracy in America*, by Alexis de Tocqueville, from which Bellah derived his title, *Habits of the Heart*. De Tocqueville used the term to describe attitudes, notions, opinions, and ideas that "shape mental habits" and are "the sum of moral and intellectual dispositions of men in society." Mores, according to Bellah, seem to involve not only ideas and opinions, but also habitual practices with respect to religion, political participation, and economic life. De Toqueville, writing in the 1830s, used a new term, "individualism," to describe the way, in which Americans lived, a way exemplified by Benjamin Franklin. Individualism is more moderate and orderly than egoism, which predates the use of individualism, but yields the same results. According to de Toqueville, "Individualism is a calm and considered feeling which predisposes each citizen to isolate himself from the mass of his fellows and withdraw into the circle of family and friends; with this little society formed to his taste, he gladly leaves the greater society to look after itself" (cited in Bellah, pp. 37, 38).

Bellah reports that de Toqueville was especially interested in those forces that would work to return people from their isolation and into social communion. Immersion in private economic pursuits was one of the forces that drove people away from a life of civic responsibility and into their own privatized spheres. At the same time, civic responsibility and involvement in public affairs was seen as the best antidote to individual isolation. De Toqueville was concerned that an overemphasis on individualism, self-reliance, and economic affluence would result in the rejection of their contemporaries, their ancestors, and their descendants. "Each man," contended de Toqueville, "is thrown back on himself alone, and there is danger that he may be shut up in the solitude of his own heart" (cited in Bellah, p. 37).

Bellah asserts that the growth of individualism is contrary to, and therefore, destructive to the basic commitment to community values. Bellah and his colleagues presuppose that community affiliation, whether in the form of neighborhood, family ties, or institutional membership (including the church), is an essential source of individual identity. Their research uncovered increasing tendencies for individuals to define themselves beyond the bounds of traditionally recognized communities of moral deliberation, a place where they face more uncertainty regarding their sense of self-worth. Consequently, the only standard remaining against which one can be measured are the measures established by the market economy: levels of income, consumption, and one's ability to conform to the means for achieving that end. Bellah notes that this is the curious paradox of nonconformity in American society. As individuals reject conformity to traditional sources of community standards and personal identity, they are simultaneously conforming to standards of status and achievement (Bellah, p. 149). Living under such compulsion leaves little room for attention to the common good, the needs of others, or to questions that would naturally evolve from the process of moral deliberation.

American society is becoming fragmented, highly individualized, and "ghetto-ized" into a diverse range of cultural enclaves, including those created by disparities in wealth and income. Witness the recent proliferation of privatized, gated communities, and other exclusive housing developments in the United States that are accessible only to the very affluent. The exclusiveness of these neighborhoods demonstrates the lengths individuals will go to avoid the costs of living in a broad-based community. They illustrate, further, how difficult it is to find common ground for moral deliberation and discussion of the common good. Coupled with the decline in political party affiliation, increasingly low voter turn out, and a general decline in church participation, Bellah's concerns for the disintegration of communities of moral deliberation are only magnified.

Ultimately, the roots of this moral fragmentation go much deeper than Bellah's analysis. One of the foremost ethicists of this era, Alasdaire MacIntyre, in his 1982 publication, *After Virtue*, addressed the moral crisis of the twentieth century. He asserts that the Enlightenment failed to find a common ground for exercising moral discernment and deliberation based on reason alone. MacIntyre understands this failure to have occurred because, in each era prior to the Enlightenment, all attempts to find a moral center only resulted in affirming the prevailing norms and values of the contemporary culture. Further, the Enlightenment project refused to deal with the teleological dimensions of human existence. In short, there was no acknowledgment of the duality of human nature. Enlightenment era philosophers proceeded on the assumption of the basic goodness of human nature. Consequently, any effort to formulate moral injunctions failed because the effort was always disconnected from the teleological understanding. Instead of an understanding based on assumptions about the human condition, the tendency in formulating moral injunctions is to resort to arbitrary authority for justification. For MacIntyre, arbitrary authority becomes the philosophy of emotivism, which is nothing more than the anarchy of the individual will, due to the lack of criteria for making moral or evaluative judgments. Emotivism depends on the use of the personal pronoun "I" as the individual engages in the expression of personal preference without regard to objective reason or attention to the facts. MacIntyre notes that moral discourse today is becoming increasingly shrill due to the lack of a coherent set of principles or an overarching framework in which to make ethical determinations. Participation in public discourse has become highly individualized, reflecting a fragmentation of public unity. Overall, MacIntyre is concerned with the general disintegration of public moral authority (pp. 6-61).

American culture, and indeed, the whole world, is undergoing another dramatic change with the advent of the digital revolution and the burgeoning growth of the Internet. The Internet has already redefined the idea of community. Now, it is possible for individuals who are relatively unknown to one another, separated by thousands of miles, and isolated in front of a computer screen, to enter into discussion groups about virtually any topic in the world. In some sense, these new communities may be "communities of moral deliberation." It is more likely they will reflect the characteristics of emotivism addressed by MacIntyre, the anarchy of the individual, and personal preference, rather than any deliberative process.

Sociobiologist E. O. Wilson contends that the impact of the Internet in the twenty-first century will be that the world will not be run by those who possess mere knowledge alone. As the result of science and technology, "access to factual knowledge of all kinds is rising exponentially while dropping in unit cost. It is destined to become global and democratic. Soon it will be available everywhere on television and computer screens." He contends that "we are drowning in information, while starving for wisdom. What is needed will be people who have the ability to synthesize information, to put together the right information at the right time, think critically about it, and make important choices wisely" (Wilson, p. 269). This is the task of ethics, the task of religious leaders especially, and the task of continuing theological education.

The question arises again as to who will participate in the exercise of communities in moral deliberation. Will it be the church, corporations, government, scholars, and self-appointed synthesizers of information? Is it possible that the arena of continuing theological education can play a role in facilitating this kind of conversation on the eve of the democratization of access to knowledge? How can continuing theological education provide a forum for moral deliberation?

At the turn of the century, the economy of the United States is stronger than it has ever been. The business sector is a dynamic, prosperous, and supportive force in the life of the community. Public morale seems unusually high. All of that said, we face serious concerns as a society. There is great disparity in income and resources between the rich and everyone else, especially the poor. We have not solved the problem of poverty, despite the masquerade of welfare reform. The incidence of child poverty is higher in the United States than in any other Western industrialized country. Approximately 42 million U.S. citizens are without health insurance, many of them working people. Concerns about youth violence, crime and excessively high levels of incarceration of our citizenry persist unresolved. Many in the scientific community have concluded that we face a global environmental catastrophe as the result of environmental degradation, global warming, and the loss of biological diversity. The church addresses all of these concerns and more, at different levels and to different degrees. Continuing theological education is called to provide a forum for the church's ongoing engagement of these concerns, and the scholars, community leaders, and political figures who have some say about how we will make decisions that will determine the future well-being of much of humanity.

If any larger, all encompassing purpose can be served by the collaborationist model of continuing education, it is in the realization of truth borne through the process of discovery. Wilson, like MacIntyre, recognizes the failure of the Enlightenment to find a common ground for ethical discernment and truth seeking. Nevertheless, he describes the Enlightenment with poetic appreciation. It was never, he says, a unified moment, "less a determined swift river than a lacework of deltaic streams working their way along twisted channels." The Enlightenment consisted of a variety of thinkers within the European academy, driven by the thrill of discovery and a shared "passion to demystify the world and free the mind from the impersonal forces that imprison it. They were driven by the thrill of discovery. They agreed on the power of science to reveal an orderly, understandable universe and thereby lay an enduring base for free, rational discourse" (p. 21).

Continuing theological education, especially when done collaboratively, can provide a similar framework for free, rational, discourse and its consequent thrill of discovery. Those who participate in programs that foster moral deliberation are in a good position to reflect upon the social currents of the day. When such free, open, and rational exchange occurs, the result can be an experience of concilience, the unity of knowledge. Wilson defines consilience as a "jumping together" of knowledge by the linking of facts, and fact-based theory across disciplines, to create a common groundwork of explanation" (Wilson, p. 8). When the church engages the world on common ground, seeking to listen to what the world is saying, as well as to address the world with its message of hope, the possibility exists for finding explanations for what ails us, as well as prescriptions for solving the problems.

Models of Collaboration in Continuing Theological Education

There are as many examples of collaborative programs as there are sectors of society and issues to be addressed. This list offers a sample of the kinds of collaborative programs that can be developed and, where possible, an identification of resources:

Building Communities from the Inside Out—Urban renewal and community redevelopment programs from the Institute for Policy Research at Northwestern University has been used extensively in communities around the country. The individuals responsible for this program format, John P. Kretzmann and John L. McKnight, are excellent speakers and resource persons. Dr. John P. Kretzmann has strong ties to the faith community and is available as a resource person for the church.

Funding of nonprofit social service organizations—Fund-raising is a critical issue for church based social service organizations such as Lutheran Social Services, Catholic Charities, United Methodist children's homes and others. The first two organizations cited comprise the two largest private, nonprofit organizations in the U.S. with more than 50 percent of their multibillion dollar budgets coming from federal sources. This community issue has political, theological and sociological dimensions.

Care of Creation—There are numerous resources within the secular academy and the theological community for addressing environmental concerns. Various denominations have formulated public statements about the care of creation and Christian responsibility for environmental stewardship. Two theologians who have given this the most attention are the Reverend Dr. Paul Santmire, pastor, Holy Trinity Lutheran Church in Akron Ohio, and Dr. Larry Rasmussen, the Reinhold Niebuhr Professor of Social Ethics at Union Theological Seminary in New York. Another highly qualified individual is Dr. David Orr, Professor of Environmental Studies at Oberlin College.

Global Hunger and Development—Bread for the World, Church World Services, Lutheran World Relief, and Catholic Relief Services are endowed with extensive expertise in addressing global hunger. Additionally, business, including food producers and commodity brokers, all need to be part of any conversation on the future of the world's food supply.

Interprofessional Educational Programming

It is an expectation that ministers and professional leaders in the church participate in continuing education. However, it has only been in recent years that denominations have begun to identify more clearly their expectations and accountability for participation in lifelong learning. That is not the case with other professions that are accountable to state licensure boards, professional associations, and specific expectations for a defined amount of continuing education in order to maintain professional certification. This is an important dimension of continuing theological education programs that involve collaboration with other organizations, agencies, and institutions. Professionals in many other fields, such as social work, education, and various health care fields, are required to earn Continuing Professional Education credits or contact hours. Attorneys must take Continuing Legal Education units (CLEs). Collaborative programs can then serve the needs of a number of constituencies at once.

Professional associations and state licensure boards normally have specific expectations for the kinds of program offerings that will satisfy their requirements for continuing education contact hours. Including other professions in a continuing education offering creates the opportunity to engage in joint development of goals, objectives, and program format. Joint undertakings will challenge program planners to look critically at the needs and interests and professional development agendas of other professions and thus be exposed to different approaches to addressing human needs and solving the pressing social problems of our era.

The Future of Collaboration in Continuing Theological Education

It is important to recognize that, despite a reigning attitude of disparagement in the secular sphere, the church has something to contribute to the surrounding community. The secular realm will reap benefits as the church offers its resources as a historic community of moral deliberation. Secular society is in desperate need of a forum where it is appropriate to exercise moral discernment in a free and open exchange that will include diverse perspectives and the opportunity to engage critically across lines of difference.

The turn of the century represents a time of both great challenge and opportunity for the church's educational enterprise, especially in the area of continuing theological education. Challenge and opportunity are offered because of the amount of rapid change underway in the church, the culture, and the world. At this writing there are dramatic changes underway in the field of education and specifically, in the area of continuing education. For one thing, the term "continuing education" itself is in decline. More and more people today describe their participation in such programs as a process of "lifelong learning." Reflecting more than simply a name change, this new terminology denotes a change in attitude, outlook, and practice that is consistent with a dramatic paradigm shift that is underway in the arena of organized learning.

One significant change is related to educational technology. As technology becomes less expensive and more accessible, it will become increasingly a part of the tools available for congregations to use in their educational enterprise. One possibility for the future of continuing education is the blurring of distinctions between seminaries, continuing education centers, and congregations. Not only will congregations be recipients of programming, but they will also become program providers, resource centers, and collaborators in continuing theological education. As congregations become "teaching congregations" the base for collaboration, cooperation, and participation with a broad range of people will expand considerably. Within ten years it is likely that numerous congregations around the world, most graduate schools, seminaries, learning centers, businesses, and nonprofit organizations will be equipped with video conferencing capacity and the ability to share resources on the Internet. As this transition to digital connections occurs, opportunities for bridges within and among communities will multiply. In the very near future, collaboration in continuing theological education will not be the exception, but the norm, for program planning and presentation. It will occur with regularity in the digital realm as well as in face-to-face formats. Developing an understanding of the importance and potential of collaboration with a variety of partners in continuing education, as well as the skills to make the collaborative process productive and just, is crucial to the future of all manner of centers of continuing education, and incumbent upon theological institutions.

References

Bellah, Robert N., Richard Marsden, William M. Sullivan, Ann Swidler, and Steven M. Tipton. *Habits of the Heart: Individualism and Commitment in American Life*, Berkeley: University of California Press, 1985.

Carter, Stephen L. *The Culture of Disbelief: How American Law and Politics Trivialize Religious Devotion*. New York: Basic Books, 1993.

Hall, Douglas John. *Thinking the Faith: Christian Theology in a North American Context*. Minneapolis: Fortress Press, 1989.

Lynn, Elizabeth and Barbara G. Wheeler, "Missing Connections: Public Perceptions of Theological Education and Religious Leadership." Auburn Studies, No. 6, Sept. 1999. Auburn Theological Seminary.

MacIntyre, Alasdaire. *After Virtue*. Notre Dame, Ind.: University of Notre Dame Press, 1984.

Schlesinger, Arthur M. Jr. *The Disuniting of America: Reflections on a Multicultural Society*. New York: W.W. Norton, 1992.

Thiemann, Ronald. *Constructing a Public Theology: The Church in a Pluralistic Culture*. Louisville: Westminster/John Knox Press, 1991.

Wilson, E. O. *Consilience: The Unity of Knowledge*. New York: Alfred A. Knopf, 1998.

Chapter 20

Religion at the Cutting Edge: Stepping Boldly into a New Millennium

Mike Maus and John Maus

The World Wide Web is playing an important and rapidly growing role in helping laypeople think about their faith. Access to the World Wide Web gives us access to a richer church life.

—Michael Klein

Many Detroit boys back in the 1950s made a late-summer sport of riding their bikes to the nearest car dealer and boosting each other up to peek at the newest models. Often the cars were covered with tarpaulins, but the outlines were clear and, occasionally, one fender could be seen. The feeling was palpable. A glimpse of a DeSoto's taillight assembly in a finned fender made the heart race!

In their time, those cars were at the cutting edge of technology. They had wraparound windows and push-button transmissions and engines so powerful that if a driver "slammed the pedal to the metal," passengers could get whiplash injuries!

But, nothing ever seems to stay the same. The DeSoto's fins did not last long (nor did the DeSoto, for that matter). Gasoline for a while was hard to get, and Americans had a fling with trying to conserve it by reinventing the automobile engine as a more efficient power source. Cars became smaller. Their seats provided better support. Seat belts, then air bags and side-impact bars of steel, provided increased measures of crash protection. The cutting edge of technology moved on to "better, smaller, safer" and left behind the values of power and beauty that had become obsolete.

Business innovates by taking advantage of technology (and imagination) to respond to the demands of the marketplace. And, the results often are better, more efficient, more attractive products priced within the reach of the "target" consumers. The end effect of technological innovation in business is to make profitable products available to the widest possible markets.

Companies work hard to understand what they do best and how their strengths fit the needs of the marketplace. Mission statements and vision statements guide companies as they set annual goals; executives and staff are held accountable for success or failure in accomplishing what they set out to do. Plans are made in concert with an evaluation of available financial and human resources, as well as available technology.

The church once focused on mission and had vision. Prophets counted. So did dreamers. The early church thought of the future, talked about it, and lived into it on the vision of its prophets and dreamers. The early church helped its members deal with the realities of the day and gave hope, comfort—and often direction—for the future. Now, however, the church is a collection of institutions for which vision seems to be less important. The prophets have been replaced by bureaucrats whose sense of mission is practical and protective. That is the case in some businesses and nonprofit organizations, too. James Baldwin once wrote, "Most of us are about as eager to be changed as we were to be born, and go through our changes in a similar state of shock" (cited in Marty, 1998, p. 8).

But, whether churches or businesses embrace or avoid change, technology changes; its changes affect how churches work and companies do business. As recently as the mid-1980s, most offices had a telephone and a typewriter on the desk; today there is hardly an office without a personal computer. In fact, in most business offices, it is hard to find a typewriter. Not so in many church offices, where the typewriter remains a mainstay along with other equipment that technological change left behind years ago. Robert Nash puts it bluntly:

> The most advanced piece of technology in most children's Sunday school classes is a flannel board. Church bulletins in the 1990s look surprisingly similar to those of the 1950s. Worship is a stagnant and endless litany. Preachers drone on to half-empty

sanctuaries, mistakenly assuming that their congregants are even listening at all. And we continue to "do church" as if people will endure this tedium forever. (Nash, 1997, p. 2)

Today's technologies have moved communication from the realm of shouting across a room to whispering across the planet, and have changed transportation from the bicycle to the space shuttle. Computing technology has gone from the abacus to virtual reality. All of these have combined to change our notions of what constitutes community. The church can be a vital part of this technological revolution by taking advantage of the new media and accepting—and making the most of—its role in the new communities in which people find themselves.

The Information Superhighway and the Church

There has been a lot of talk about the information superhighway in recent years, bringing to mind the building of freeways in and between major cities. Especially in the cities, freeways cut wide swaths, often displacing the poor and decimating historic neighborhoods. In rural areas as well, the wide, multi-lane, limited-access highways split farms and separated neighbors, forcing people to go out of their way to plow their fields or take cookies to friends or get to church.

Computer owners and Internet users, the people who ride on the information superhighway, like those who benefited from, without getting disrupted by, the interstate highway system, are predominantly white, well educated, and hardly poor. They reside largely in the suburbs or exurbs, the places *to* which freeways go. Minority populations, in places *through* which freeways go, have fewer computers and less access to the Internet. However, unlike the freeways, the benefits and costs of the information superhighway may not be so permanently and inequitably divided. New computers today sell for as little as $300—a big change from the $3,000 we paid for our first PC—and Internet access can be had for free in many places. Or a consumer can pay for the Internet access and receive the computer for free, just by agreeing to a two to three year contract. It is even possible to agree to read some advertisements each time a computer is used, and in return, both the computer and the Internet access are free. The poor have not yet gained equal access to the Internet, but the possibility of their having access is not beyond the realm of the imagination.

There is a positive side to this technology, even if access has currently created technological haves and have-nots. The mystery writer Robert Parker says the interstate highways created a "transcontinental neighborhood," while the Internet and World Wide Web have created a "global neighborhood" (p. 33). People use the Web to chat over electronic back fences, exchange information, read the Bible, study for degrees, and care for one another in ways unimagined even a generation ago. The Internet makes it possible to form communities that have nothing to do with physical location, political system, race, sex, or any of the other myriad ways we have of separating an "us" from a "them." It also links families, bringing parents and children, grandparents and grandchildren, together to talk with each other, rather than just to or at each other, and often over great distances. One couple we know has six daughters and sons who live literally all over the world. All are regular travelers on the *information highway* and are in contact with each other almost daily. It is also that way in our family. We use email to keep in touch, to share ideas, to brighten each other's days, to reach out and say, "I love you." If we, and others can do it, why can't the church?

An Opportunity for Education

The church has made a start. Ecunet, started in the eighties by church people with a vision of using the Internet as a tool for communication and ministry, helps the church to reach out and share ideas. Individuals can—and do—do this as well: a quick search (in July, 1999) found more than forty thousand homepages (World Wide Web sites created by individuals) that mention the Bible. But most churches, like many individuals, seem to choose to do otherwise, to stick with old forms of communication although better, more efficient ones are available.

Many small churches struggle to survive perhaps even more than they seek to serve. In the years that many smaller (as well as larger) churches have been losing members to golf courses, televisions, and alarm clocks that seem to work only Monday through Friday, a generation has been coming of age that sees the church, especially the institutional church, as irrelevant. In general, people who have grown up with the VCR and the personal computer and, more recently, the Internet and World Wide Web, do not spend much time in church, certainly not as much as their parents do, or their grandparents did.

But, it does not have to be that way. Loren Mead says churches must "reinvent" themselves if they are to grow into the future. While Mead believes that "institutional structures and forms developed to support one vision of our mission are rapidly collapsing," he also senses that new forms can and will emerge (p. 5). This reinventing will have to go beyond the institutional structures of denominations and seminaries to the pastors and leaders themselves. Change is a juggernaut that is coming, whether we are ready for it or not, and the only way to avoid being overrun by its wheels is to learn and never stop learning.

This is why creativity and adaptability in education is crucial. Seminaries and similar institutions must continually reinvent their curricula, so that their graduates are prepared for the world they enter—no longer is the "same old stuff" taught by "the usual suspects" going to help pastors, lay leaders, and congregations meet the challenges of the changing world of communications. Continuing education offerings must be extensive and relevant, and pastors and leaders must take advantage of them. This is another area where the church can learn from business: many companies expect to spend 10 percent of an employee's salary and 10 percent of the employee's time on training. In other words, they train their workers for five weeks and at great expense each year. If business did not benefit from such training expenses, it would not make them. And, if business benefits from something like this, the church can benefit as well.

For example, providers of continuing education could find ways to help students learn how to encourage more direct and intentional cooperation between pastors and businesspersons in their congregations. Much is to be learned from folks who work in offices, factories, schools, and stores, many of whom work daily with computers and the Internet. But, before pastors reach out, their "comfort level" has to improve; they need greater confidence before they can begin to learn. Continuing educators could offer seminars on current technology, getting business people and innovators who create and use the new technologies to share their experience and expertise.

The church has done this before, with other technology. No less a visionary than Martin Luther looked at the technology of his day, the recently developed printing press, and "caught a glimpse of the enormous implications of the shifts that it would bring. He knew that the church would have to make use of this transformative development" (Sample, p. 93). It may be obvious, but still it must be said: the church must imagine the implications of cultural changes and diligently work to put them to use in appropriate ways or it risks being moved further from mainline to sideline. Continuing education programs for clergy and laity should play a significant role in the imagining process.

The church can take advantage of the emerging medium as a tool in its daily life. It also can examine and address the ethical issues raised by the new technologies. There are signs that the generation that is growing up comfortable with computers is doing this, especially when it comes to understanding "church" and where they will go for support when troublesome ethical and moral issues demand their attention.

George Barna, a respected surveyor of American religious life who approaches the task from an evangelical perspective, puts the opportunity (or challenge) in stark terms, at least as far as the traditional sense of "church" is concerned. He says that "one out of six teens (16 percent) said that within the next five years they expect to use the Internet as a substitute for their current church-based religious experience. This notion was most common among teenagers who currently attend church regularly. African American teens were four times more likely than white teens to expect to rely on the Internet for their future religious experience (31 percent vs. 8 percent respectively)." Even more disquieting for the traditional church was Barna's finding that "12 percent of the adult population is already using the Internet for religious purposes." Barna himself says that his "research indicates that by 2010 we will probably have 10 to 20 percent of the population relying primarily or exclusively upon the Internet for its religious input. Those people will never set foot on a church campus because their religious and spiritual needs will be met through other means—including the Internet."

This creates major challenges for local churches—and for the people who educate their leaders—as they plan for mission in the new century. Preachers and leaders interpret the gospel in all that they do in the life of the church. In the past, this has been fairly straightforward: taking something from the printed page, studying it, and sharing it with others in a way that helped them understand its meaning. This usually was done in worship, with the congregation gathered, or in classes or other small groups; it was a community effort. In general, there was an opportunity to discuss what was being read and interpreted with others. This task has new dimensions as computers and the Internet make it possible to share the Word of God in ways unimagined only a generation or two ago, and as individuals access the Scriptures by themselves, outside the traditional "community." Most of the people who will do that are today's younger generation, who have grown up with computers and are comfortable with using the Internet for a variety of wholesome purposes. One of the possibilities to which Barna points is that "within the next 15 years, a majority of Americans will be completely isolated from the traditional church format."

The church has a window of opportunity here. If continuing educators and others help it learn to use the tools, the church can challenge the minds of Web users and strengthen their values. Younger, more affluent, better-educated persons comfortable with the Web can find stories of faith on church Web sites. Visitors can be directed to a religion-based site (denominational, local church Web page, independent). The church will be competing in a crowded marketplace filled with talented people who are not necessarily in tune with the message of the church. Since this is where younger people who should be the church's future will be found, the church must understand the implications of the new technology and become comfortable with its use. Continuing educators as cultural interpreters can help here, as can businesspersons. The key is to make the church's messages and ministries more accessible and audience-friendly, and to learn more about how the technology can help make the church a more effective communicator.

The influence of computers and the Internet will be even more dramatic as computers become smaller and are integrated into the appliances that many people use every day. In a keynote speech to a computer conference in June 1999, Microsoft's chief operating officer said that in the near future computers would be in appliances from refrigerators to washing machines (Herbold, June 23, 1999). By the time he spoke, we already were accustomed to computers that tell us the time, control our televisions, maintain the temperatures in our homes, diagnose what is wrong with our cars, guide our airline flights, even audit our tax returns. But in washing machines?

What does all this have to do with church and ministry? Have you been in many church offices lately? The ones we have visited, admittedly not numbering in the hundreds or even dozens, but still seeming fairly typical, are crowded and usually have an overworked staff trying to make do with equipment that is inadequate to the tasks. As computers get smaller (and more powerful), they will take up less space in an office, allowing the staff to have more room in which to work. Connected to the Internet, either by modem or by a higher-speed link, a pastor will be able to link to the library at the Vanderbilt University Divinity School to get the week's lectionary readings. He or she can go to the Sermonshop meeting on Ecunet to participate in a discussion of the readings and exchange ideas for the upcoming sermon. The staff person (paid or volunteer) in the less crowded office will be able to manage the membership rolls and finances, and handle the preparation of the worship program and regular mailings more efficiently.

Church school teachers will mine the Internet—either from their home computers (40 percent of all U.S. homes had computers by 1998, and the number was growing rapidly), or from the computer in the church office—for resource materials. They will use search engines to find resources to strengthen their teaching, from classroom materials to Bible study guides and even things for younger children that relate to the theme of a particular day.

The Internet is much more than a source for resources. It is an opportunity for interactivity that can encourage greater participation in the thinking and interpreting work that characterizes much church activity. Online forums, for example, allow people to publicize their thoughts and interact with others who share their interests. One particular kind, a moderated forum, sends all messages to one person who can add his or her own comments before publishing messages for others' reading and response. This model sounds a lot like the minister who uses a parishioner's question as the basis for a sermon, but with the added benefit of a question-and-answer session after the sermon. It also allows a fairly free-flowing discussion to follow the sermon, thus increasing the interaction between pulpit and pew. All this can take place with the speed of the Internet, dealing with multiple questions at once and responding quickly.

In business as well as in the church, reinventing really focuses on an ability to recognize, even anticipate the need for change. Businesses engaged in reinventing often focus on understanding the culture in which the company does business—churches doing the same need likewise to focus on the culture in which the members of the church live. Similarly, providers of continuing education must focus on courses that are relevant in their students' culture(s). Just as it is not enough for a business to understand the products that it sells, it is not enough for the church to understand the Scriptures, nor for an educator to understand the course he or she teaches. A real effort must be made to understand the consumers, church members, and students and their needs. None can survive by following a "We've always done it this way" approach. To insist on preserving the familiar for its own sake is to make all but certain that the company, church, or school will quickly lose strength and eventually will die.

Brian D. McLaren, author of *Reinventing Your Church*, says his argument grew out of a struggle "to learn what it means to be a Christian, and lead a Christian church, in a postmodern way, in a postmodern world, with a message that transforms a culture first by truly entering it, understanding it, and embracing it with compassion" (McLaren, February 23, 1999). McLaren warns that the church often speaks "an outmoded language," works in "outmoded structures," and thinks "in outmoded paradigms." He really seems to be saying that the church does not speak to people in languages they can understand.

If open systems, ones that are not proprietary, are the way of the future as they have been the engine that has driven development of computers and software in recent years, what about open churches and open Scriptures? In the church's early days, the Bible was accessible only to a select few. Priests, since they were trained to read, were the deliverers and interpreters of Scripture. Gutenberg changed that. His press made it possible to print Bibles that would be available to ordinary people, at least those who could read. More recently, the computer opened new doors to the Scriptures, again for those whose literacy (and economic circumstances) make it possible for them to take advantage of it. The World Wide Web, assuming its stunning growth continues, will do the same thing. A challenge for the church, and for the people who educate those who will lead the church into the future, is to imagine the opportunities for ministry opened by this new, more compact, more affordable technology.

Esther Dyson, an Internet pioneer who works to encourage a broad and deep understanding of its many ramifications, says "The Net matters because people use it as a place to communicate, conduct business, and share ideas, not as a mystical entity in itself" (Dyson, p. 6). But for many in the church, mainly in the pastorate and lay leadership, the Internet *is* a "mystical entity" that they despair of understanding with about the same degree of energy that they claim they never will be able to program a VCR unless they have a teenager's help.

Okay. For the moment, let us accept that this *is* all kid stuff (even though we know it is much more than that). Let's accept that the Internet is a lot like the average VCR in that only a younger person can understand it and "get" what it is all about. If that's the case, think about the opportunity that this presents for a church which more often than not has a Sunday morning majority of folks with gray or even white hair. If only the young "get" the Net, it seems like a real opportunity for the church to use the Net to "get" the young. Downes and Mui's argument that "Technology is now the central driver of the business economy" is one way for the church to begin to recognize what is "out there" in the world where many of its people spend their work days (Downes and Mui, p. 73). They also suggest that one way to redefine the business environment (and we would argue the church environment as well) is to "hire the children." Why? Because "Young people, especially children, implicitly understand digital technology in a way that the rest of us can only watch and admire" (Downes and Mui, p. 158). Dyson's claim that "The Net offers us a chance to take charge of our own lives and to redefine our role as citizens of local communities and of a global society" also applies to the life of the church and thus is a challenge to educators (Dyson, p. 2).

The church must take charge of its life and begin to accomplish the redefinition, the re-imagining, of its mission. This is Mead's challenge to the church that wants to live into the future. For him, the principal setting for this task is the congregation. But in the borderless age of the Internet, local has global dimensions and thus requires an understanding of what it means to be people of faith that goes far beyond neighborhood study groups and potluck suppers. Essentially, the Internet is an opportunity for a centralized institution like the church to decentralize, which Dyson cites as "the greatest structural impact of the Net." "Things and people," she says, "no longer depend on a center to be connected" (Dyson, p. 8). Think what that means for most of the churches in the United States. For years, these institutions that were important parts of the center of the American culture generally have been losing authority as well as members. Now comes the Net and the World Wide Web to decentralize things even further and probably destabilize them even more.

Here is a very real opportunity for the church, or at least for individual churches, pastors and leaders who understand the technology and are willing to adopt—and adapt—it to serve their purposes. The concept of congregation takes on a whole new meaning, just as the concept of international borders has been redefined by an electronic communications network that makes fortified borders less relevant and, in many cases, utterly useless.

Still, what we are talking about here is a bit like jumping into the deep end of a pool without knowing how to swim. Decentralization can be disturbing and disorienting, but it also can be seen as opening new opportunities for learning. Decentralization changes long-established patterns, patterns that in the case of the church as well as the university and the seminary have served fairly well, in some cases for centuries. While decentralization can create problems for the church, it also opens new possibilities for people unable to travel or resistant to going to a campus or a big city. It could prove to be an opportunity for the church to get beyond old borders and to reach out in new ways, using pioneering work being done by the Association of Theological Schools, denominations, and individual churches. As computers and the Internet become even more affordable in the new century, churches and seminaries that use them creatively are more likely to survive than those that insist on doing communication, ministry, and education in the same old ways. This time of change offers a real opportunity for the church as an institution and a local center to refocus itself and gain a new understanding of mission.

Mead talks of the poles of parish and congregation as the extremes of the church, extremes that usually exist in tension with each other. Parish is neighborhood, area, geography that goes beyond the particularities of denomination to include all of the parts of life. "The word stands for the fact that the church cannot separate itself from its social context, from realms of politics and economic life. It is engaged indissolubly with the world" (Mead, p. 44). Congregation, on the other hand, is people, individuals, and believers whose life together is structured "within the framework of faith. Where parish implies first a relationship to society, congregation implies first a separation from it" (Mead, p. 45). But, the Internet blurs the distinction between the two. As Dyson says, "one benefit of the Internet is that it allows the formation of communities independent of geographies" (Dyson, p. 32). Thus, as the church reinvents itself and comes to a new understanding of mission, it will live and work in an environment where old borders and boundaries have little meaning, except as relics of an earlier historical period. Pastors and leaders must learn soon to use the new tools wisely and well.

The writer and critic Jon Katz describes the challenge for business, which really is the challenge for the church and those who educate its people for ministry: "The Net isn't destroying such institutions as Wall Street and journalism so much as challenging them to behave differently—to be more interactive, to offer more choices, to listen harder" (Katz, p. 99).

The Net is not destroying the church, either, but it certainly is providing new possibilities for meeting people and strengthening their spiritual lives—if it will learn to do what Katz suggests. Think of this: there are more than twice as many churches as public schools in the United States. What if those churches committed themselves to be centers for training, community development, and communication among all sorts of people? They could reinvent their ministries by putting these new tools to work productively and imaginatively. As the price of computers drops and capabilities grow, and the office clutter they cause is reduced by the steady reduction in the space they need, they become more than just affordable tools; they are necessary elements for effective ministry.

Dyson says, "The one thing required of you is to make use of the Net's powers. They are like a Bible on a shelf or an exercise machine in a den—not worth much unless you do something with them" (Dyson, p. 280). People of faith use their Scriptures to support their growth; there is no support, no growth, if the Scriptures are left to gather dust. If the church fails to use the computer and the Internet, it leaves the Bible on the shelf and abandons the prospects of revitalized mission and service. If educators in seminaries and other institutions remain resistant to the use of computers and the Internet, they will become even more irrelevant to the very people they must reach and teach. For the church to meet the new millennium's challenges, its people—clergy and lay— must know how to use the tools and be bold to do so.

References

Baldwin, James. Cited in Martin E. Marty, *Context*, April 15, 1998, p. 8.

Barna, George, "The Cyberchurch Is Coming," April 20, 1998, material quoted from a news release available at http://www.barna.org/PressCyberChurch.htm

Downes, Larry, and Chunka Mui. *Unleashing the Killer App: Digital Strategies for Marketplace Dominance*. Boston: Harvard Business School Press, 1998.

Dyson, Esther. *Release 2.0*. New York: Broadway Books, 1997.

Herbold, Robert. Speech at *PC Expo*. New York, N.Y., June 23, 1999.

Katz, Jon. "How the Net Changed America" in *Yahoo Internet Life*. September, 1999.

Klein, Michael. "The Church on the Web" in *The Christian Century*. August 11-18, 1999.

McLaren, Brian D. Comments about his book, *Reinventing Your Church*. Grand Rapids: Zondervan, 1998, posted on the amazon.com Web site, Feb. 23, 1999.

Mead, Loren. *The Once and Future Church*. Washington, D.C.: The Alban Institute, 1991.

Nash, Jr., Robert N., *An 8-Track Church in a CD World*. Macon, Ga.: Smith & Helwys, 1997.

Parker, Robert B. *Night Passage*. New York: Jove Books, 1998.

Sample, Tex. *The Spectacle of Worship in a Wired World*. Nashville: Abingdon Press, 1998.

Chapter 21

What Might the Future Be?

D. Bruce Roberts and Robert E. Reber

As the preceding chapters indicate, the continuing education movement among clergy and laity is a vast and complex one. It is barely fifty years old, loosely organized, and reflects the vagaries of church life. Although at a considerable disadvantage in the church's educational ecology, the movement has demonstrated considerable creativity and growth. We are confident that it can grow and become even more important in the coming decades. Whether this growth will prove fruitful will depend, however, upon those of us who are committed to developing programs of quality. To foster the professional development and personal growth of church leaders we must answer affirmatively six key questions.

First, in a society where participation in professional continuing education and adult education is growing every year, will religious institutions provide attractive opportunities for lifelong learning for their leaders?

The churches lag behind the rest of society in recognizing the importance of serving their constituencies on a lifelong basis. Given the priorities of most churches today, there is a possibility that the gap will continue to widen. If this happens, the churches will become increasingly irrelevant in meeting the educational needs and interests of their members, which will likely result in the further privatization of religion and the abdication of the role of religion in public life. The future of the churches depends upon the ongoing education of clergy and laity so that they may give leadership within congregations, religious institutions, and society at large. We need a learned clergy and a learned laity to meet the demands and challenges of local church and community life and of being God's people in the world.

Second, will we shift from a dominant emphasis on education for children to a commitment to lifelong learning for all church members?

In many congregations, the educational emphasis is on children. Great amounts of energy, not to mention anxiety, are consumed in recruiting teachers, reviewing and purchasing curriculum, constructing and maintaining buildings, organizing and running Sunday schools for children. Often it is difficult to recruit teachers for these enterprises precisely because the adults do not feel adequately prepared to teach anything about Christian faith.

Not only are we losing youth and young adults, adults are leaving old-line denominational churches in droves, in spite of evidence that there is a high degree of religious commitment in this society. There is ample data to conclude that our educational efforts with children and youth do not take, and do not result in lifelong commitment to discipleship. No matter how high quality our curricula, youth leave church during their college years because church is boring!

We boldly suggest that the key to reversing this trend is not to improve youth programs but instead to implement quality adult education. To retain members across generations, clergy must create and lead innovative, engaging, relevant, and energizing programs for adults—young and old. Parents must receive training and encouragement to become the primary religious educators for their children. There is an urgent need for continuing educators to prepare clergy and lay leaders in knowledge and skills of lifelong education so that persons of all ages may share in the excitement and life-giving vibrancy of a genuine learning community.

Third, will we engage the vast number of persons with theological and religious interests who do not currently participate in educational programs because of economic, social, or racial barriers?

Churches remain segregated by race/ethnicity and class. We have thus far made little effort to reach out to those who are different. We have rarely been creative or committed to working with those who have been turned off and even bored by our educational endeavors. Our rhetoric about being inclusive has not changed our reality of division and conflict.

To move beyond the current situation both inside and outside religious institutions, careful study and experimentation will be needed. Delivery systems will have to change and we will have to involve people from many different sectors into planning processes with us. If every seminary, conference, retreat center, or congregation would take on just one educational project a year, short or long term, that addresses explicitly the needs of those who might come but who are not yet a part of the community, what a difference it would make.

Fourth, will we respond to the pervasive hunger for the spiritual life that so many North Americans express and often explore outside the confines of established theological institutions and local congregations?

The Gallup organization is preparing to publish a study on the "Spiritual Pulse of the Nation." Quoting from that study, D. Michael Lindsay, in a recent address to the Princeton Consultation on Spirituality and Congregational Life, sponsored by Princeton and Auburn Theological Seminaries, said that their data suggest that 82 percent of the American public reports wanting to grow spiritually. In a similar study done in 1994, 58 percent reported wanting to grow spiritually. That is rather phenomenal growth in five years! Yet, the figures cohere with casual observations. For instance, bookstores have greatly expanded sections dealing with spirituality, particularly in areas dealing with meditation and contemplative prayer. In addition, a group of management and planning consultants with which we are familiar draws its members from those who work primarily in business and not-for-profit institutions. Each of these persons thinks of himself or herself as a change agent for good in the society and to be engaged in a spiritual activity and quest. Yet, not one of them belongs to a church! They perceive church as an institution with an agenda not conducive to their spiritual development and irrelevant to their quest.

Continuing educators must help congregational leaders, lay and clergy, find ways of engaging people in spiritual quests that are at once novel *and* appropriate to Christian faith. While the Christian tradition has many resources for the spiritual life, many other religious traditions have resources that are helpful and appropriate for Christian appropriation as well. We must take the risk of leading persons in spiritual practices that help them discern and participate in the will of God in our time.

Fifth, will we persuade religious leaders to respond to the extraordinary and multifaceted challenges to the quality of life on this planet, whether ecological, technological, religious, or political?

The content of much professional and adult education today avoids these concerns. Yet public awareness is increasing and many church members also belong to the numerous citizen groups and organizations concerned with plant and animal life, protecting the environment, recycling, building bridges of peace around the world, eliminating hunger, providing health care, defending human rights, and so forth. The awareness of the interconnectedness of the planet and all forms of life continues to grow. At the same time, violence plagues our society, filling our television screens and movies, characterizing political, religious and ethnic relationships, and destroying family and community life. Unfortunately, such issues remain at the periphery of continuing theological education. We must engage these critical issues of justice, peace, health, and ecological wholeness in educational contexts if we desire to make a qualitative difference in the lives of individuals and the places where they live and work and worship.

Finally, will we foster and support innovation and experimentation in continuing and professional education that will make a qualitative difference in congregations and in the preparation of future church leaders?

It is increasingly clear that there will not be one "right" answer to any of the questions that face churches and continuing theological educators. We must keep reminding ourselves that there are as many "right answers" to the issues and problems that face us as there are contexts in which we work. Ronald Heifetz challenges us to focus on the "adaptive" work in our organizations, continuing to pose the questions that require changes in our values, beliefs, and behavior, while resisting the technological or quick-fix solutions. Not having one "right" answer available to us is frightening on the one hand, but freeing on the other; we know that solutions must be invented in our various contexts, through innovations and experiments that are evaluated and mined for new insights. Continuing educators are challenged not only to be innovative in the practice of continuing theological education, but also to help clergy and lay leaders learn how to learn through reflective practice, experimentation and evaluation, and innovative trial and error. In a recent speech, a judicatory executive in the Midwest suggested that churches would need to find new ways to do ministry in our culture, or be prepared to be considered irrelevant or "quaint." Similarly, Rabbi Edwin Freedman once suggested that what is needed in times like ours is explorers who risk going against the prevailing worldview to seek new paths and new directions. As continuing educators today, who face an uncertain future, we too, will need to become explorers, finding new ways to delivering our programs, forging new partnerships and alliances, allocating funds in new ways that encourage innovation, while maintaining sustained focus on given audiences and issues over time. The challenge is before us!

We believe that the articles in this book indicate the enormous possibilities and challenges for continuing theological education. What is required is a willingness to take risks, to get involved in new ideas and partnerships, to experiment and to communicate what we are learning in our educational experiments and innovations. The health of our institutions, whether it be local church, seminary, conference center or judicatory continuing education, will depend on our willingness to think and act systemically and creatively.